AF553907

SOIL QUALITY AND CONTAMINATION

SOIL QUALITY
AND
CONTAMINATION

Edited by

Dr. Pawan Kumar 'Bharti'
Centre for Agro-Rural Technologies (CART-India)
20, Jamaalpur Maan, Raja Ka Tajpur
Distt.- Bijnore (UP) – 246 735 (India)
E-mail: gurupawanbharti@rediffmail.com

&

Dr. Avnish Chauhan
Department of Applied Science, College of Engineering
Teerthanker Mahaveer University, Bagarpur
Moradabad (UP) – 244 001
E-mail: avnishchauhan_in@yahoo.co.in

Associate Editors

Dr. Sandeep Gupta
A.K.G. Eng. College, Ghaziabad (UP) (India)

&

Dr. Pawan Kumar
J.M. Environet Pvt. Ltd., Gurgaon, Haryana (India)

DISCOVERY PUBLISHING HOUSE PVT. LTD.
NEW DELHI-110 002

Published by:
Tilak Wasan
DISCOVERY PUBLISHING HOUSE PVT. LTD.
4383/4B, Ansari Road, Darya Ganj
New Delhi-110 002 (India)
Phone : +91-11-23279245, 43596064-65
Fax : +91-11-23253475
E-mail : discoverypublishinghouse@gmail.com
sales@discoverypublishinggroup.com
parul.wasan@gmail.com
web : www.discoverypublishinggroup.com

***First Edition:* 2013**

ISBN: 978-93-5056-361-8

Soil Quality and Contamination

© 2013, Editors

All rights reserved. No part of this publication should be reproduced, stored in a retrieval system, or transmitted in any form or by any means: electronic, mechanical, photocopying, recording or otherwise, without the prior written permission of the author and the publisher.

This book has been published in good faith that the material provided by authors is original. Every effort is made to ensure accuracy of material, but the publisher and printer will not be held responsible for any inadvertent error(s). In case of any dispute, all legal matters are to be settled under Delhi jurisdiction only.

Printed at:
Aditi Fine Art Press
Delhi

Preface

In recent years, the rapid growth of industrialization and development pose negative impacts on lithosphere, atmosphere and hydrosphere. It is essential to know the status of physico-chemical parameters and other pollutants discarding from various industries in to surface water, ground water, soil and crop plant vegetation for health safety of regional people, which may help in recent research in the field of soil and water pollution by industries and for advance alarming against pollution to public, NGOs. The present book deals with the physico-chemical assessment and quality evaluation of agriculture soil, which may change the soil fertility and affect the agricultural plant productivity.

Agricultural soil requires sufficient irrigation for high production in agricultural fields. Irrigation water with poor quality can result in the alteration of physico-chemical characteristics of irrigated agricultural soil. Several minerals such as chloride, sulphate, bicarbonate, sodium, calcium and magnesium in irrigation water may change the soil quality with its continuous application on soil. These minerals contained in the irrigation water can build up the soil's trophic level and ultimately influence the agriculture productivity.

This book provides comprehensive coverage of the fundamental principles and current practices and trends in the field of soil characterization, soil quality and contamination.

This book updates the subject matter, illustrations and problems to incorporate new concepts and issues related to soil pollution, soil quality and contamination from various sources.

Particularly thanks are due to all contributors and publisher for their contribution, cooperation and assistance.

I hope this book will be of benefit to both present and future colleagues, who teach, study and working in the field of environmental pollution, soil pollution, agronomy, industrial pollution and agricultural sciences.

Dr. Pawan Kumar 'Bharti'

Contents

List of Contributors

1. **Avnish Chauhan,** Department of Applied Science, College of Engineering, Teerthanker Mahaveer University, Bagarpur, Moradabad (UP) – 244001
2. **A.K. Chopra,** Department of Zoology and Environmental Science, Gurukula Kangri University, Haridwar, Uttarakhand, India
3. **Charles Ikenna Osu,** Department of Pure and Industrial Chemistry, University of Port-Harcourt, Rivers State, Nigeria
4. **E. I. Moyin-Jesu,** Agronomy Department, Federal College of Agriculture, Akure, Ondo State, Nigeria
5. **Jaibir Singh Pharswan*,** Department of History and Archaeology, H.N.B. Garhwal University, Srinagar (Garhwal)-246 174, Uttarakhand, India
6. **Jagmohan Singh Negi**, Herbal Research and Development Institute, Mandal, Gopeshwar (Chamoli)- 246 401, Uttarakhand, India
7. **Pawan Kumar,** 1. Department of Zoology and Environmental Science, Gurukula Kangri University, Haridwar-249404 & 2. J.M. Environet Pvt. Ltd., Gurgaon, Haryana, India
8. **Pawan Kumar Bharti,** Centre for Agro-Rural Technologies (CART-India), 20, Jamaalpur Maan, Raja Ka Tajpur, District-Bijnore (UP)-246735, India
9. **Sandeep Gupta,** Department of Applied Sciences, A.K.G. Eng. College, Ghaziabad (UP), India
10. **Triloki Nath Vaish,** Hi-Tech Engineering College, Ghaziabad (UP), India
11. **Vinay Kumar Daksh,** Hari Vihar Colony, Behind Jaat College, Mawana, Meerut (UP), India
12. **Yogamber Singh Farswan,** Department of History and Archaeology, H.N.B. Garhwal University, Srinagar (Garhwal)-246 174, Uttarakhand, India

1

Soil Quality Assessment in the Vicinity of an Industrial Area

—*Pawan Kumar 'Bharti', India*

ABSTRACT

In India, the industrial effluents have contributed a major source of pollution. Textile industrial effluent when discharged into a large pond and through pond ultimately percolated to the ground water. Thus, contaminated ground water has deteriorated immensely the drinking utilities, post agriculture irrigation and impacts on soil systems and crop productivity. The aim of this study is to emphasize on the physico-chemical parameters of soil and alterations due to irrigation with contaminated ground water affected by textile industrial effluents, on agricultural land.

Key words: *Soil quality, Textile industrial effluent, agriculture soil, physico-chemical parameters*

Introduction

In recent years, the rapid growth of industrialization and development pose negative impacts on lithosphere, atmosphere and hydrosphere. The composite effluent from textile industries may affect the quality of surface water, soil, ground water and plant tissues. Toxic pollutants may percolate down via soil profile and reach in ground water, which ultimately cause the health hazards among human being and livestock after consumption as daily drinking requirements. The waste water without any treatment may cause adverse effect on the health of human, domestic animals, wildlife and environment (Sharma *et al.*, 1999). Thus, contaminated ground water has deteriorated immensely the drinking utilities, post agriculture irrigation and impacts on soil systems and crop productivity.

Ground water contaminated by textile effluents, has deteriorated immensely the post agriculture irrigation, drinking utilities and impacts on soil systems. For prevention of ground water pollution, it is very essential to treat industrial wastewater before discharging in to the surface water, because through the surface water pollutants may reach in ground water by leaching process via soil profile.

It is essential to know the status of physico-chemical parameters and pollutants discarding from textile industries in to surface, ground water, soil and crop plant vegetation for health safety of regional people, which may help in recent research in the field of soil and water pollution by industries and for advance alarming against pollution to public, NGOs and GOs. The present paper deals with the physico-chemical parameters assessment of agriculture soil, which may change the soil fertility and agricultural plant productivity.

The main source of water on earth is rain and a large quantity of rain water goes to nearest water body by run-off method and rest amount percolate down in earth crust according to soil character. Lost rain water by run-off process is known as run away water, while rest water delay in soil and reach in water table. Generally, soil occupied four types of water, chemical bonded water (bounded with soil particles), hygroscopic water (remain on soil particle's surface), capillary water (between the soil particles and available for plants) and gravitational water (percolated down in to aquifers). All the four categories are shown in figure given below (Kaushik, 2006).

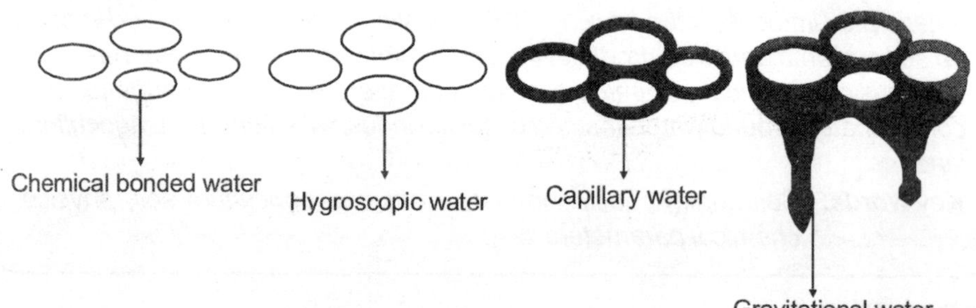

Fig. 1.1: Different types of Soil Water

Waste water of dye houses generally discharged openly into Binjhole pond water, thus polluted the surface water quality of the region (Malik *et al.*, 2006). After delaying for a long period of time the salt contents may remain in agriculture soil for a long period and alter the nature and quality of soil. Soil particles bound a huge amount of salts due to adsorptive nature, which remain in capillary water and easily available for plants. The excess of salts may create some problems to soils, i.e. salinity and water logging.

Agricultural soil requires sufficient irrigation for high production in agricultural fields. Irrigation water with poor quality can result in the alteration of physico-chemical characteristics of irrigated agricultural soil. Several minerals such as chloride, sulphate, bicarbonate, sodium, calcium and magnesium in irrigation water may change the soil quality with its continuous application on soil. These minerals contained in the irrigation water can build up the soil's trophic level and ultimately influence the agriculture productivity (Malik and Bharti, 2007).

Historical Resume

The contaminated ground water used in irrigation purposes may harmful for soils of agriculture fields and ultimately effects on productivity of agriculture crop plants, and soil macrobiotic community also.

Many workers from India and abroad have been discussed various aspects of agricultural soil pollution in term of characteristics of affected agricultural soils and bottom sediments from time to time. Some of important contribution made in the field of industrial pollution, with references to physical, chemical and biological parameters of contaminated agricultural irrigated soil and bottom sediment soils by different authors of country and abroad.

Aggarwal and Mehrotra (1952) surveyed the soil and soil water affected by effluent in some selected regions of Uttar Pradesh. Doneen (1954) reported the stalinization of soils of salts in irrigation waters. Richards (1954) evaluated the quality of saline and alkali soils and gave a technique for the improvement of these sick soil systems in the agricultural sector for good performance of agriculture productivity.

Singh and Bhumbla (1968) analyzed the effect of quality of irrigation water on soil properties. Singh *et al.*, (1969) reported the salinity problem in soil of high water table areas of north India. Singh and Sharma (1971) studied on the effects of saline irrigation waters on physico-chemical properties of some soils of Rajasthan. Bhargava *et al.*, (1972) evaluated the characteristics of some typical saline sodic soils occurring in Karnal district of Haryana. Sharma and Parihar (1973) evaluated the effect of depth and salinity of ground water on evaporation and soil salinization. Dowedy and Larson (1975) reported the availability of some metals in various vegetable crops in a polluted region in the vicinity of an industrial area.

Ajmal and Khan (1985) analysed the effects of textile waste on physico-chemical properties of soil and seed germination. The BOD, COD and total solids, Cl, SO_4, Na, Ca and Mg concentrations in the effluents were found to be very high. Minhas and Gupta (1992) indicated the effects of wastewater irrigation in agriculture soils and found sodicity due to the poor water quality. Singh *et al.*, (1994) highlighted the degradation of water and soil quality of Parwanoo area with respect to heavy metals. Srinivasan and Murali (1996) carried out some studies on effect of industrial pollutants on properties of soils. Pujari and Sinha (1999) studied on the water and soil quality of some villages of Attabira area irrigated by bargarg main canal originated from Hirakund reservoir of Orissa.

Yadav *et al.*, (2002) highlighted the post irrigation impact of domestic sewage effluent on composition of soils, crops and ground water in Kurukshetra district. Shrivastava *et al.*, (2003) collected soil samples from surface of the soil from different agriculture fields in the Khandesh region and Tapi River sediment samples were also collected from five different stations which were 7-8 km away from each other and detected the concentrations of heavy metals have been determined by ICP-AES.

Malik and Bharti (2007) studied on soil quality of irrigated agricultural fields in a textile industrial area of Panipat city. Gharaibeh *et al.*, (2007) found the impact of field application of treated wastewater on hydraulic properties of vertisols.

Trevors and Saier (2007) described the regulation of pollution in various environmental components viz. water, air and soil. Mico *et al.*, (2007) described the comparison of two digestion methods for the analysis of heavy metals by flame atomic absorption spectrophotometer.

Kumar *et al.*, (2012) highlighted the pollution of various environmental components including soil system.

Study Area

Mainly ground water is use for irrigation purposes in most part of country and also in Haryana state. However, Yamuna is flowing in this region for irrigation utilization in agriculture sector of entire area but mostly agriculture farm holders have their own tube wells for facility.

In Panipat city, Dye houses are situated on Jatal road in industrial area, these are quite famous for handloom business. Textile dying industries in Panipat region consume large quantities of water and discharge it into a common effluent drain, which ends up in to a large pond situated near Binjhole village. Since last five or six years, it was noticed that ground water quality is degrading day by day of the regions and local people think that the dye waste water is the major source of environmental pollution in area.

Methodology

Soil samples were collected from different selected sites. During the sampling, the nomination (for labeling and identification) of soil samples was applied properly and carefully.

The physico-chemical analysis of soil sample were made of the entire collected samples following the method outlined in a standard method for examination of water and wastewater APHA (2005), Trivadi & Goel (1984) and Bharti (2012).

Observations

Experimental Site

Physico-chemical parameters of agriculture soils

Temperature (°C):

Temperature of agricultural soil was recorded maximum 27.87 ± 3.56 in summer 2005 and minimum 17.40 ± 3.92 in winter 2005-06 ranged between

11.3 to 31.5°C. The highest value of temperature in agricultural soil was found 31.5°C during June 2006 and lowest 11.3°C in January 2006.

Water holding capacity (%)

Water holding capacity of agricultural soil was recorded maximum 43.75 ± 0.49 in summer 2005 and minimum 36.13 ± 4.92 in monsoon 2005 ranged between 31.58 to 44.35%. The highest value of water holding capacity in agricultural soil was found 44.35% during June 2006 and lowest 31.58% in September 2005.

Bulk density (g/cm^3)

The bulk density of agricultural soil was recorded maximum 1.24 ± 0.04 in monsoon 2006 and minimum 1.15 ± 0.03 in summer 2005 ranged between 1.08 to 1.31 g/cm^3. The highest value of bulk density in agricultural soil was found 1.31 g/cm^3 during October 2005 and lowest 1.08 g/cm^3 in January 2006.

Soil moisture (%)

The soil moisture of agricultural soil was recorded maximum 10.76 ± 2.26 in monsoon 2006 and minimum 3.52 ± 1.04 in summer 2005 ranged between 2.75 to 12.2%. The highest value of soil moisture in agricultural soil was found 12.2% during August 2005 and lowest 2.75% in May 2005.

pH

pH of agricultural soil on pH scale was recorded maximum 7.63 ± 0.15 in monsoon 2006 and minimum 7.11 ± 0.01 in summer 2007 ranged between 7.1 to 7.9. The highest value of pH in agricultural soil was found 7.9 during October 2006 and lowest 7.1 in April 2005.

Electrical Conductivity (mho/cm)

Electric conductivity of agricultural soil was recorded maximum 27.73 ± 1.66 in monsoon 2006 and minimum 24.18 ± 1.12 in winter 2005-06 ranged between 22.3 and 30.0 mho/cm. The highest value of Electric conductivity in agricultural soil was found 30.0 mho/cm during June 2005 and lowest 22.3 mho/cm in December 2005.

Chloride (µg/g)

Chloride concentration in agricultural soil was recorded maximum 734.33 ± 112.01 in summer 2005 and minimum 499.50 ± 37.47 in summer 2007 ranged between 416.0 to 871.0 µg/g. The highest value of chloride in agricultural soil was found 871.0 µg/g during June 2006 and lowest 416.0 µg/g in January 2006.

Potassium (µg/g)

Potassium concentration in agricultural soil was recorded maximum 36.50 ± 0.71 in summer 2007 and minimum 31.00 ± 1.00 in monsoon 2005 ranged between 30.0 to 37.0 μg/g. The highest value of potassium in agricultural soil was found 37.0 μg/g during March 2007 and lowest 30.0 μg/g in August 2005.

Sodium (μg/g)

Sodium concentration in agricultural soil was recorded maximum 599.0 ± 36.77 in summer 2007 and minimum 192.0 ± 91.99 in monsoon 2005 ranged between 133.0 to 665.0 μg/g. The highest value of sodium in agricultural soil was found 665.0 μg/g during April 2005 and lowest 133.0 μg/g in September 2005.

Control Site

Physico-chemical Parameter of Agriculture Soil

Temperature (°C):

Temperature of soil at control site was recorded maximum 27.83 ± 2.70 in summer 2005 and minimum 17.50 ± 3.48 in winter 2005-06 ranged between 11.8 to 31.0°C. The highest value of temperature in soil was found 31.0°C during June 2006 and lowest 11.8°C in January 2007.

Water holding capacity (%)

Water holding capacity of soil at control site was recorded maximum 44.18 ± 0.74 in summer 2005 and minimum 36.81 ± 1.89 in winter 2006-07 ranged between 32.17 to 45.0%. The highest value of water holding capacity in soil was found 45.0% during June 2005 and lowest 32.17% in September 2006.

Bulk density (g/cm^3)

The bulk density of soil at control site was recorded maximum 1.22 ± 0.01 in monsoon 2006 and minimum 1.11 ± 0.051 in summer 2006 ranged between 1.05 to 1.25 g/cm^3. The highest value of bulk density in soil was found 1.25 g/cm^3 during October 2006 and lowest 1.05 g/cm^{3}in January 2006.

Soil moisture (%)

The soil moisture of soil at control site was recorded maximum 11.06 ± 1.86 in monsoon 2006 and minimum 3.73 ± 1.29 in summer 2005 ranged between 2.8 to 12.82%. The highest value of soil moisture in soil was found 12.82% during August 2006 and lowest 2.8% in May 2005.

pH

pH of soil at control site was recorded maximum 7.47 ± 0.058 in monsoon 2005 and minimum 7.23 ± 0.15 in summer 2005 ranged between 7.1 to 7.6. The highest value of pH in soil was found 7.6 during October 2006 and lowest 7.1 in April 2005.

Electrical conductivity (mho/cm)

Electric conductivity of soil at control site was recorded maximum 23.75 ± 0.27 in summer 2006 and minimum 23.00 ± 0.163 in winter 2006-07 ranged between 22.5 to 24.1 mho/cm. The highest value of Electric conductivity in soil was found 24.1mho/cm during April 2006 and lowest 22.5 mho/cm in September 2005.

Chloride (µg/g)

Chloride concentration in soil at control site was recorded maximum 529.33 ± 114.47 in summer 2005 and minimum 313.80 ± 64.32 in winter 2005-06 ranged between 225.0 to 671.0 µg/g. The highest value of chloride in soil was found 671.0 µg/g during June 2006 and lowest 225.0 µg/g in January 2006.

Potassium (µg/g)

Potassium concentration in soil at control site was recorded maximum 34.50 ± 0.71 in monsoon 2005 and minimum 30.33 ± 2.52 in winter 2006-07 ranged between 28.0 to 36.0 µg/g. The highest value of potassium in soil was found 36.0 µg/g during April 2005 and lowest 28.0 µg/g in August 2005.

Sodium (µg/g)

Sodium concentration in soil at control site was recorded maximum 380.00 ± 12.73 in monsoon 2005 and minimum 95.35 ± 37.01 in winter 2006-07 ranged between 11.0 to 468.0 µg/g. The highest value of sodium in soil was found 468.0 µg/g during April 2005 and lowest 11.0 µg/g in October 2005.

Discussion

Soil's physico-chemical parameters may demonstrate the pollution status in the industrial region, so, physical and chemical characteristics are important for the assessment of contamination and pollution load.

Physico-chemical parameters of agriculture soil

The temperature of soil greatly affects the physical, biological and chemical processes occurring in soil system. Biological decomposition can come to a near stand still, thereby limiting the rate at which nutrients such as nitrogen, phosphorus, sulphur and calcium are made available. Absorption and transport of water and nutrient ions by higher plants are adversely affected by low temperature (Brady, 1995). The temperature of field soils is not subject to radical human regulation. However, two kinds of management practices have significant effects on soil temperature, those that keep some type of cover or mulch on the soil and those that reduce excess soil moisture. There is not any significant variation in the temperature of agricultural soil (17.4-27.8°C) and control soil (17.5-27.8°C). The chemical processes and activities of microorganism which convert plant nutrients into available forms are also materially influenced by temperature. Removal of excess water from soil may facilitate changes in soil temperature. Humus content, good tillage, dark color of soil are the some other factors which influence the soil temperature (Miller and Turk, 2002).

The phenomenon of capillarity is a common one, the classic example being the movement of water up a wick when the lower end is immersed in water. Capillary forces are at work in all moist soils. However, the rate of movement and the rise in height are less than one would expect on the basis of soil pore size. One reason is that soil pores are filled with air, which may be entrapped, showing down or preventing the movement of water by capillary. Usually the height of the rise resulting from capillarity is greater with fine textured soils if sufficient time is allowed and the pores are not too small. This is readily explained on the basis of the capillary size and the continuity of the pores. With sandy soils the adjustment is rapid but so many of the pores are non-capillary that the height of rise can not be great (Brady, 1995). Water holding capacity is a property as to water quantity is absorbed or retained by given amount of soil (Ramani and Srivastava, 1989). Water held in the soil pores with varying degrees of tenacity depending on the amount of water present and the size of pores in soils. Depending on the soil, as much as one forth to two thirds of the moisture may remain in the soil after the plants have wilted or died due to the lack of soil water. Water holding capacity was found similar in agricultural soil (36.1-43.7%) and control soil (36.8-44.2%) with much difference between soil and sediment. Yuandong *et al.*, (2006) described the similar trend of water holding capacity on the basis of soil texture and chemical composition in the agricultural soil system.

Bulk density relates to the combined volumes of the solids and pore spaces, soils with a high proportion of pore space to solids have lower bulk densities than those that are more compact and have less pore space. Consequently, any factor that influences soil pore space will affect bulk density. Mainly soil texture and compactness strongly influence the bulk density of soils (Brady, 1995). The pore space of a soil is that portion of the soil volume occupied by air and water. The amount of pore space is determined by the arrangement of the solid particles. If the particles lie close together, as in stands or compact sub-soils, the total porosity is low. If they are arranged in porous aggregates, as is often the case in medium textured soils high in organic matter, the pore space per unit volume will be high. Soil aeration may influence the availability of nutrients to plants (Miller and Turk, 2002). The bulk density was found similar between agricultural soil (1.15-1.24 g/cm^3) and control soil (1.10-1.22 g/cm^3) Bulk density was similarly described by Yuandong *et al.*, (2006) and Krebs *et al.*, (1999) in soil environment.

The structure of the soil influences its moisture content. A well granulated soil has more total pore space than one with poor granulation or one that has been compacted. The reduced pore space may be reflected in a lower water holding capacity. The compacted soil also has to higher proportion of small and medium sized pores, which tend to hold the water with greater tenacity than do the larger pores. Moisture content of agricultural soil (3.5-10.7%)

and control soil (3.7-11.06%) were found similar during the study. Rainwater leaching have made more efficient if antecedent moisture content of the soil profile was increased by saline water irrigation just before the onset of monsoons. On a wet soil, a rainfall event is expected to displace the salts to a greater depth. Conservation and proper utilization of rainwater for leaching salts is also utmost important.

The measurement of soil pH shows the acidity and basic nature of the soil. The soil is acidic if the pH is lower, while the higher pH means that soil is basic. The pH value was observed slightly high (7.11-7.63) in agriculture land, which shows that agriculture land is going to alkaline in nature which confirms that agriculture land again disturbed by its proper pH values whereas due to the decay of organic matter has produced the acidic properties of soil. If the decomposition of organic matter is there in soil, it will turn the pH low, other wise some foreign substances may alter the soil nature and properties towards alkaline (Nongkynrih *et al.*, 1996). Initial soil pH is an important property of the soil because of its influence on the infiltration rate of the soil (Gupta *et al.*, 1989). There are several causes of minor fluctuation in soil pH. For instance, the movements of salts into and out of soil moisture moves up and down the profile will influence pH. Similarly, the pH of mineral soils declines during the crop-growing season as a result of the acids produced by microorganisms and by the roots of higher plants. When soil temperatures are low, an increase in pH often is noted because biotic activities during these times are considerably slower.

pH of soil significantly influences other soil chemical properties as well as biological organisms. High pH of textile industrial effluent can hampers plant crop growth (Sial *et al.*, 2006). The soil pH significantly affects the availability of most of the chemical element of importance to plants and microbes. Likewise, the tendency for toxic levels of element such as iron, manganese, aluminum to be established at low pH and deficiencies of iron and manganese at high pH have been mentioned. Continuous application of effluents with high pH will render the soils unfit for further cultivation (Sial *et al.*, 2006). Soil pH was found slightly alkaline in agricultural soil (7.1-7.6) and control soil (7.2-7.4). Similar trend of pH fluctuation have been described by Kasem and Singh (1999) in agricultural soil environment.

Electric conductivity is the measure of current carrying capacity, which gives a clear idea of soluble salts present in soil. Conductivity generally depends upon the dilution of suspension. However, the salt composition is high in the water having high electric conductivity, but it may be beneficial for those soils having a lack or deficiency of some salts. The electric conductivity of agricultural soil and control soil was found in the range of 24.1-27.7 and 23.0-23.7 mho/cm respectively with some minor fluctuations. Electric conductivity has positive correlation with all heavy metals viz. Cd (0.3965) Cu (0.9454), Fe (0.4198), Mn (0.9076), Ni (0.8286), Pb (0.8596) and Zn (0.7586) in agricultural soil.

Chloride was found very high in effluent drain sediment and slightly low as with similar fluctuation in pond bed sediment, but in agricultural soil and soil near textile industries chloride was found comparatively low because of the high settlement of chloride in drain sediment from textile industrial effluent; while rest was reach in agricultural soil by various contacts. The chloride in agricultural soil and control soil was found 499.5-734.3 and 313.8-529.3 µg/g respectively with some minor fluctuations. Chloride has positive correlation with all heavy metals viz. Cd (0.3654) Cu (0.8479), Fe (0.3249), Mn (0.7254), Ni (0.6603), Pb (0.6972) and Zn (0.7744) in agricultural soil environment. Manchanda (1990) has also reported that pulse crops such as pea, mungbean, gram, lentil, and broadbean suffered more due to toxic accumulation of chloride, when irrigated with Cl ion then SO_4^{-2} dominant (70%) water of more salinity.

Potassium is extremely mobile with in the plant and helps regulate the opening and closing of stomata in the leaves and the uptake of water by root cells. At any one time most of the potassium is in the primary mineral and non-exchangeable forms. The exchangeable potassium is the chief source of available potassium in soil (Jha and Pandey, 1984). Potassium plays many essential roles in plants. It is an activator of dozens of enzymes responsible for such plants processes as energy metabolism, starch synthesis, nitrate reduction, and sugar degradation. To maintain the level of exchangeable and soil solution potassium high enough to encourage good crop production, chemical fertilizer are used. Potassium may deficient in alkaline soil and an excess of potassium may delay maturity of plant. In some crops it may tend to accumulate in the leaf and stem rather then in the grain (Miller and Turk, 2002). The potassium in agricultural soil and control soil was found almost in uniform pattern 31.0-36.5 and 30.3-34.5 µg/g respectively with some minor fluctuations. Potassium has slightly positive correlation with many heavy metals viz. Cd (0.6852) Cu (-0.1689), Fe (0.7116), Mn (0.0611), Ni (0.2623), Pb (0.2369) and Zn (-0.6269) in agricultural soil. Korfali and Davies (2004) and Soltan (1999) have been exhibited a clear idea about the fluctuations in potassium concentrations in soil system.

Sodium in alkali soils results in a deflocculation of the colloids and hence in a breaking down of the soil structural units. This puddle condition renders the soil more or less impervious and retards entrance of irrigation and rain water impedes drainage. In heavy textured soil, the penetration of roots may be restricted by the deflocculated zone. Aeration is also much reduced, setting up aeration conditions and resulting in the formation of reduced compounds which are toxic to plants (Miller and Turk, 2002). The highly alkaline soil was due to the presence of sodium carbonate. Large quantity of adsorbed sodium repressed the availability of several nutrients especially, iron, manganese and phosphorous (Miller and Turk, 2002). The occurrence of sodium in agricultural soil and control soil was found very high 192.0-

Table 1.1: Seasonal Variation of Physico-chemical Characteristics of Soil near Textile Industries

Parameters	Unit	Summer 2005		Monsoon 2005		Winter 2005-06		Summer 2006		Monsoon 2006		Winter 2006-07		Summer 2007	
		Mean	SD	Mean	SD	Mean	SD	Mean	SD	Mean	SD	Mean	SD	Mean	SD
Temperature	°C	27.667	3.456	25.833	2.517	17.160	3.866	26.050	4.063	26.133	2.003	18.075	3.969	19.750	2.475
WHC	%	42.590	0.476	34.997	4.926	35.800	2.814	42.203	1.288	35.693	4.836	35.000	2.386	38.930	1.018
Bulk density	mg/cm3	1.203	0.021	1.273	0.021	1.274	0.048	1.213	0.015	1.280	0.026	1.295	0.030	1.225	0.021
Soil moisture	%	3.377	1.027	10.600	2.360	5.210	1.166	3.670	0.853	10.760	2.249	5.513	1.603	4.605	0.856
pH		7.700	0.100	7.800	0.100	7.920	0.084	7.800	0.082	7.833	0.058	7.850	0.058	8.050	0.071
EC	mho/cm	30.833	1.041	29.667	1.457	26.120	0.944	30.075	1.680	30.267	1.201	26.750	1.012	27.050	1.061
Cl	µg/g	769.333	140.479	721.000	86.000	551.600	35.211	716.500	172.055	739.333	96.862	567.250	32.253	552.000	8.485
Na	µg/g	424.000	117.656	100.333	86.489	264.600	159.054	461.750	94.132	133.667	73.921	228.000	125.748	503.500	13.435
K	µg/g	33.333	1.528	30.333	1.528	33.000	1.581	34.500	1.291	31.000	1.000	32.750	0.957	33.500	2.121

Table 1.2: Seasonal variation of Physico-chemical Characteristics of Agricultural Irrigated Soil

Parameters	Unit	Summer 2005		Monsoon 2005		Winter 2005-06		Summer 2006		Monsoon 2006		Winter 2006-07		Summer 2007	
		Mean	SD	Mean	SD	Mean	SD	Mean	SD	Mean	SD	Mean	SD	Mean	SD
Temperature	°C	27.867	3.556	26.200	2.551	17.400	3.922	26.375	4.328	26.567	2.601	18.325	4.105	19.750	3.182
WHC	%	43.747	0.485	36.127	4.920	36.942	2.828	43.188	1.220	36.767	4.868	36.443	2.857	41.190	0.905
Bulk density	mg/cm3	1.147	0.025	1.217	0.031	1.194	0.086	1.148	0.034	1.240	0.040	1.218	0.085	1.175	0.035
Soil moisture	%	3.517	1.040	10.643	2.424	5.272	1.178	3.668	0.820	10.763	2.264	5.550	1.429	4.645	1.181
pH		7.300	0.200	7.563	0.185	7.324	0.319	7.330	0.215	7.633	0.153	7.453	0.301	7.110	0.014
EC	mho/cm	27.667	2.082	26.500	1.323	24.180	1.117	27.450	1.873	27.733	1.662	24.538	0.912	25.600	0.566
Cl	µg/g	734.333	112.010	641.667	69.292	514.800	71.521	683.500	148.586	673.000	71.631	535.500	69.150	499.500	37.477
Na	µg/g	537.333	125.085	192.000	91.995	363.400	157.267	566.750	101.385	200.000	72.062	329.000	124.887	599.000	36.770
K	µg/g	35.000	2.000	31.000	1.000	34.400	1.517	36.000	1.414	31.000	1.000	33.750	1.258	36.500	0.707

Table 1.3: Seasonal variation of Physico-chemical Characteristics of Soil at Control Site

Parameters	Unit	Summer 2005		Monsoon 2005		Winter 2005-06		Summer 2006		Monsoon 2006		Winter 2006-07		Summer 2007	
		Mean	SD	Mean	SD	Mean	SD	Mean	SD	Mean	SD	Mean	SD	Mean	SD
Temperature	°C	27.833	2.701	26.500	2.500	17.500	3.482	26.325	4.369	26.933	2.503	17.800	4.537	19.500	2.404
WHC	%	44.183	0.742	37.733	5.519	37.500	2.670	43.720	0.916	37.843	5.826	36.810	1.890	41.295	2.029
Bulk density	mg/cm3	1.107	0.051	1.207	0.012	1.168	0.076	1.125	0.017	1.220	0.010	1.183	0.070	1.180	0.042
Soil moisture	%	3.733	1.286	10.683	1.994	5.630	0.972	3.825	1.147	11.063	1.857	6.010	1.532	4.440	1.329
pH		7.233	0.153	7.467	0.058	7.310	0.167	7.250	0.058	7.467	0.058	7.400	0.141	7.250	0.071
EC	mho/cm	23.633	0.153	23.100	0.557	23.040	0.182	23.750	0.265	23.300	0.436	23.000	0.163	23.650	0.212
Cl	μg/g	529.333	114.474	446.667	62.067	313.800	64.317	483.000	148.272	458.333	58.969	336.750	69.014	314.500	47.376
Na	μg/g	338.000	124.864	95.333	37.005	183.800	143.796	356.250	91.940	104.000	35.384	145.500	105.583	380.000	12.728
K	μg/g	33.000	2.646	30.333	2.517	33.200	0.837	34.000	1.414	30.667	2.082	33.250	1.708	34.500	0.707

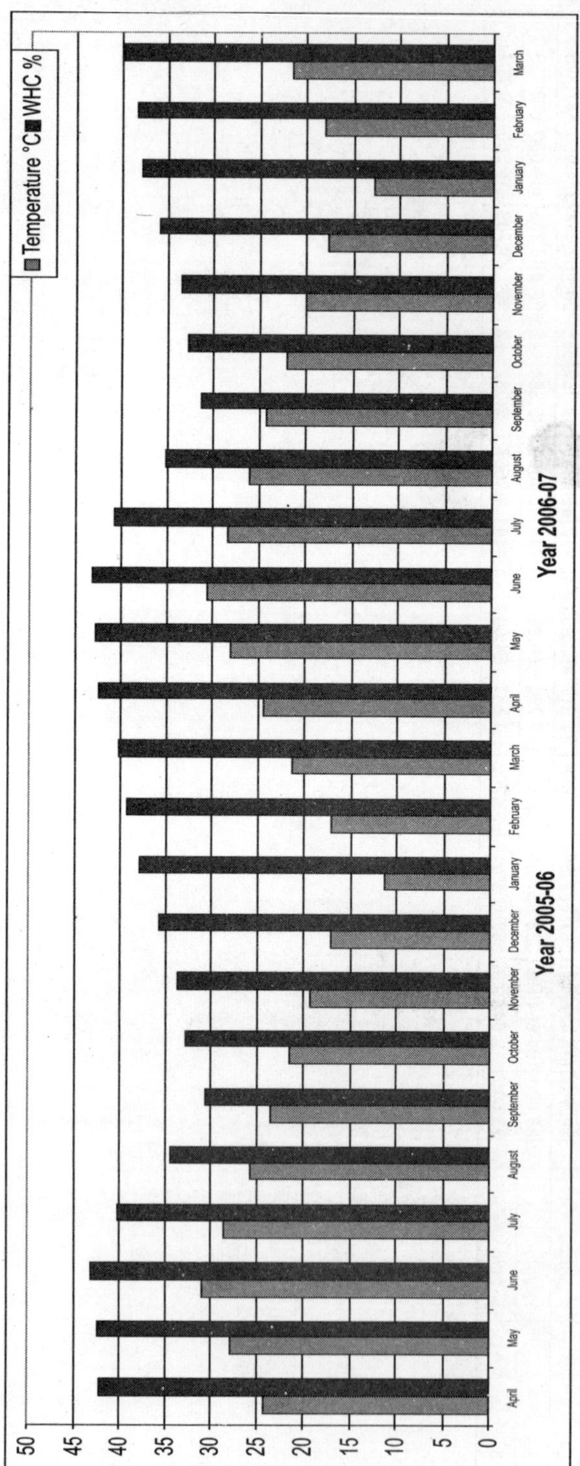

Fig. 1.2: Monthly variation of temperature and WHC in soil near textile industries

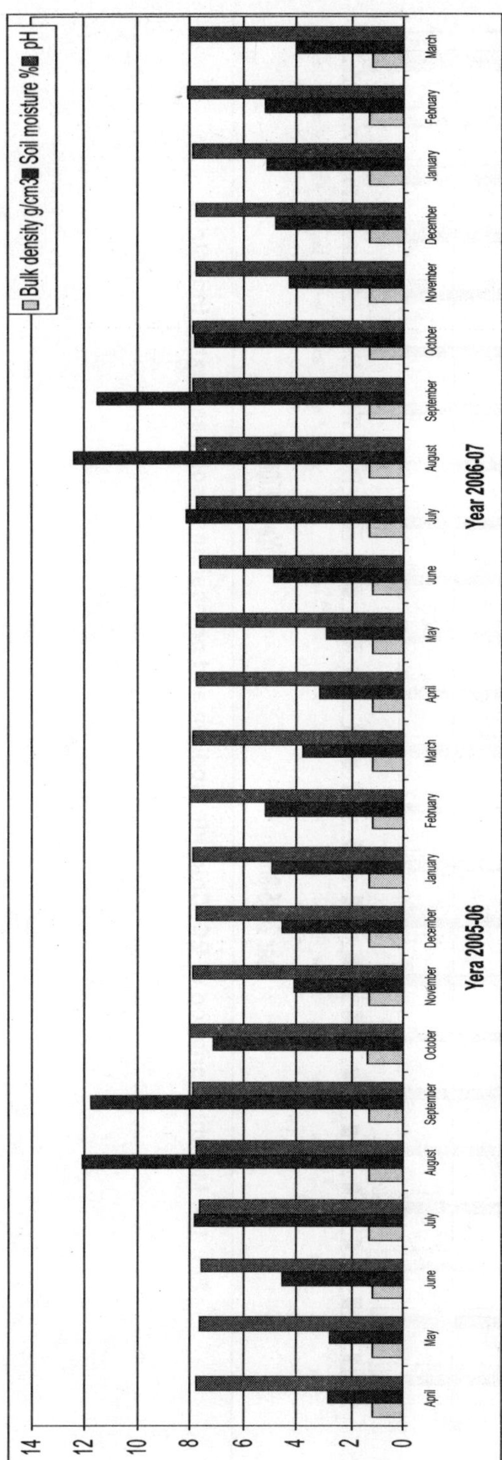

Fig. 1.3: Monthly variation of bulk density, soil moisture and pH in soil near textile industries

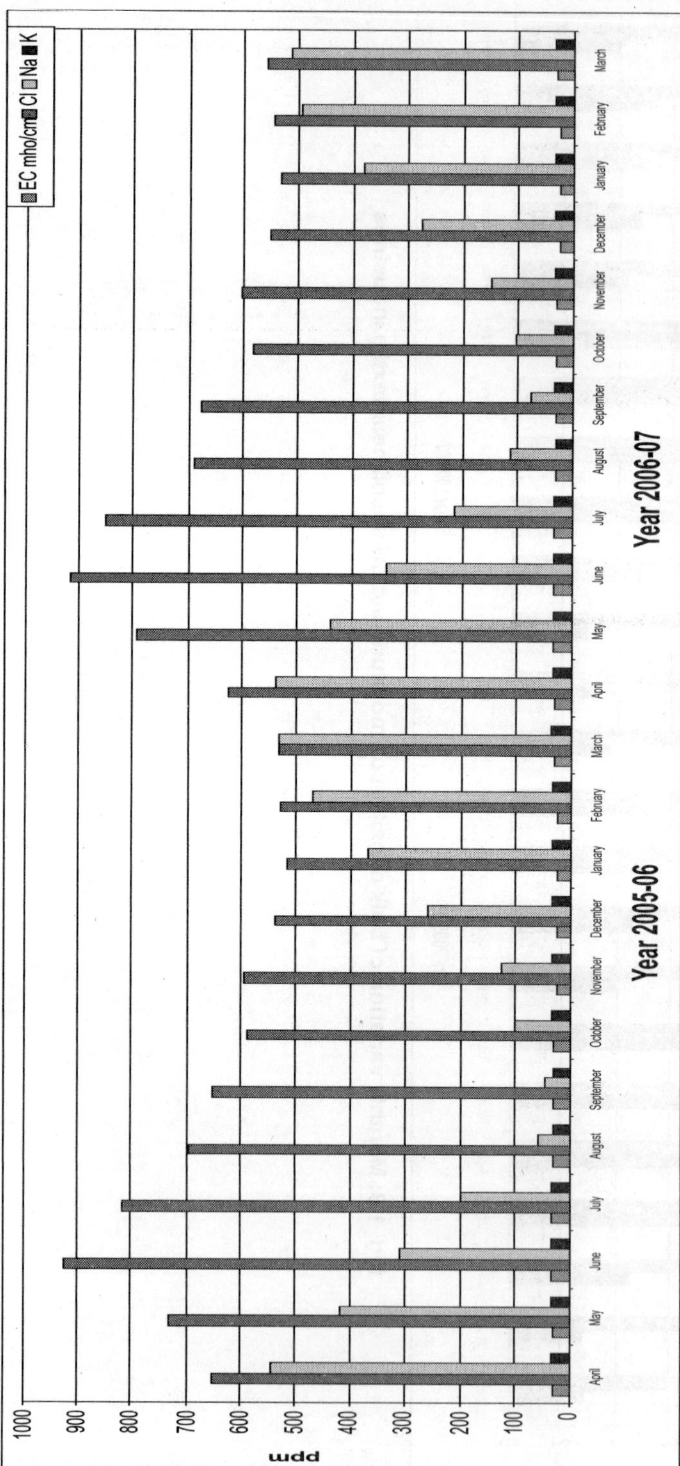

Fig. 1.4: Monthly variation of EC, Chloride, sodium and potassium in soil near textile industries

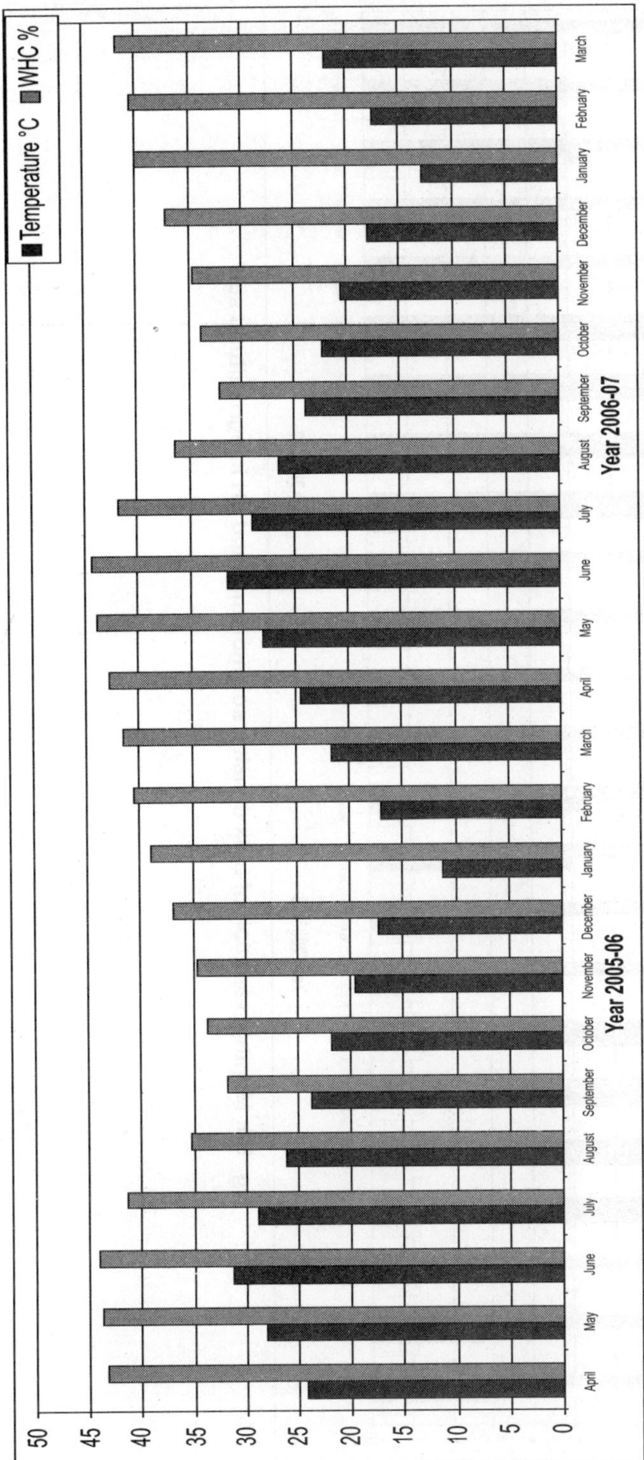

Fig. 1.5: Monthly variation of temperature and WHC in agricultural soil

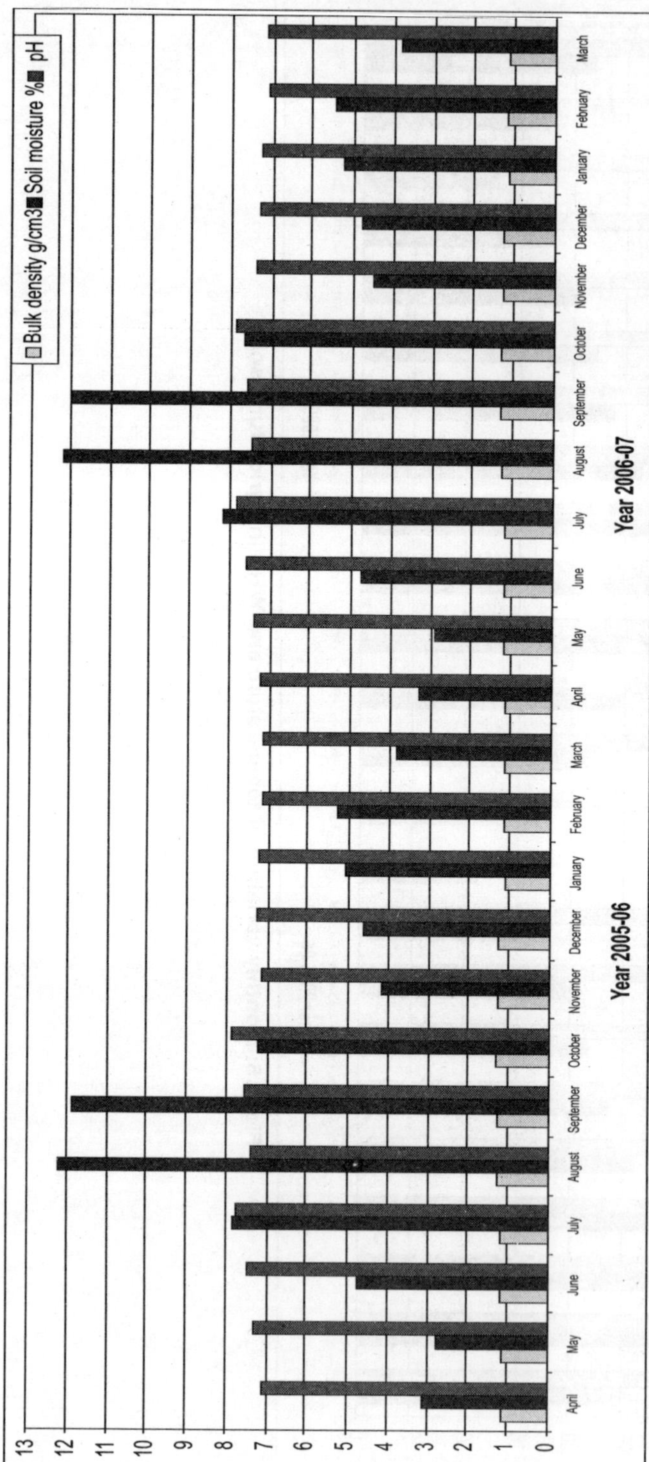

Fig. 1.6: Monthly variation of bulk density, soil moisture and pH in agricultural soil

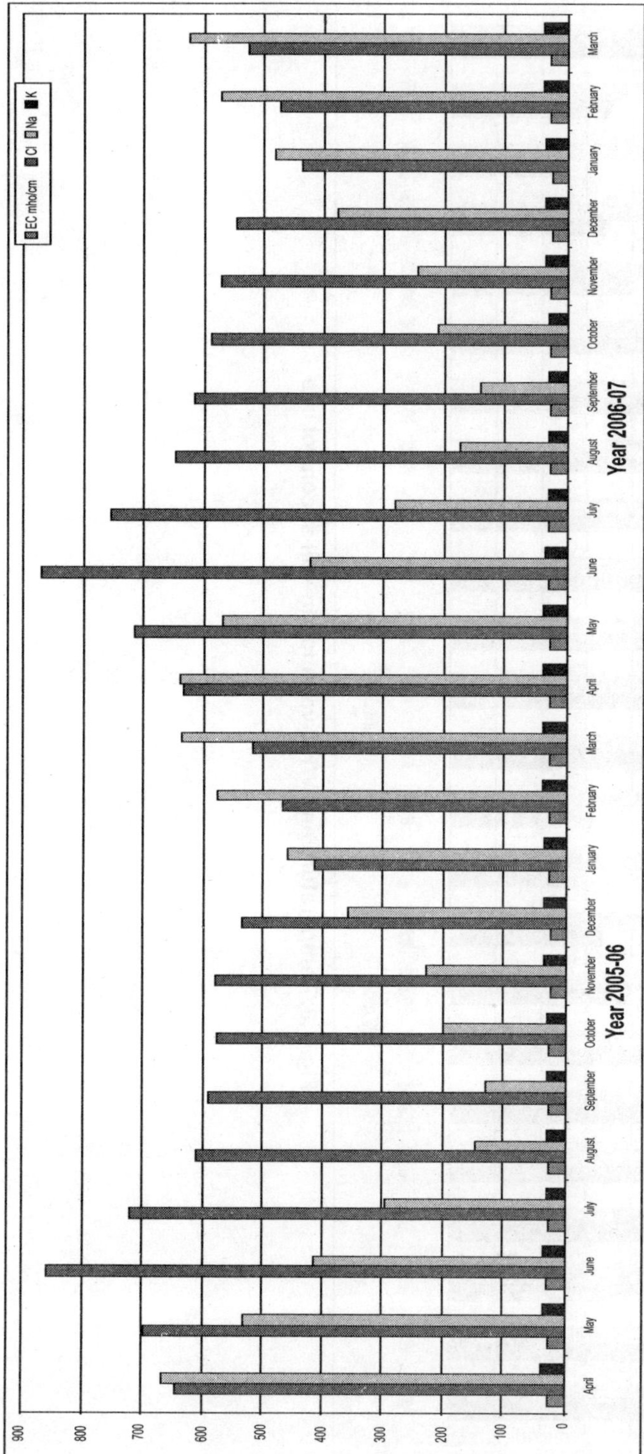

Fig. 1.7: Monthly variation of EC, Chloride, sodium and potassium in agricultural soil

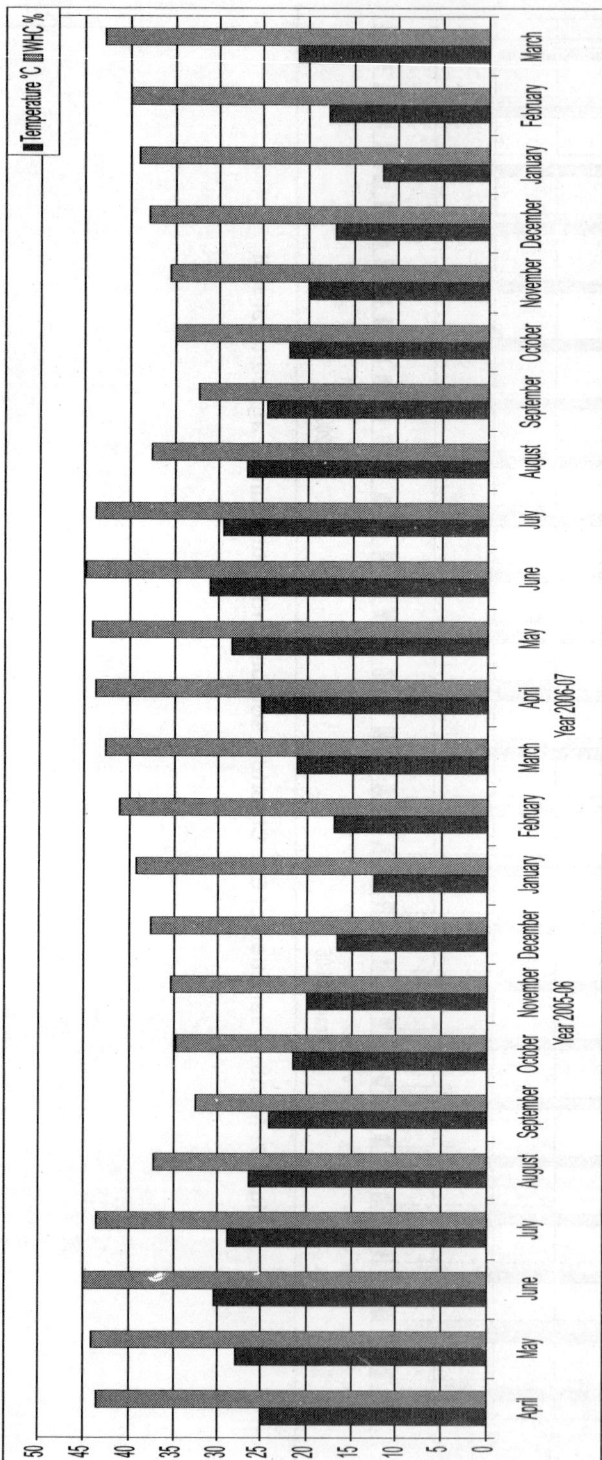

Fig. 1.8: Temperature and WHC variation in soil at control site

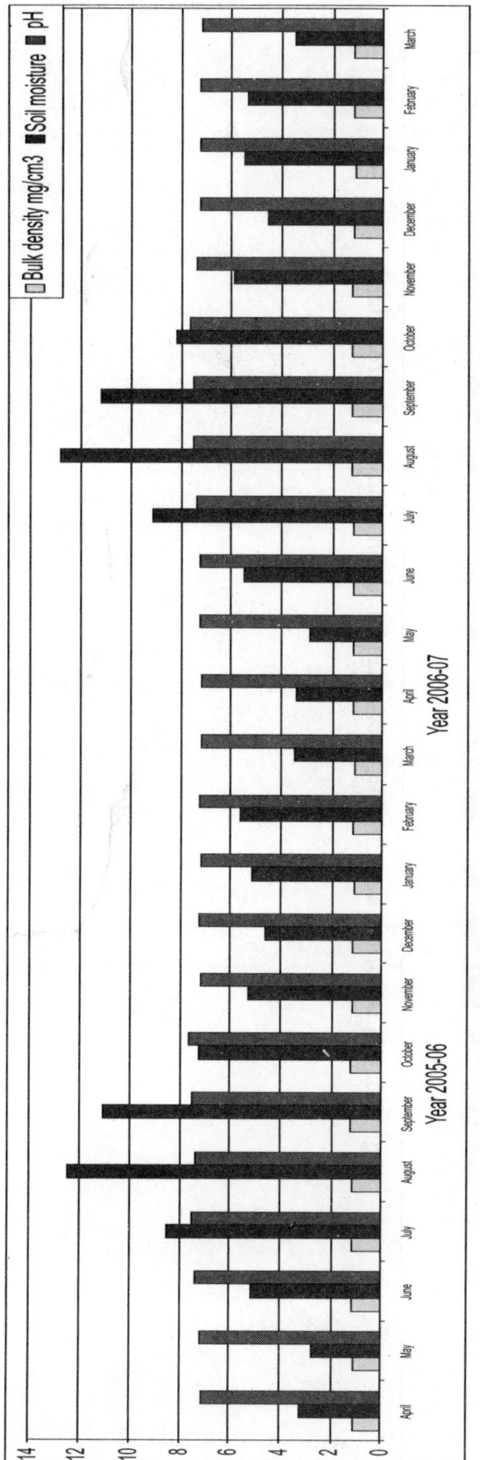

Fig. 1.9: Bulk density, soil moisture and pH variation in soil at control site

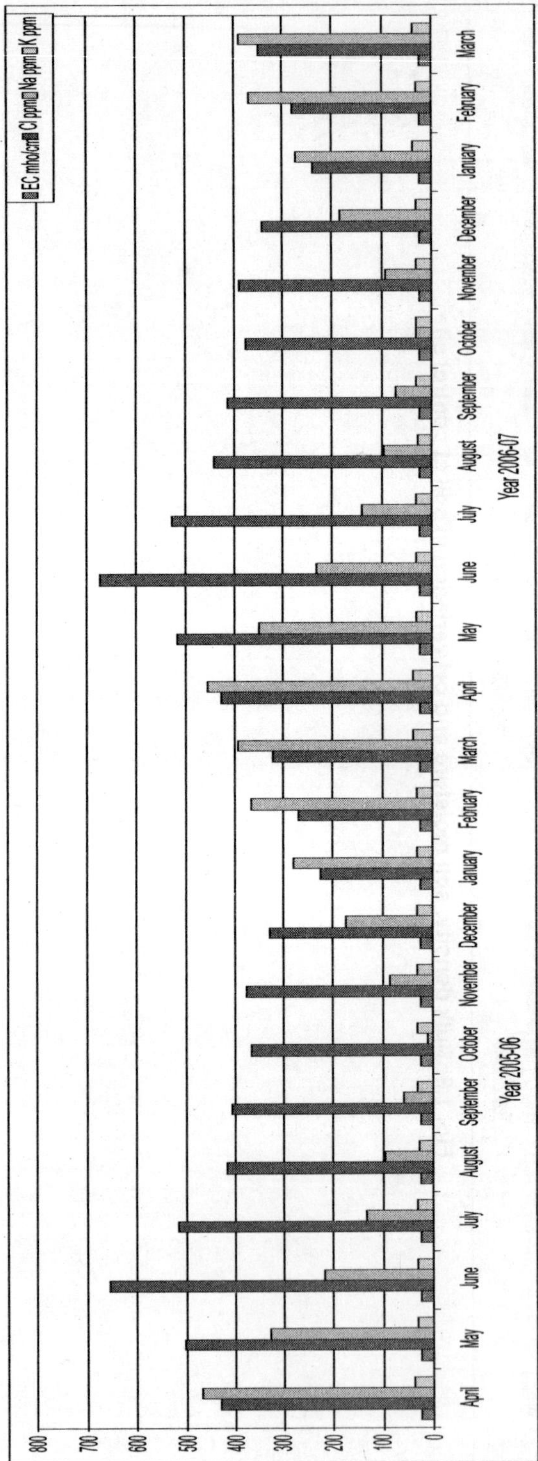

Fig. 1.10: EC, Chloride, sodium and potassium variation in soil at control site

599.0 and 95.33-380.0 μg/g respectively with some minor fluctuations. Sodium has slightly positive correlation with many heavy metals viz. Cd (0.7499) Cu (0.0853), Fe (0.8436), Mn (0.3169), Ni (0.4813), Pb (0.4876) and Zn (-0.4581) in agricultural soil. Similar observations were made by Soltan (1999) and Korfali and Davies (2004) in agricultural soil system. Desalination of soil is usually accomplished by impounding of water at the surface of the alkaline soil. The relationship in between reduction of salts and exchangeable sodium from a given depth of soil and the amount of leaching water for the sandy loam soil (Minhas and Khosla, 1986). The amount of soluble salts in soil can be reduce to safe limits for agriculture crops by leaching (Rao *et al.*, 1987).

Table 1.4: Mean values (±SD) of physico-chemical Characteristics of Soil at Control and Experiment Sites

Parameters	Unit	2005-06				2006-07			
		Control Site	SD	Experimental sites	SD	Control Site	SD	Experimental sites	SD
Temperature	°C	22.625	5.527	22.558	5.707	22.942	5.694	23.042	5.397
WHC	%	39.646	4.205	38.825	4.271	39.645	4.165	39.136	4.169
Bulk density	mg/cm3	1.157	0.066	1.180	0.066	1.179	0.051	1.203	0.059
Soil moisture	%	6.242	3.052	6.054	3.163	6.493	3.179	6.220	3.144
pH		7.321	0.156	7.361	0.262	7.358	0.124	7.428	0.258
EC	mho/cm	23.242	0.380	25.742	1.960	23.392	0.425	26.404	1.976
Cl	μg/g	401.583	116.923	601.667	119.654	413.417	116.613	614.667	121.975
Na	μg/g	217.667	148.153	386.667	189.092	223.833	141.224	395.500	182.030
K	μg/g	32.583	2.193	33.917	2.314	32.917	2.021	34.000	2.335

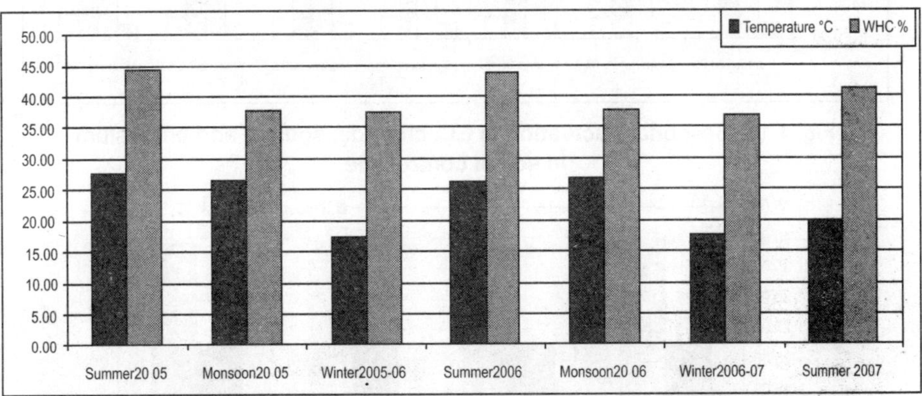

Fig. 1.11: Seasonal fluctuation in temperature and WHC in soil at control site

The effects of water quality parameters on the changes in physico-chemical characteristics of soils and crop productivity have been studied and evaluating the suitability of water for irrigation, however, integration of the interactive and interdependent processes of various water quality indices with soils have required to obtain comprehensive knowledge of the whole system. It

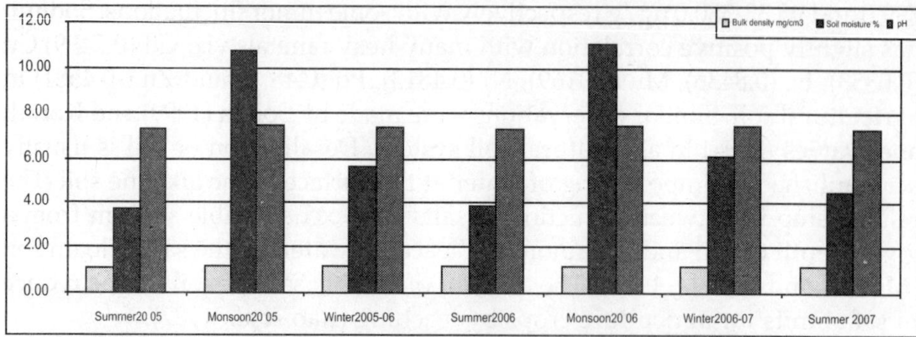

Fig. 1.12: Seasonal fluctuation in bulk density, soil moisture and pH in soil at control site

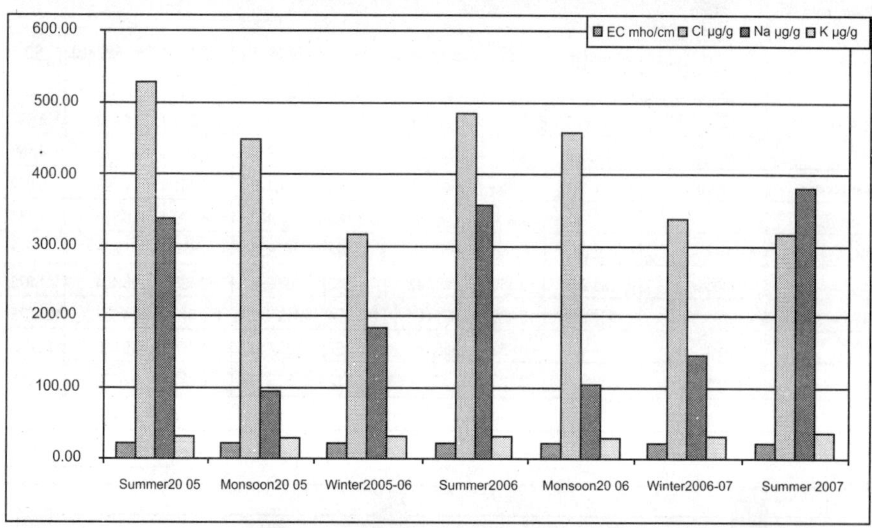

Fig. 1.13: Seasonal fluctuation in EC, chloride, sodium and potassium in soil at control site

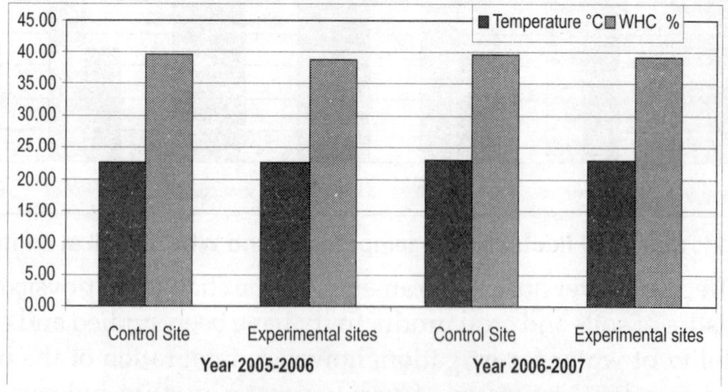

Fig. 1.14: Mean values of temperature and WHC in soil at control and experimental site

requires the development of computerized models for providing a quantitative description of the dynamic behavior of soils upon interaction with irrigation water quality and its relation with crop productivity. Modeling efforts should go a long way in making generalizations based on the experience gained under specific conditions and extrapolation of experimental findings to different locations and seasons in the study area.

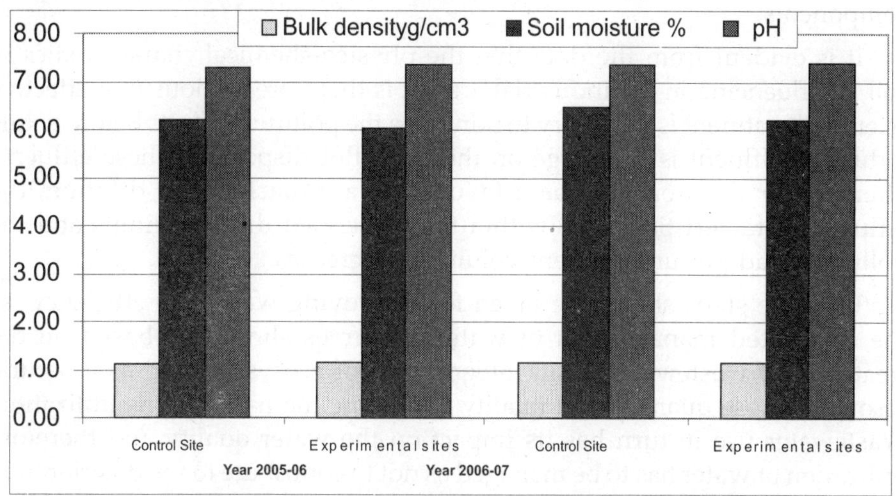

Fig. 1.15: Mean values of bulk density, soil moisture and pH in soil at control and experimental site

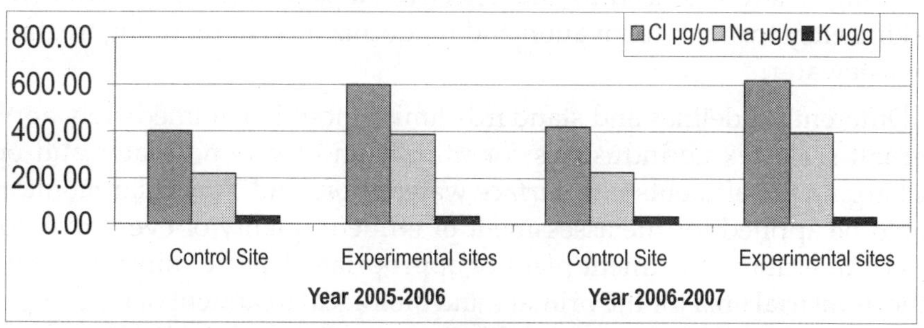

Fig. 1.16: Mean values of EC, chloride, sodium and potassium in soil at control and experimental site

Conclusion

The present study reveals that there was slightly changes in soil quality as compared with control site. The source of pollution is only the textile industries of area. Thus, textile industrial effluents discharging from dye houses contaminated the surface water, drain sediment, pond sediment and ground water also.

Textile industrial effluent or contaminated ground water has been altered the physico-chemical parameters of agricultural soil. It was indicated that the comparison of agricultural soil to control soil that some characteristics were influenced by contaminated irrigated ground water. Few salts in agricultural soil were found slightly higher than control soil. So, some appropriate measures for the amendment and control of textile pollution should be adopted by industrialists, municipality, government, NGOs and local people also at various levels for the protection of environmental components.

It is evident from the data that the physico-chemical characteristics of soil is influencing in the industrial area. It is therefore obvious that effective scientific treatment is necessary to minimize the pollution effects before textile industrial effluent is discharge on the land. But disposal of these effluents after proper dilution may be a favourable approach. After dilution, the effluent characteristics come within the prescribed disposal limits and the pollution load per unit effluent volume is decreases.

Effective steps should be taken for improving water use efficiency, as the integrated management of water resources should be based on the treatment of wastewater as an integral part of ecosystem and as a natural resource whose quantity and quality determine the nature of its utilization. Wastewater use in turn has its impact on the water quality and therefore utilization of water has to be managed as not to contribute to the deterioration of water quality. Secondly, conjunctive use of ground water and surface water resources needs to be planned in the irrigation project from the beginning. There is a need to take effective steps for improving wastewater use efficiency through renovation and modernization of recycling treatments of wastewater.

Different guidelines and standards limits should be immediately applied in small scale textile industries for utilization of ground water and open discharging the effluents into surface water or on land. A regular monitoring should be applied for the assessment of effluent quality of every dye house outlet. An effluent treatment plant of appropriate capacity must be installed in the industrial area for the primary and biological treatment of for composite effluent from textile industries. Unlike most organic pollutants, heavy metals are generally refectory and cannot be degraded or readily detoxified biologically. Hence the safe and effective disposal of wastewater containing heavy metals is always a challenge to industrialists and environmentalists, since cost-effective treatment alternative are not available (Manahan, 1984).

Beside this, water supply of the industrial sector should be managed and regularly analyzed the suitability of drinking water quality. Ground water safety measures are immediately necessary in the industrial region. Restoration of affected agricultural soil is still an environmental aspect for Haryana state. Almost agricultural soils were noticed alkaline already, however, the soil in the industrial area of selected location was not so alkali, but its pH was more than 7. All the above observation and data indicated that the qualities of effluents sometimes do not meet the CPCB, BIS, MINAS and WHO specified norms. The effluents may also cause various health problems among the human being through contaminated ground water supply by municipal tube wells water scheme. In order to achieve the standards it is suggested to install the effluent treatment plants for the treatment of composite effluents of the textile industries.

REFERENCES

Aggarwal, R.R. and Mehrotra, R.R. (1952): Soil survey and soil water in Uttar Pradesh, *Suptd. Printing and Stationery*, Aallahabad, pp: 361-372.

Ajmal, M. and Khan, A.U. (1985): Effects of a textile factory effluent on soil and crop plants, *J. Env. Poll.*, 37(2): 131-137.

APHA (2005): Standard methods for the examination of water and waste water, *American Public Health Association,* 21st edition, 1015, Fifteenth Street, NW, pp: 1170.

Bhargava, G.P.; Singhla, S.K. and Abrol, I.P. (1972): Characteristics of some typical saline sodic soils occurring in Karnal district Haryana state, Report No. 2, Division of soils and agronomy; *CSSRI, Karnal*, pp: 35.

Bharti, P. K. (2012): Groundwater Pollution, *Biotech Books*, Delhi, pp: 243.

Brady, N.C. (1995): The nature and properties of soils, Prentice Hall of India Pvt. Ltd., New Delhi, pp: 621.

CPCB (2003): Ground Water, *Central Pollution Control Board, Parivesh Bhawan,* Delhi, pp: 56.

CPCB (2003): Parivesh: Ground water, *Central Pollution Control Board,* Delhi-32, July, pp: 40.

De, A.K. (2002): Environmental Chemistry, *New Age International (P) Limited Publishers*, pp: 392.

De, A.K. (2005): Adsorption of cadmium and zinc on coal fly ash, *J. Ind. Poll. Control,* 21 (1): 27-30.

Doneen, L.D. (1954): Stalinization of soils of salts in irrigation waters, *Trans. Geophys. Union,* 35: 943-952.

Dowedy, R.H. and Larson, W.E. (1975): The availability of sludge borne metals in various vegetable crops, *J. Env. Qual.*, 4: 278-282.

Eckenfelder, W.W. and Bornad, J.L. (1971): Treatment cost relationship for industrial waste, *Chemical Engg. Progress*, 67(9): 76.

Fakayode, S.O. and Onianwa, P.C. (2002): Heavy metal contamination of soil, and bioaccumulation in Guinea grass (*Panicum maximum*) around Ikeja industrial Estate, Lagos, Nigeria, *Environmental Geology,* 43: 145-150.

Fetter, C.W. (1994): Applied Hydrology, 3rd edition, Macmillan, New York.

Florence, T.M. (1982): The speciation of trace elements in waters, *Talanta*, 29: 345-369.

Forstner, U. (1985): chemical forms and reactivities of metals in sediments in chemical methods for assessing bioavailable metals in sludge and soils, In: Leschber, R., Davies, R.D. and Hermite, L.P. (Eds), *Elsevier, London,* pp: 1-30.

Forstner, U. and Wittman, G.T.W. (1981): Metal pollution in the aquatic environment, second ed. *Springer, Berlin*, pp: 486.

Forstner, U.; Ahlf, W.; Calmano, W.; Kersten, M. and Schoer, J. (1990): Assessment of metal mobility in sludge and soild wastes, In: Metal speciation in the environment (Eds.- Broeckaert, J.A.C; Gucer, S. and Adams, F.) Springer, Berlin, pp: 1-41.

Fransson, Åsa (2007): A case study to verify methods for estimating transmissivity distributions along boreholes, *Hydrogeology Journal*, 15: 307–313,

Fraser, B.G. and Williams, D.D. (1998): Seasonal boundary dynamics of a ground water/ surface-water ecotone, *Ecology*, 79(6): 2019-2031.

Frostner, U., and Wittman, G.T.W. (1979) Metal pollution in the aquatic environment, *Berlin Germany, Springer- Verlag.*, pp: 545.

Gardner, W.R. (1957): Some steady state solutions of the unsaturated moisture flow equation with application to evaporation from a water table, *Soil Sci.*, 85: 228-232.

Garg, V. K; Sharma, I.S. and Bishnoi, M.S. (1998): Fluoride in under ground water of Uklana town, District Hisar, Haryana, *Poll. Res.* 17(2): 149-152.

Garg, V.K. and Kaushik, P. (2006): Influence of short-term irrigation of textile mill wastewater on the growth of chickpea cultivars, *Chemistry and ecology*, 22(3): 193-200.

Garg, V.K. and Kaushik, P. (2006): Influence of short-term irrigation of textile mill wastewater on the growth of chickpea cultivars, *Chemistry and Ecology*, 22(3): 193-200.

Garg, V.K.; Chaudhary, A.; Deepshikha and Dahiya, S. (1998): An appraisal of ground water quality in some villages of district Jind, *Indian J. Environmental Protection*, 19(4): 267-272.

Gharaibeh, M.A.; Eltaif, N.I. and Bayan Al-Abdullah (2007): Impact of Field Application of Treated Wastewater on Hydraulic Properties of Vertisols, *Water Air Soil Pollut*, DOI- 10.1007/s11270-007-9423-z.

Goltenboth, F. (1994): Impact of textile factory in Salatiga on Ledok river system, Central Java, *J. Environ. Toxicol.*, South East Asia, pp: 301-317.

Gomez-Serrano, Garcia-Macias, A., Espinosa-Mansilla, A. and Valenzuela-Calahorro (1998): Adsorption of mercury, cadmium and lead from aquoes solution on heat treated and sulphurized activated carbon. *Wat. Res.,* 32:1-4.

GoogleEarth (2006): Software for satellite imagery, available at http://www.google.com.

Gopal, B. (1994): Conservation of inland water in India: An overview. Verh. Internet. Verein. *Hydrobiologia*, 384: 267.

Govindan, V.S. and Sundarlingam, V.S. (1979) Studies on treatment of textile mill waste water by stabilization pond method. *J. Pollution Control*, 5 (2):137-145.

Gray, C. W. and Mclaren, R. G. (2006): Soil factors affecting heavy metal solubility in some New Zealand soils, *Water, Air and Soil Pollution*, 175: 3-14.

Groff, K.A. (1993): Textile waste. *Environmental Research.* 65: 421.

Gupta, R.K., Singh, R.R. and Abrol, I.P. (1989): Influence of simultaneous changes in sodicity and pH on hydraulic conditions of an alkali soil, *Soil Science,* 147: 28-33.

http//:www.engg.ksu.edu as access on 16 november, 2006

Jayabaskeran, K. J. Sree Ramulu U. S. (1996): Distribution of heavy metals in soil of various sewage farms in Tamil Nadu, *J. Indian Soc. Soil. Sci.*, 44: 401-404.

Jha, M.N. and Pandey, P. (1984): Impact of growing eucalyptus and soil monocultures on soil in natural sal area of Doon valley, *Ind. For.*, 110: 16-18.

Kaushik, M.P. (2006): Vanaspati Vigyan, Prakash Prakashan, Muzaffarnagar, 834.

Korfali, S.I. and Davies, B.D.E. (2004): The relationship of metals in river sediments (Nahr-Krebs, R.; Gupta, S.K.; Furrer, G. and Schulin, R. (1999): Gravel sludge as an immobilizing agent in soils contaminated by heavy metals: A field study, *Water, Air and Soil Pollution*, 115: 465-479.

Kumar, P.; Singh, V. and Bharti, P.K. (2012): Environmental Pollution, In: Environmental Pollution and Biological Diversity, (Eds.- Bharti, P.K., Chauhan, A. and Kumar, P.), *Discovery Publishing House*, Delhi, pp: 1-17.

Malik, D.S. and Bharti, P. K. (2007): Soil quality of irrigated agricultural fields in textile industrial area of Panipat city, *Asian Journal of Experimental sciences*, 21 (2): 445-451.

Malik, D.S.; Bharti, P.K. and Grover, S. (2006): Alteration in surface water quality near textile industries at Panipat (Haryana), *Environment Conservation J.*, 7(2): 65-68.

Manahan, S. (1984): Environmental Chemistry, Brooks/Colei, CA, USA, pp: 638.

Manchanda, H.R. (1990): Significance of the type of salinity for growing pulses under saline conditions, *Indo-Pak workshop on Soil Salinity and Water Management*, Feb, 10-14, pp: 2-3.

Mico, C; Recatal, L.; Peris, M. And Sanchez, J. (2007): A comparison of two digestion methods for the analysis of heavy metals by flame atomic absorption spectroscopy, *Spectroscopy Europe*, 19 (1): 23-26

Millar, C.E. and Turk, L.M. (2002): Fundamentals of soil science, Biotech Books, Delhi-35, pp: 462.

Minhas, P.S. and Gupta, R.K. (1992): Quality of irrigation water – assessment and management, Publication and Information Division, ICAR, *Krishi Anusandhan Bhawan, Pusa, New Delhi*, pp: 123.

Minhas, P.S. and Khosla, B.K. (1986): Solute displacement in a silt loam soil as affected by the method of water application under different evaporation rates, *Agric. Wat. Mgmt*, 12: 63-75.

Nemerow, N.L. (1971): Industrial water pollution: origins, characteristics and treatment, Addision, *Wesley Publishing* Co., pp: 532.

Nightingale, H. I. (1987): *Wat. Res. Bull.*, 23: 663.

Nongkynrih, P.; Dkhar, P.S. and Khathing, D.T. (1996): Micronutrients elements in acid alfisols of Meghalaya under rice cultivation, *J. Soil Si.*, 44(3): 455-457.

Numberg, H.W. (1984): The volumetric approach in trace metal chemistry of natural waters and atmospheric precipitation, *Analyst. Chim. Acta*, 164: 1-21.

Obiri, Samuel (2007): Determination of Heavy Metals in Water from Boreholes in Dumasi in the Wassa West District of Western Region of Republic of Ghana, *Environ Monit Assess*, 130: 455–463

Padmavathiamma, P.K. and Li, L.Y. (2007): Phytoremediation Technology: Hyper-accumulation Metals in Plants, *Water Air Soil Pollut.*, DOI- 10.1007/s11270-007-9401-5.

Palanivelu, K.; Priya, M.N.; Selvan, A.M. and Natesan,U. (2006): Water quality assessment in the tsunami affected coastal areas of Chennai, *Current Science*, 91 (5): 583-584.

Pujari, G.K. and Sinha, B.K. (1999): Studies on the water and soil quality of some villages of Attabira area irrigated by Bargarg main canal originated from Hirakund reservoir of Orissa, *J. of Env. and Poll.*, 6(1): 71-76.

Ramani, K.V. and Srivastava, M.S. (1989): Effect of flyash from thermal power station on soil, *BHEL J.* 10: 1-4.

Rao, K.V.G.K.; Gupta R.K. and Kamra, S.K. (1987): Reclamation of waterlogged high SAR saline soil, CSSRI, Karnal, A feasibility report for *CIRB, Hissar, CSSRI, Karnal*, pp: 21.

Reddy, K.J. and Jianping Lin (2000): Nitrate removal from ground water using catalytic reduction, *Water Res.* 34 (3): 995-1001.

Riohards, L.A. (1954): Diagnosis and improvement of saline and alkali soils, US Deptt. Agri., edited Handbook, No. 60: 160.

Sharma, D.R. and Parihar, S.S. (1973): Effect of depth and salinity of ground water on evaporation and soil salinization, *Indian J. Agric. Sci.*, 43: 582-586.

Sharma, K.P.; Sharma, K.; Bharadwaj, S.M. and Chaturvedi, R.K. (1999): Environmental impact assessment of textile printing industries in Sanagar, Jaipur: A case study. *J. Int. Bot. Soc.* 78: 71-74.

Shrivastava V.S. and Patil B.H. (2003): Metallic and some physico-chemical studies of soil and aquatic sediments, *Eco Env Conserv*, 9(1): 75-77

Sial, R.A.; Chaudhary, M.F.; Abbas, S.T.; Latif, M.I. and Khan, A.G. (2006): Quality of effluent from Hatter Industrial Estate, *Journal Zhejang Univ. Science B*, pp: 974-980

Singh, B. and Bhumbla, D.R. (1968): Effect of quality of irrigation water on soil properties, *J. Res.* (Punjab Agri. Univ.), 5: 166-171.

Singh, K.N.; Bains, S.S. and Dayanand (1969): Salinity problem in high water table areas- An appraisal, *Indian J, Agron.*, 14: 31-34.

Singh, K.S. and Sharma, R.P. (1971): Studies on the effects of saline irrigation waters on physico-chemical properties of some soils of Rajasthan, *J. Indian Soc. Soil Sci.*, 18: 345-356.

Singh, T.B.; Jadon, S.P.S. and Mishra, G.J. (1994): Degradation of water and soil quality of Parwanoo area with respect to heavy metals, *IJEP*, 14 (4): 282-287.

Soltan, M.E. (1999): Evaluation of ground water quality in Dakhla oasis (Egyptian Western Desert), *Environmental Monitoring and Assessment*, 57: 157-168.

Souther, R.H. and Alsapaugh, T.A. (1957): Biological treatment of mixture of textile wastes and domestic sewage. *Textile*, 2 (1): 135-139.

Srinivas, C.; Piska, R.S. and Reddy, R. (2002): Ground water pollution due to the industrial effluents in Kothur industrial area, Mahaboonagar, A.P., *Asian J. Micobiol. Biotech. Env. Sci.*, 4(3): 39-42.

Srinivasan, M. and Murali, M. (1996): Some studies on effect pollutants on properties of soils, *IJEP*, 16(7): 522-523.

Stetzenbach; Klaws, J.; Irene M. Farnham; Vernon F. Hodge and Kevin H. Johannesson (1999): Using multivariate stastical analysis of ground water major cation and trace element concentrations to evaluate ground water flow in a regional aquifer, *Hydrol. Process.* 13: 2655-2673.

Tan, K.H. and Nopamornbodi, O. (1981): Electron microbeam analysis and scanning electron microscopy of soil-root interfaces, *Soil Sci.*, 131: 100-106.

Taylor, S.R. (1964): Abundance of chemical elements in the continental crust – A new table, *Geochim. Cosmochim. Acta.* 28: 1273-1275.

Thorat, P.R. and Pathade, G.R. (2001): Textile waste: Characterization and treatment, In: Environmental Pollution and management of wastewaters by microbial techniques (Eds.- Pathade, G.R. and Goel, P.K.), ABD Publishers, Jaipur, India, pp: 316-325.

Trevors, J.T. and Saier Jr., M.H. (2007): Regulation of Pollution, *Water Air Soil Pollut,* DOI 10.1007/s11270-007-9344-x.

Trivedi, R.K. and Goel, P.K. (1984): Chemical and biological methods for water pollution studies Karad, *Environmental publication,* pp: 1-251.

Va´zquez, N.N.; Gil, M.A.; Esteves, J. L. and Narvarte, M. A. (2007): Monitoring Heavy Metal Pollution in San Antonio Bay, Rý´o Negro, Argentina, *Bull. Environ. Contam. Toxicol.,* DOI 10.1007/s00128-007-9084-z.

Vaidge, A.A. and Datye, K.V. (1982): Environment pollution during chemical processing of synthetic fibers, *Colourage,* 14: 3- 10.

Wainwright, John and Mulligan, Mark (2004): Environmental modeling, *John Wiley & Sons Ltd.* pp: 408.

WHO (2006) Standards for drinking water, available at http//:www.lenntech.com

Widyanto, L.S. (1975): The effect of industrial pollutants on the growth of water hyacinth (Eicchornia crassipes Mart Solm.), In: *Proceedings of the third Indonesian Weed Science Conference,* Bandung, pp: 328.

Wint, A. (1981): The disposal of toxic wastes, In: Industrial Effluent Treatment Vol-I (Eds.- Watler, J.K. and Wint, M.), pp: 1-19.

Yadav, R.K.; Goyal, B.; Sharma, R.K.; Dubey, S.K. and Minhas, P.S. (2002): Post-irrigation impact of domestic sewage effluent on composition of soils, crops and ground water- a case study, *Environment International,* 28: 481-486.

Yu, F-Y; Li, C-W and Kang, S-F. (2005) Color, dye and doc removal, and acid generation during fenton oxidation of dyes, *Environmental Technology,* Vol-26: 537-544.

Yuandong, Z.; Shirong, L. and Jiangming, M. (2006): Water-holding capacity of ground covers and soil in alpine and sub-alpine shrubs in western Sichuan, China, *ACTA Ecologica Sinica,* 26(9): 2775-2782.

2

Elemental Analysis of Archaeological Soil Samples of Khajnawar through Atomic Absorption Spectrophotometer (AAS)

—*Jaibir Singh Pharswan, India*
—*Yogamber Singh Farswan, India*
—*Jagmohan Singh Negi, India*

ABSTRACT

The study was carried out in the soils of excavated site of Khajnawar, District Saharanpur (Uttar Pradesh), India. The aim of present study was to estimate the intensity of occupation in different phases through elemental analysis of soil by using Atomic Absorption Spectrophotometer. Based on the estimated result it has been observed that besides phosphorus (P), other elements like Calcium (Ca), Magnesium (Mg), Sodium (Na), Potassium (K) and Iron (Fe) provided the valuable information to reconstruct the intensity of occupation at the archaeological site during different elements indicated that the occupational activity was rich in the different phases of settlement.

Key words: *Ancient occupation, Excavation, Trace elements, Archaeological, AAS*

Introduction

Apart from the use of phosphate analysis on this broader scale, it was noticed that there are several other major and minor elements like, Sodium (Na), Magnesium (Mg), Manganese (Mn), Barium (Ba), Strontium (Sr), Potassium (K), Iron (Fe), Calcium (Ca), Zinc (Zn) etc., which are significantly useful to infer various aspects of past settlement. To estimate these elements, the method of trace element analysis has become an authentic and applied technique in archaeological science during 1970s. Some studies have been carried out on this discipline by Bradley (1980), Lavy (1980), Stimmell et al., (1984), Eidt (1984), Davies et al., (1988), Linderholm and Lundberg (1994). Later on, it has also been established that human activities, such as building fires, depositing refuse and excrement on the soil and interment of men and animals alter the chemistry of natural soil of a habitation (Arrhenius, 1929, 1931; Treganza and Cook, 1948; Dietz, 1957; Jackson, 1958; Deetz and Dethlefsen, 1963; Black, 1965; Cook and Heizer, 1965) and unavailability of food, ecological conditions and environmental degradation, change the morphology and behaviour of the animal (Bowen and Dymond, 1955; Robinson, 1963; Bang and Baud, 1972; Aitken, 1976; Schoeninger, 1979; Hare,1980; Currey, 1984; Hatch and Geidel, 1983; Toots and Voorhes, 1965; Tuross et al., 1989). These assumptions were concluded with the application of phosphate analysis in the soil and estimation of carbon and nitrogen isotope ratios in faunal remains respectively.

On the basis of earlier work, much could be done in the field of faunal morphological analysis and trace elements in archaeological soils and bones of Indian archaeological sites. Though a lot of work on the potential of the trace element analysis has been done word-wide, but such techniques has not been employed in Indian archaeological context, only a few studies has been carried out on the dynamics of trace elements in soil and bones of Indian archaeological sites (Farswan and Nautiyal, 1997, Farswan et al. 2001; Pharswan and Farswan, 2007,10).

Materials and Methods

Description of the Site

The archaeological site Khajnawar was excavated by department of History and Archaeology, H.N.B. Garhwal University, Srinagar (Uttarakhand), India in 2004. This is located on the left bank of Hindan a tributary of river Yamuna near the village Khujnawar, district Saharanpur, Uttar Pradesh. A large number of potteries, a wall of Kushana period and a coin of medieval period was recovered from the first year excavation. Besides this a large number of animal remains were also recorded. All the collected samples were numbered sequentially using permanent markers, recorded in analytical data book and packed in air-tight polythene bags separately. During sampling, use of necked hands was totally avoided, as it create the favorable condition to change the elemental composition of soil. All the specific features of the archaeological site and modern settlement were also noted for the better understanding of elemental levels in different places and locations. Samples were collected from Khajnawar at site I and II.

Collection and Selection of Soil Samples

Collection and selection of soil samples for the chemical analysis depends on their nature as well as type of study we would like to do. In general historical cultural habitational site a systematic sampling was done vertically and horizontally (Griding method) from each cultural layer, at least a distance of 30 cm gap (Edit, 1973; Nautiyal and Farswan, 1992). Some samples from outer periphery of each type of archaeological site were also collected, as these are helpful in correlating the results of a particular site. Before starting the sampling, a plan of sampling was also drawn, this was used to see the pattern of results obtained at different points and locations.

Determination of Hydrogen Ion Concentration

The hydrogen ion concentration (pH) is determined basically to check the acidity and alkalinity in the soil or state of preservation of archaeological site and artifacts as well. As the higher level of acidity and alkalinity adversely affects the preservation status of archaeological material (Deetz and Dethlefsen, 1963; Heidenreich and Konard, 1973; Eidt, 1977). Therefore, before collecting the samples for present study, soil pH of archaeological site was measured with the help of field pH meter. For the estimation of soil pH a paste of soil sample with distilled water was prepared up to saturation level, this paste is allowed to stand for one hour and the pH of the paste is measured through the pH meter. Soil pH was estimated in each and every location of archaeological settlement considered for the present study and the results obtained are mentioned in Table1.

Pretreatment of Soil Samples and Chemical Analysis

To remove the moisture, all collected soil samples were dried in hot air oven separately (in different vials and crucibles) at least overnight at 100°C. Oven dried samples were grinded mechanically with the help of hand mortar and passed through 2 mm sieves. In every stage of processing (pretreatment and chemical analysis) the soil samples were marked with their respective recorded numbers. All the collected samples were also recorded in laboratory analytical data book.

Estimation of Organic Phosphorus

Phosphorus in the soil is found in different forms i.e. organic, inorganic, available and total phosphorus, but in archaeological view point we only considered the organic phosphorus or anthropogenic phosphorus. To estimate different phosphorus, different techniques are used which are as:

(a) Estimation of Total Phosphorus

0.5 gm of each soil sample was taken in a Kjeldahld flask of 300 ml capacity and the paste of soil was made with the help of one or two drop of distilled water. Then, concentrate perchloric acid ($PClO_4$) and nitric acid (HNO_3) in 1:1 ratio was added in each sample and all the samples were placed into digestion unit (Kjeldahld extraction unit) at 80°C. Digested up to the level of white precipitation and allowed to cool. After cooling, 21 milliliter of dilute Sulphuric acid (H_2SO_4) was added in each flask and heated up to 10 minutes. All the heated samples were filtered through whatman No. 42 filter paper and diluted up to volume of 250 milliliter with the help of deionised (distilled) water. 50 ml of each sample was then taken in to a volumetric flask and 5-6 drops of stannous chloride ($SnCl_2$ $2H_2O$) solution and 2 ml of ammonium molybdate ($(NH_4)_6$ Mo_7O_{24} $4H_2O$) solution was added in every sample. Finally the absorbance or transmittance of blue colour appeared in each sample was measure through Spectrophotometer (Spectronic-20) at 690 nm wavelength. Before analysis, spectrophotometer was calibrated with blank solution (solution of deionised water with addition to stannous chloride and ammonium molybdate solution), and to avoid any error, spectrophotometer was also calibrated after the gap of 10 analyses. Simultaneously the transmittance or optical density of the various dilutions of the standard potassium orthophosphate ($KH_{2-}PO_4$) was also determined as a blue phosphomolybdate complex in sulphuric acid at 690 nm wavelength. The values obtained in milligram per liter were plotted graphically (3 log scale graph) and a standard curve was drawn. With the help of standard curve, concentrations of phosphorus in different soil samples were calculated in milligram per liter or percentage.

(b) Estimation of Available Phosphorus

For the analysis of available fraction of phosphorus, 1 gm of each soil sample was taken into a 250 milliliter conical flask and 200 milliliter of 0.002 N H_2SO_4 was added in each sample and all these samples were placed on a rotary shaker for at least half an hour. After shaking with 0.002 N $H_2SO_{4,}$ all of them were filtered with the help of Whatman 42 filter paper. After that 50 milliliter of each sample was taken into a 50 milliliter capacity volumetric flask, and 2 milliliter of ammonium molybdate solution and 5-6 drops of stannous choloride solution was added in every flask and passed through spectrophotometer (spectronic-20) at 690 nm wavelength and the absorbance or transmittance of each sample was recorded. All the steps of estimation in spectrophotometer were followed according to the methods of estimation of total phosphorus.

(c) Estimation of Organic Phosphorus

The organic fraction of phosphorus was calculated by subtracting the value of available phosphorus from the value of total phosphorus.

Elemental Analysis in Archaeological Soil

All the collected samples considered for the study were oven dried, grinded mechanically and sieved through 2 millimeter screen sieve. After sieving 200 milligram of each sample was taken into polythene vial and 20 milliliter of 1 molar hydrochloric acid was added to each vial. These samples were kept at room temperature (26 degree Celsius) for 21 days (3 weeks) which were agitated regularly everyday. The resulting solution of each sample was filtered and the elemental composition (Ca, Fe, Na, K, Mg and P) of the solution was measured through Atomic Absorption Spectrophotometer (AAS). A reference sample was also run with each set of samples for the verification of data. Concentrations of aforesaid trace elements are recorded in ppm.

Results and Discussion

All the samples were collected from the archaeological site khajnawar (U.P.). A systematic sampling was done vertically and horizontally from each cultural layers by using grinding method as suggested by Nautiyal et al., (1992), Farswan and Nautiyal (1997). The hydrogen ion concentrations (pH) of soils at different locations were measured on the site and in laboratory also. The estimated levels of pH indicated that all the archaeological sites were well preserved because the pH concentration in these sites (Table 1) are ranging in between 5.7 to 7 (slightly acidic to slightly alkaline in nature), which is favourable for the better preservation of archaeological artifacts. As described in introduction that the aims of present study was to reconstruct the intensity of occupation in different cultural phases and locations of ancient settlements of this area, through elemental analysis of anthropogenic soil. It is clarified from earlier studies that phosphorus analysis has become an archaeological tool for locating archaeological sites and intensity of occupation (Proven, 1971; Proudfoot, 1976; Eidt, 1977; Bakkevig, 1980; Conway, 1983; Woods, 1984; Deotare et al., 1988; Deotare, 1990; Nautiyal et al., 1992; Farswan and Nautiyal, 1997). In present investigation we have also estimated the concentration of phosphorus along with other trace elements. For such purpose the technique of spectrophotometer is used, and different fractions of phosphorus (available, total and organic) were estimated for every soil samples considered. The estimated and calculated mean values are mentioned in Table (2 and 3), which indicated interesting pattern of distribution in different locations, i.e. hearth, butchering, cooking, tool making, refuse deposition area, floor area and burial grounds. These results are also verifying the results of earlier studies.

Besides phosphorus, concentration of trace element Calcium (Ca), Iron (Fe), Magnesium (Mg), Sodium (Na), Potassium (K) were also estimated in all the soil samples through Atomic Absorption Spectrophotometer (AAS) and the analytical results recorded in parts per million (ppm) are presented in Tables (2 and 3). It is verified from the analytical results that the concentration of different trace elements such as Calcium (Ca), Magnesium (Mg), Potassium (K), Iron (Fe), and Sodium (Na) estimated from various archaeological anthropogenic soil samples are in accordance to the patterns of phosphorus enrichment, estimated from the same samples. The range of concentration of all these trace elements (Ca, Mg, K, Fe, Na along with P) at various locations (cooking and hearth, refuse deposition area, butchering area, tool making area, floor area and burials areas) of different archaeological sites are significantly higher as compared to the controlled or reference soil samples which are collected from outer periphery of the site (Table 2 and 3). Similar patterns of ubiquity are also seen in other studies made by Heidenreich and Navratil (1973), Heidenreich and Konard (1973) and Konard et al., (1983) in the distribution of Ca, P and Mg at the Robitaille and Munsungun Lake. As they have used these established values of Ca, Mg and P in exploring both internal site patterns and to compare series of sites, and a detailed task of identifying hearths. Linderholm and Lundberg (1994) have also estimated considerably a higher concentration of Fe and P in the feature and dwelling samples as compared to the controlled samples, Farswan et al., (2001) has also carried out a systematic study of elemental analysis of recently excavated Indian Harappan site Dholavira and identified various cultural phases, and locations of the settlement.

Table 2.1: Hydrogen Ion Concentration (pH) of Khajnawar Soil Sample

Location	Site	pH Value of the Soil Sample				
		Layer I	Layer II	Layer III	Layer IV	Layer V
Khajnawar	I	6.3	5.9	5.8	6.5	7.0
	II	6.5	5.7	6.2	6.8	6.7

Table 2.2: Mean values of concentration of different elements in the soil samples of Khajnawar, U.P. from Site I, (E2=100)

Elements	Concentration of elements (in ppm E2)					
	Humus	Layer I	Layer II	Layer III	Layer IV	Natural
Ca	302.10	525.85	491.40	575.28	495.78	310.23
K	18.06	77.67	81.67	73.25	89.89	19.34
Na	16.32	42.12	41.67	45.66	46.75	16.45
Mg	29.50	55.65	60.87	59.56	61.77	31.98
P	15.75	63.35	58.43	60.12	57.77	13.04
Fe	53.05	111.75	109.56	103.09	113.02	58.50

In case of our investigation, though we have estimated the same pattern of distribution of different elements in occupationally rich locations of different settlements. Here generally we have excavated or recovered single phase settlement in every archeological settlement. But the analytical results obtained are significant higher at different culturally occupied locations specially floor levels, hearth areas, garbage areas & cooking areas, which was verified by stratigraphy and recovered archaeological artifacts form every archaeological sites of this region. To refine and strengthen the results, we have established Spearman Rank correlation in between different elements, to see the level of significance of each element. Besides this, in analytical order other elements like, Strontium (Sr), Barium (Zn) and Manganese (Mn) were also analyzed in same archaeological sample but no any remarkable difference in the levels of those elements has been noticed between controlled and archaeological soil samples, therefore, those elements were not included in the present study. Finally we can state that besides traditional technique of phosphorus analysis, estimation of other elements like Mg, Ca, Fe, Na, K and P can be used in locating the activity areas of the ancient occupational settlement and patterns of occupational activities of the archaeological site.

Table 2.3: Mean values of concentration of different elements in the soil samples of Khajnawar, U.P. from Site I (E2=100)

Elements	Concentration of elements (in ppm E2)					
	Humus	Layer I	Layer II	Layer III	Layer IV	Natural
Ca	322.10	520.85	488.45	575.28	493.58	315.23
K	18.06	73.65	82.67	61.42	79.79	15.54
Na	16.30	43.32	40.67	45.56	45.75	15.45
Mg	29.25	58.65	62.87	55.50	60.77	29.98
P	15.75	58.55	64.43	67.22	58.57	15.04
Fe	57.17	109.65	106.50	108.25	109.12	58.25

REFERENCES

Aitkens, J. M. (1976): Factors affecting the distribution of zinc in the human skeleton. Calcified Tissue Research, 20: 23-30.

Arrhenius, O. (1929): Die phosphate method I & II. *Zeitschrift fur Pflanzenernahrung, ungung and Bodenkunde,* Teil A 14: 121-140 & 185-194.

Arrhenius, O. (1931): Markanalysen in Arkeologienstjanst, *Geol. Foren. Forha ndilnger.*

Bakkevig, S. (1980): Phosphate analysis in archaeology, problems and recent progress. Norwegian Archaeological Review, 13(2): 73-100.

Bang, S. and Baud, C. A. (1972): Topographic distribution of sr and its incorporation into bone mineral substance in vivo, Proceedings of Sixth Annual International Conference on X-Ray Optics and Microanalysis (G. Shinoda Ed.), 841-845. University of Tokyo Press.

Black, C. A. (1965): Methods of soil analysis. University of Wisconsin Press, Madison.

Bowen, H. J. M. and Dymond, J. A. (1955): Strontium and barium in plants and soils. Proceedings of the Royal Society of London Series B, 144: 355-368.

Bradley, R. I. (1980): Trace elements in soils around Dyfed, Wales, Geoderma, 24: 17-23.

Conway, J. S. (1983): An investigation of soil phosphorus distri-bution within occupational deposits from a Roman British hut- group. Journal of Archaeological Science, 10: 117-128.

Cook, S. F. and Heizer, R.F. (1965): Studies on the chemical analysis of the archaeological sites. University of California publications in Anthropology, 2: 1-102.

Davies, B. E., Bintliff, J. L., Gaffney, C. F. and Waters, A. T. (1988): Trace metal residues in soil as markers of ancient site occupancy in Greece, in Trace substances in environmental health XXII, (ed. D. D. Hemp Hill,), a symposium, Columbia, MO, pp. 391-398.

Deetz, J. and Dethlefsen, E. (1963): Soil pH as a tool in archaeological interpretation. American Antiquity, 29(2): 242-243.

Deotare, B. C. (1990): Chemical study of anthropic soils from chalcolithic tuljapur garhi. Man and Environment XV, (2): 61-62.

Deotare, B. C., Kshirsagar, A. A. and Gogate, V. D. (1988): The study of soils, bones and pottery, in excavation at inamgaon, Vol. I, Part II, (M. K. Dhawalikar, H. D. Sankalia and Ansari, Z. D. Eds.), Archaeochemistry, pp.963-990.

Dietz, E. F. (1957): Phosphorus accumulation in soil of an Indian habitation site. American Antiquity, 22: 404-409.

Eidt, R. C. (1984): Advances in abandoned settlement analysis: application to prehistoric anthrosols in Colombia. South America. Milwaukee.

Farswan, Y.S. and Nautiyal, V. (1997): Investigation of phosphorus enrichment in the burial of Kumaun (mid-Central) Himalaya, India. Journal of Archaeological Science, 24: 251-258.

Hare, P.E. (1980). Organic Geochemistry of Bone and its Relation to the Survival of Bone in the Natural Environment. *in Fossils in the Making*. Vertebrate Taphonomy and Paleoecology. In Behrensmeye, A.K., and A.P. Hill (eds), *Fossils* in the *Making: Vertebrate Taphonomy* and *Paleoecology*, pp208-219.

Hatch, J. W. and Geidel, R. A. (1983): Tracing status and diet in prehistoric Tennessee. Archaeology, 56-59.

Heidenreich, C. E., Konard, V. A. and Navratil, S. (1973): Soil analysis at the Robitaille site. Ontario Archaeology, 20: 25-62.

Jackson, M. L. (1958): Phosphorus determinations for soils. Soil Chemical Analysis.

Konard, V. A. Robson, Bonnichsen and Vickie Clay, (1983): Soil chemical identification of ten thousands years of prehistoric activity areas at the Munsungun Lake Thoroughfare, Maine. Journal of Archaeological Science, 10: 13-28.

Levy, R. (1980): Sources of soluble calcium and magnesium and their effects on sodium adsorption ratios of solutions in two soils of Israel. Geoderma, 23: 113-123.

Linderholm, J. and Lundberg, E. (1994): Chemical characteri-zation of various archaeological soil samples using main and trace elements determined by I.C.P. Spectroscopy. Journal of Ar-chaeological Science, 21: 303-314.

Nautiyal, V., Farswan, Y.S. and Rawat, J.S. (1992): Phosphorus analysis of soil from archaeological sites in the mid-Central Himalaya and Ganga-Yamuna doab. Man and Environment, XVII(1): 41-50.

Pharswan, Jaibir Singh and Farswan, Yogamber Singh (2007): Phosphorus analysis in soils of central Himalaya. Journal of Meerut University History Alumni, 7:53-68.

Pharswan, Jaibir Singh and Farswan, Yogamber Singh (2010): Methodology and techniques of soil analysis in archaeology. Research Journal of Social Sciences, 2: 15-19.

Proudfoot, N. (1976): The analysis and interpritation of soil phosphorus in archaeologacal contents, in *geoarchaeology* (D. A.Davidson and M. K. Shackley Eds.) pp. 93-113. London: Duckworth.

Provan, D. M. J. (1971): Soil phosphate analysis as a tool in archaeology. Norwegian Archaeological Review, 4: 37-50.

Robinson. J. T. (1963): Adaptive radiation in the australo-pithicus and the origin of man. In: Aferican Ecology and Human Evolution. Howell, F.C. and Bouriers, eds. Aldine Publ. Co., Chicago, pp. 385-416.

Schoeninger, M. J. (1979). Diet and status at chalcatzingo: some impirical and technical aspects of strontium analysis. American Journal of Physical Anthropology, 51: 295-310.

Stimell, C. A., Han Cook, R. G. U. and Dadies, A.M. (1984): Chemical analysis of archaeological soil from Yagi site, Japan. In (J.B. Lambert, Ed.) Archaeological Chemistry-III Advances in Chemistry Series 205. Washington, DC: Chemical Society, pp. 79-96.

Toots, H. and Voorheis, M. R. (1965): Strontium in fossil bones and the reconstruction of food chains. Science, 149: 854-855.

Treganza, A. E. and Cook, S. F. (1948): The quantitative investi-gation of aboriginal sites: complete excavation with physical and archaeological analysis of a single Mound. American Antiquity, 13: 187-197.

Tuross, N., Behrensmeyer, A. K. and Eanes, E. D. (1989): Strontium increases and crystallility changes in taphonomic and archaeological bone. Journal of Archaeological Science, 16: 661-672.

Woods, W. I. (1984): Soil chemical investigation in Illinois archaeology: Two example studies, in Archaeologi-cal Chemistry-III (ed. J. Lambert). American Chemical Society,Washington DC, pp. 67-77

3

Analysis of Soil Quality of Agriculture Land in Haridwar Region

A Case Study

—Avnish Chauhan, India

Introduction

Soil can be defined as the solid material on the Earth's surface that results from the interaction of weathering and biological activity on the parent material or underlying hard rock. The study of soils as naturally occurring phenomena is called pedology (from the Greek word *pedon*, meaning soil or earth).

Pedology takes into account:

- Factors and processes of soil formation
- Soil characteristics
- Distribution of soil types

The importance of soil may be realized from the fact that about 80% of Indian population is directly or indirectly engaged in agriculture practices. In India is under tremendous pressure because of ever increasing of population and the population is more than 1.21 billion. Soils are truly wonderful and are major support systems of human life and welfare and also provide anchorage for roots, hold water long enough for plants to make use of it and hold nutrients that sustain life – otherwise the Earth's landscape would be as barren as Mars. Soils are home to myriad micro-organisms that accomplish a suite of biochemical transformations - from fixing atmospheric nitrogen to the decomposition of organic matter and to armies of microscopic animals as well as the familiar earthworms, ants and termites. In fact, most of the land's biodiversity lives in the soil, not above ground.

In permanent agricultural systems, soil fertility is maintained through applications of manure, other organic materials, inorganic fertilizers, lime and the inclusion of legumes in the cropping systems, or a combination of these. In many parts of the world the availability, use and profitability of inorganic fertilizers have been low whereas there has been intensification of land-use and expansion of crop cultivation to marginal soils. As a result, soil fertility has declined and it is perceived to be widespread, particularly in sub-Saharan Africa including Ethiopia (Pieri1, 1989; Henao and Banante, 1999 and Belachew and Abera, 2010).

"The eternal truth that soil and water are the two basic capitals of humankind and natural forest are the mothers of rivers and the factories for manufacturing soil" stated by Sunder Lal Bahuguna (1987).

Few years ago, *Our Common Future,* the report of the World Commission on Environment and Development, stated: "If human needs are to be met, the Earth's natural resources must be conserved and enhanced. Land use in agriculture and forestry must be based on a scientific assessment of land capacity and the annual depletion of topsoil."

Soils developed from volcanic parent materials such as ash and pumice have unique morphological, physical, and chemical attributes. They are characterized by properties such as low bulk density, high water-retention capacity, an exchange complex dominated by variable charge surfaces, and high anion-retention capacity (Msanya, 2007). The soil is a key component of natural ecosystems because environmental sustainability depends largely on a sustainable soil ecosystem (Adriano et al., 1998). When soil is polluted, the ecosystem is altered and agricultural activities are affected.

Soil Composition

Soil is made up of three main things and these are clay, humus and sand. There are also many small organisms that live in the soil, and most of these are useful to the plants.

Clay

Clay is made from the breakdown and recombination of silicate rocks. It is made up of alternating layers of silicon oxides then aluminium oxides, with various cations such as Ca2+ loosely bound in between the layers. Anions adsorb onto the oxide surfaces, with doubly and triply charged cations sticking better than singly charged ones. Clays are the main source of nutrients in the soil.

Humus

This is any organic matter in the soil—i.e. the products of the decay of plants and animals. It is mostly made up of aromatic compounds. Over time it breaks down to carbon dioxide and water so it needs to be continually replaced. Humus is important in regulating the amount of water in the soil.

Sand

This is solid particles of ground up rock. A small amount of sand is necessary to ensure the correct water content in the soil. Soil pollution is a widely recognized global environmental threat (Makino, 2010).

Result and Discussion

Monthly data on various physico-chemical properties of soil samples collected from polluted and control areas have been presented in the Tables 23-34.

Soil Carbon

Soil carbon is the generic name for carbon held within the soil, primarily in association with its organic content. Soils contain carbon (C) in both organic and inorganic forms. In most soils (with the exception of calcareous soils) the majority of C is held as soil organic carbon. Soil carbon improves the physical properties of soil. It increases the cation exchange capacity (CEC) and water-holding capacity of soil. Carbon, as it relates to the organic matter of soils, is a major component of soil and catchment health. The amount of soil organic carbon depends on soil texture, climate, vegetation and historical and current land use/management. During 2005-06, organic carbon in the soil samples collected from control site ranged between 2.99±0.15% (June) to 3.14±0.12% (April) and 3.22±0.11% (March) to 3.38±0.09% (Nov.) at sites 1 and 3, respectively, whereas at polluted site it ranged between 2.74±0.07% (June) to 2.93±0.08% (April) and 2.88±0.07% (Jan.) to 2.98±0.09% (Oct.) at sites 2 and 4, respectively.

During 2006-07, organic carbon in the soil samples collected from control site ranged between 3.01±0.15% (April) to 3.14±0.17% (Feb.) and 3.21±0.17% (Jan.) to 3.39±0.13% (May) at sites 1 and 3, respectively, whereas at polluted site it ranged between 2.73±0.13% (Feb.) to 2.97±0.09% (July) and 2.87±0.09% (Jan.) to 2.98±0.11% (May) at sites 2 and 4, respectively.

During 2007-08, organic carbon in the soil samples collected from control site ranged between 3.03±0.11% (April) to 3.12±0.12% (Feb.) and 3.27±0.15% (April) to 3.39±0.14% (Dec.) at sites 1 and 3, respectively, whereas at polluted site it ranged between 2.81±0.09% (March) to 2.92±0.11% (Dec.) and 2.90±0.11% (April) to 2.97±0.13% (Jan.) at sites 2 and 4, respectively.

Soil Organic Matter

The term soil organic matter is used to describe the organic constituents in the soil (tissues from dead plants and animals, products produced as these decompose and the soil microbial biomass).The constituents of soil organic matter can be divided into non-humic substances, which are discrete identifiable compounds such as sugars, amino acids and lipids, and humic substances, which are complex largely unidentifiable organic compounds. Organic matter can be considered a pivotal component of the soil because of its role in physical, chemical and biological processes. Many of these functions interact. For example, the high cation exchange (nutrient holding capacity) properties of organic matter are a major means by which organic matter is able to bind soil particles together in a more stable structure. Organic matter does not have an anion (negative) exchange capacity, and is therefore not able to bind anions like phosphate and sulphate. However, organic matter is a substantial reservoir for phosphorus and sulphur, as well as nitrogen. These elements are bound within the organic structure, and are released to the soil solution when microbes break down organic matter. During 2005-06, organic matter in the soil samples collected from control site ranged between 5.16±0.11% (June) to 5.41±0.13% (April) and 5.55±0.12% (March) to 5.83±0.14% (Nov.) at sites 1 and 3, respectively, whereas at polluted site it ranged between 4.73±0.05% (June) to 5.04±0.09% (April) and 4.97±0.09% (Jan.) to 5.13±0.08% (Oct.) at sites 2 and 4, respectively.

During 2006-07, organic matter in the soil samples collected from control site ranged between 5.19±0.16% (April) to 5.42±0.18% (Feb.) and 5.53±0.16% (Jan.) to 5.84±0.13% (May) at sites 1 and 3, respectively, whereas at polluted site it ranged between 4.70±0.13% (Feb.) to 5.12±0.13% (July) and 4.95±0.11% (Jan.) to 5.14±0.07% (May) at sites 2 and 4, respectively.

During 2007-08, organic carbon in the soil samples collected from control site ranged between 5.22±0.17% (April) to 5.38±0.11% (Feb.) and 5.64±0.13% (April) to 5.84±0.13% (Dec.) at sites 1 and 3, respectively, whereas at polluted site it ranged between 4.84±0.08% (March) to 5.03±0.11% (Dec.) and 4.99±0.11% (April) to 5.12±0.08% (Jan.) at sites 2 and 4, respectively.

Soil Nitrogen

Soil nitrogen exists in three general forms - organic nitrogen compounds, ammonium (NH_4^+) ions, and nitrate (NO_3^-) ions. At any given time, 95-99% of the potentially available nitrogen in the soil is in organic forms, either in plant and animal residues, in the relatively stable soil organic matter or in living soil organisms, mainly microbes such as bacteria. This nitrogen is not directly available to plants, but some can be converted to available forms by microorganisms. The majority of plant-available nitrogen is in the inorganic (sometimes called mineral nitrogen) NH_4^+ and NO_3^-forms. Nitrogen content in the soil samples collected from control site ranged between 0.211±0.08% (May) to 0.220±0.04% (April) and 0.229±0.09% (Dec.) to 0.251±0.06% (Nov.) at sites 1 and 3, respectively, whereas at polluted site it ranged between 0.191±0.06% (Nov.) to 0.203±0.06% (Sep.), 0.188±0.05% (May) to 0.207±0.05% (Feb.) at sites 2 and 4, respectively.

During 2006-07, nitrogen in the soil samples collected from control site ranged between 0.210±0.05% (April) to 0.223±0.09% (Nov.) and 0.227±0.06% (June) to 0.253±0.05% (Nov.) at sites 1 and 3, respectively, whereas at polluted site it ranged between 0.210±0.05% (April) to 0.223±0.09% (Nov.) and 0.189±0.04% (May) to 0.209±0.05% (Feb.) at sites 2 and 4, respectively.

During 2007-08, organic carbon in the soil samples collected from control site ranged between 0.217±0.07% (April) to 0.227±0.06% (Jan.) and 0.227±0.07% (Dec.) to 0.237±0.09% (Feb.) at sites 1 and 3, respectively, whereas at polluted site it ranged between 0.189±0.04% (Dec.) to 0.197±0.06% (Feb.) and 0.192±0.04% (April) to 0.197±0.04% (Jan.) at sites 2 and 4, respectively.

Soil pH

pH is a measure of how acidic or basic things are and is measured using a pH scale between 0 to 14, with acidic things having a pH between 0-7 and basic things having a pH from 7 to 14. For instance, lemon juice and battery acid are acidic and fall in the 0-7 range, whereas seawater and bleach are basic (also called "alkaline") and fall in the 7-14 pH range. Pure water is neutral, or 7 on the pH scale. The pH of soil or more precisely the pH of the soil solution is very important because soil solution carries in it nutrients such as Nitrogen (N), Potassium (K), and Phosphorus (P) that plants need in specific amounts to grow, thrive, and fight off diseases. If the pH of the soil solution is increased above 5.5, Nitrogen (in the form of nitrate) is made available to plants. If the soil solution is too acidic plants cannot utilize N, P, K and other nutrients they need. In acidic soils, plants are more likely to take up toxic metals and some plants eventually die of toxicity (poisoning). During 2005-06, pH in the soil samples collected from control site ranged between 7.38±0.23 (Sep.) to 7.53±0.16 (Feb.) and 7.38±0.15 (May) to 7.57±0.20 (Jan.) at sites 1 and 3, respectively, whereas at polluted site it ranged between 7.04±0.11 (Sep.) to 7.21±0.10 (Dec.) and 7.01±0.12 (Nov.) to 7.20±0.11 (Dec.) at sites 2 and 4, respectively.

During 2006-07, pH in the soil samples collected from control site ranged between 7.37±0.23 (Jan.) to 7.58±0.23 (July) and 7.38±0.27 (May) to 7.57±0.29 (Jan.) at sites 1 and 3, respectively, whereas at polluted site it ranged between 7.11±0.17 (Jan.) to 7.22±0.15 (June) and 7.01±0.12 (Nov.) to 7.20±0.19 (Dec.) at sites 2 and 4, respectively.

During 2007-08, pH in the soil samples collected from control site ranged between 7.51±0.14 (Feb.) to 7.59±0.18 (Dec.) and 7.57±0.16 (April) to 7.61±0.15 (Jan.) at sites 1 and 3, respectively, whereas at polluted site it ranged between 7.11±0.14 (Feb.) to 7.16±0.16 (April) and 7.04±0.10 (Dec.) to 7.10±0.18 (March) at sites 2 and 4, respectively.

Available Phosphorus

Phosphorus (P) is an essential element classified as a macronutrient because of the relatively large amounts of P required by plants. Phosphorus is one of the three nutrients generally added to soils in fertilizers. During 2005-06, available phosphorus in the soil samples collected from control site ranged between 0.27±0.07% (March) to 0.37±0.08% (Nov.) and 0.24±0.06% (Nov.) to 0.36±0.08% (Feb.) at sites 1 and 3, respectively, whereas at polluted site it ranged between 0.21±0.03% (March) to 0.30±0.06 (Dec.) and 0.19±0.02% (Aug.) to 0.28±0.09% (Feb.) at sites 2 and 4, respectively.

During 2006-07, available phosphorus in the soil samples collected from control site ranged between 0.28±0.03% (April) to 0.39±0.06% (Jan.) and 0.25±0.06% (Nov.) to 0.38±0.07% (May) at sites 1 and 3, respectively, whereas at polluted site it ranged between 0.20±0.07% (May) to 0.33±0.07% (Dec.) and 0.20±0.06% (Dec.) to 0.29±0.05% (March) at sites 2 and 4, respectively.

During 2007-08, available phosphorus in the soil samples collected from control site ranged between 0.35±0.05% (Jan.) to 0.39±0.09% (Feb.) and 0.30±0.06% (Dec.) to 0.37±0.09% (April) at sites 1 and 3, respectively, whereas at polluted site it ranged between 0.25±0.04 (Jan.)% to 0.28±0.06% (Feb.) and 0.23±0.04% (Dec.) to 0.32±0.06% (April) at sites 2 and 4, respectively.

Potassium

Potassium is an essential element for healthy plant and animal growth. In plants, one of its most important functions is regulation of stomatal opening. This controls the rate of assimilation of carbon dioxide and the rate of transpiration. In animals, potassium helps maintain water balance and regulate neuromuscular activity. Only 0.1 to 0.2 percent of all of the potassium in soil is in soil solution and available for uptake by plants. This potassium is present as K^+ ions, and is in equilibrium with the exchangeable potassium. During 2005-06, potassium in the soil samples collected from control site ranged between 13.52±0.92% (April) to 15.48±1.10% (Dec.) and 16.69±1.21% (Dec.) to 19.57±1.35% (August) at sites 1 and 3, respectively, whereas at polluted site it ranged between 11.74±0.77% (May) to 13.92±1.01% (Dec.) and 13.89±1.08% (Dec.) to 16.67±1.15% (Oct.) at sites 2 and 4, respectively.

During 2006-07, potassium in the soil samples collected from control site ranged between 5.19±0.16% (April) to 5.42±0.18% (Feb.) and 14.79±1.09% (Feb.) to 16.40±1.17% (Nov.) at sites 1 and 3, respectively, whereas at polluted site it ranged between 12.40±0.77% (Aug.) to 13.98±0.94% (May) and 13.19±0.93% (July) to 15.41±1.01% (Dec.) at sites 2 and 4, respectively.

During 2007-08, potassium in the soil samples collected from control site ranged between 15.89±1.01% (Feb.) to 16.81±1.09% (Dec.) and 16.89±1.12% (Dec.) to 17.33±1.20% (March) at sites 1 and 3, respectively, whereas at polluted site it ranged between 13.88±0.89% (Feb.) to 14.47±0.88% (Jan.) and 15.59±1.06% (Dec.) to 15.92±1.03% (March) at sites 2 and 4, respectively.

C:N Ratio

During 2005-06, C:N ratio in the soil samples collected from control site ranged between 13.84±1.13 (June) to 14.50±1.28 (May) and 13.47±1.01 (Dec.) to 14.56±1.09 (May) at sites 1 and 3, respectively, whereas at polluted site it ranged between 14.04±1.05 (June) to 14.82±1.04 (Jan.) and 13.98±0.97 (Feb.) to 15.79±1.20 (May) at sites 2 and 4, respectively.

During 2006-07, C:N ratio in the soil samples collected from control site ranged between 14.79±1.09 (Feb.) to 16.40±1.17 (Nov.) and 13.38±0.83 (Dec.) to 14.74±0.77 (Jan.) at sites 1 and 3, respectively, whereas at polluted site it ranged between 12.40±0.77 (Aug.) to 13.98±0.94 (May) and 14.80±0.93 (April) to 15.87±0.83 (Dec.) at sites 2 and 4, respectively.

During 2007-08, C:N ratio in the soil samples collected from control site ranged between 15.89±1.01 (Feb.) to 16.81±1.09 (Dec.) and 16.89±1.12 (Dec.) to 17.33±1.20 (March) at sites 1 and 3, respectively, whereas at polluted site it ranged between 13.88±0.89 (Feb.) to 14.47±0.88 (Jan.) and 15.59±1.06 (Dec.) to 15.92±1.03 (March) at sites 2 and 4, respectively.

C:P Ratio

During 2005-06, C:P ratio in the soil samples collected from control site ranged between 8.31±0.68 (Nov.) to 11.45±0.48 (March) and 9.07±0.41 (Feb.) to 14.08±0.53 (Nov.) at sites 1 and 3, respectively, whereas at polluted site it ranged between 14.04±1.05 (June) to 14.82±1.04 (Jan.) and 9.22±0.76 (Nov.) to 13.70±0.53 (March) at sites 2 and 4, respectively.

Table 3.1: Monthly mean Values of some Chemical Parameters of Soil Collected from Urban Area during 2005-2006

Months	Parameters											
	Organic Carbon (%)			Organic Matter (%)			Nitrogen (%)			pH		
	Control (Site-1)	Polluted (Site-2)	D%	Control (Site-1)	Polluted (Site-2)	D%	Control (Site-1)	Polluted (Site-2)	D%	Control (Site-1)	Polluted (Site-2)	D%
	2005-2006											
December	3.05± 0.12	2.87± 0.08	5.90	5.26± 0.13	4.96 ±0.11	10.14	0.212± 0.06	0.194± 0.02	8.49	7.46± 0.19	7.21± 0.10	3.35
January	3.11± 0.14	2.92± 0.09	6.12	5.37± 0.08	5.03± 0.07	6.33	0.215± 0.09	0.197± 0.06	8.37	7.42± 0.13	7.20± 0.12	2.96
February	3.13± 0.15	2.91± 0.12	7.03	5.39± 0.11	5.01± 0.09	7.05	0.219± 0.05	0.199± 0.04	9.13	7.53± 0.16	7.17± 0.13	4.78
March	3.09± 0.13	2.88± 0.11	6.80	5.33± 0.09	4.96± 0.03	6.94	0.217± 0.06	0.201± 0.05	7.37	7.50± 0.12	7.14± 0.09	4.80
April	3.14± 0.12	2.93± 0.08	6.69	5.41± 0.09	5.04± 0.09	6.84	0.220± 0.04	0.203± 0.03	7.73	7.49± 0.18	7.11± 0.11	5.07
May	3.06± 0.17	2.89± 0.13	5.56	5.28± 0.07	4.98± 0.04	5.68	0.211± 0.08	0.196± 0.07	7.11	7.52± 0.15	7.13± 0.16	5.19
June	2.99± 0.15	2.74± 0.07	8.36	5.16± 0.11	4.73± 0.05	8.33	0.213± 0.09	0.198± 0.08	7.04	7.47± 0.17	7.10± 0.14	4.95
July	3.03± 0.12	2.83± 0.09	6.60	5.23± 0.06	4.88± 0.03	6.69	0.215± 0.05	0.193± 0.06	10.23	7.42± 0.18	7.09± 0.13	4.45
August	3.05± 0.11	2.86± 0.08	6.23	5.26± 0.09	4.93± 0.05	6.27	0.214± 0.07	0.199± 0.04	7.00	7.39± 0.21	7.07± 0.15	4.33
September	3.06± 0.11	2.89± 0.08	5.55	5.29 ±0.08	4.98± 0.07	5.86	0.217± 0.08	0.203± 0.06	6.45	7.38± 0.23	7.04± 0.11	4.60
October	3.09± 0.09	2.84± 0.11	8.09	5.33± 0.09	4.89± 0.11	8.26	0.220± 0.06	0.200± 0.04	9.09	7.43± 0.17	7.07± 0.13	4.84
November	3.07± 0.12	2.77± 0.13	9.77	5.30± 0.05	4.77± 0.06	10.00	0.213± 0.05	0.191± 0.06	10.33	7.47± 0.15	7.09± 0.11	5.08

During 2006-07, C:P ratio in the soil samples collected from control site ranged between 7.82±0.47 (Sep.) to 11.95±0.53 (March) and 8.70±0.64 (May) to 13.48±0.83 (Nov.) at sites 1 and 3, respectively, whereas at polluted site it ranged between 8.29±0.51 (Dec.) to 13.63±0.78 (May) and 9.86±0.63 (March) to 14.73±0.81 (Oct.) at sites 2 and 4, respectively.

During 2007-08, C:P ratio in the soil samples collected from control site ranged between 7.97±0.66 (April) to 8.81±0.53 (Jan.) and 8.84±0.57 (April) to 11.29±0.56 (Dec.) at sites 1 and 3, respectively, whereas at polluted site it ranged between 10.23±0.76 (Feb.) to 11.60±0.80 (Jan.) and 9.06±0.62 (Dec.) to 12.86±0.63 (Dec.) at sites 2 and 4, respectively.

Table 3.2: Monthly mean Values of Some Chemical Parameters of Soil Collected from Urban Area during 2006-2007

Months	Parameters											
	Organic Carbon (%)			Organic Matter (%)			Nitrogen (%)			pH		
	Control (Site-1)	Polluted (Site-2)	D%	Control (Site-1)	Polluted (Site-2)	D%	Control (Site-1)	Polluted (Site-2)	D%	Control (Site-1)	Polluted (Site-2)	D%
					2006-2007							
December	3.05± 0.13	2.74± 0.11	10.16	5.26± 0.19	4.72± 0.14	9.70	0.211± 0.06	0.189± 0.04	10.4 3	7.41± 0.27	7.12± 0.20	3.91
January	3.09± 0.11	2.76± 0.07	10.68	5.33± 0.16	4.76± 0.11	10.69	0.214± 0.08	0.193± 0.06	9.81	7.37± 0.23	7.11± 0.17	3.53
February	3.14± 0.17	2.73± 0.13	13.05	5.42± 0.18	4.70± 0.13	13.28	0.219± 0.09	0.195± 0.08	10.96	7.47± 0.20	7.13± 0.19	4.82
March	3.07± 0.18	2.94± 0.11	4.23	5.30± 0.13	5.07± 0.18	5.09	0.215± 0.07	0.193± 0.05	10.23	7.49± 0.17	7.15± 0.13	4.54
April	3.01± 0.15	2.74± 0.12	8.97	5.19± 0.16	4.73± 0.13	8.86	0.210± 0.05	0.189± 0.04	10.00	7.53± 0.28	7.20± 0.18	4.38
May	3.02± 0.16	2.73± 0.11	9.60	5.20± 0.11	4.78± 0.09	9.62	0.211± 0.08	0.186± 0.03	11.85	7.51± 0.25	7.19± 0.16	4.26
June	3.03± 0.11	2.96± 0.09	2.31	5.22 ±0.14	5.11± 0.12	2.11	0.213± 0.06	0.189± 0.06	11.27	7.55± 0.20	7.22± 0.15	4.37
July	3.04± 0.12	2.97± 0.09	2.30	5.24± 0.18	5.12± 0.13	2.29	0.212± 0.08	0.193± 0.08	8.96	7.58± 0.23	7.18 ±0.17	5.28
August	3.06± 0.18	2.94± 0.09	3.92	5.28± 0.16	5.07± 0.15	3.98	0.216± 0.09	0.197± 0.07	8.78	7.54± 0.17	7.13 ±0.21	5.44
September	3.05± 0.15	2.92± 0.09	4.26	5.26± 0.12	5.04± 0.12	4.18	0.215± 0.05	0.190± 0.08	11.63	7.51± 0.23	7.12± 0.23	5.19
October	3.08± 0.17	2.94± 0.12	4.55	5.31± 0.11	5.07± 0.16	4.56	0.219± 0.08	0.192± 0.09	12.33	7.56± 0.24	7.11± 0.20	5.95
November	3.10± 0.13	2.92± 0.11	5.81	5.34± 0.15	5.04± 0.15	5.62	0.223± 0.09	0.187± 0.06	16.14	7.57± 0.26	7.14± 0.18	5.68

Table 3.3: Monthly mean values of Some Chemical Parameters of Soil Collected from Urban area during 2007-2008

Months	Parameters											
	Organic Carbon (%)			Organic Matter (%)			Nitrogen (%)			pH		
	Control (Site-1)	Polluted (Site-2)	D%	Control (Site-1)	Polluted (Site-2)	D%	Control (Site-1)	Polluted (Site-2)	D%	Control (Site-1)	Polluted (Site-2)	D%
					2007-08							
December	3.07± 0.12	2.92± 0.11	4.89	5.30± 0.16	5.03± 0.11	5.09	0.225± 0.09	0.189± 0.04	16.00	7.59± 0.18	7.15± 0.11	5.80
January	3.09± 0.14	2.90± 0.13	6.15	5.32± 0.19	5.00± 0.09	6.02	0.227± 0.06	0.193± 0.05	14.98	7.54± 0.17	7.12± 0.13	5.57
February	3.12± 0.12	2.87± 0.11	8.01	5.38± 0.11	4.94± 0.10	8.18	0.223± 0.08	0.197± 0.06	11.66	7.51± 0.14	7.11± 0.14	5.33
March	3.06± 0.13	2.81± 0.09	8.17	5.28± 0.13	4.84± 0.08	9.09	0.220± 0.09	0.195± 0.07	11.36	7.52± 0.13	7.13± 0.18	5.19
April	3.03± 0.11	2.83± 0.08	6.60	5.22± 0.17	4.88± 0.12	6.51	0.217± 0.07	0.193± 0.06	11.06	7.55± 0.18	7.16± 0.16	5.17

Table 3.4: Monthly mean values of some chemical parameters of soil collected from urban area during 2005-2006

Months	Parameters											
	Available Phosphorus (%)			Potassium mg/100 gm (%)			C:N			C:P		
	Control (Site-1)	Polluted (Site-2)	D%	Control (Site-1)	Polluted (Site-2)	D%	Control (Site-1)	Polluted (Site-2)	D%	Control (Site-1)	Polluted (Site-2)	D%
1	2	3	4	5	6	7	8	9	10	11	12	13
					2005-2006							
December	0.34± 0.08	0.30± 0.06	11.76	15.48± 1.10	13.92± 1.01	10.08	14.39± 1.17	14.79± 1.09	2.78	8.96± 0.51	9.59± 0.49	7.03
January	0.31± 0.06	0.28± 0.03	22.58	15.41± 1.03	12.59± 0.86	18.30	14.47± 1.23	14.82± 1.04	2.42	10.05± 0.47	10.42± 0.51	3.68
February	0.29± 0.04	0.25± 0.05	13.79	14.79± 0.89	12.12± 0.89	18.05	14.29± 1.12	14.62± 1.08	2.31	10.78± 0.41	11.62± 0.61	7.79
March	0.27± 0.07	0.21± 0.03	22.22	14.88± 0.88	12.47± 0.77	16.20	14.24± 1.28	14.33± 1.12	0.63	11.45± 0.48	13.70± 0.53	19.65
April	0.30± 0.06	0.23± 0.04	23.33	13.52± 0.92	11.88± 0.81	12.13	14.34± 1.20	14.36± 1.10	0.13	10.46± 0.50	12.71± 0.53	21.51
May	0.32± 0.04	0.27± 0.07	15.63	13.77± 0.90	11.74± 0.77	14.74	14.50± 1.28	14.74± 1.04	1.63	9.57± 0.43	10.70± 0.50	11.08
June	0.35± 0.07	0.26± 0.04	25.71	14.19± 0.84	12.33± 0.71	13.11	13.84± 1.13	14.04± 1.05	1.42	8.55± 0.45	10.55± 0.48	23.39
July	0.33± 0.05	0.23± 0.05	30.30	14.29± 0.89	12.47± 0.69	12.74	14.09± 1.22	14.66± 1.06	4.05	9.19± 0.47	12.30± 0.49	33.84

1	2	3	4	5	6	7	8	9	10	11	12	13
August	0.31± 0.04	0.27± 0.05	22.58	14.88± 0.98	13.88± 0.73	6.72	14.25± 1.25	14.37± 0.97	0.84	9.84± 0.53	10.59± 0.50	7.62
September	0.34± 0.03	0.25± 0.03	26.74	14.97± 1.02	12.98± 0.70	13.29	14.01± 1.30	14.23± 1.23	1.57	9.02± 0.61	11.55± 0.47	28.05
October	0.36± 0.07	0.28± 0.04	22.22	15.31± 0.95	12.47± 0.68	18.55	14.05± 1.09	14.20± 1.31	1.07	8.59± 0.63	10.13± 0.46	18.97
November	0.37± 0.08	0.30± 0.05	18.92	15.39± 0.91	12.89± 0.66	16.24	14.41± 1.03	14.50± 1.27	0.62	8.31± 0.68	9.22± 0.76	10.95

Table 3.5: Monthly mean values of some chemical parameters of soil collected from urban area during 2006-2007

Months	Parameters											
	Available Phosphorus (%)			Potassium mg/100 gm (%)			C:N			C:P		
	Control (Site-1)	Polluted (Site-2)	D%	Control (Site-1)	Polluted (Site-2)	D%	Control (Site-1)	Polluted (Site-2)	D%	Control (Site-1)	Polluted (Site-2)	D%
	2006-2007											
December	0.35± 0.09	0.33± 0.07	5.71	15.59± 1.04	12.93± 0.96	17.06	14.45± 0.96	14.41± 0.90	0.34	8.72± 0.59	8.29± 0.51	4.93
January	0.39± 0.06	0.29± 0.04	25.64	15.51± 1.01	12.97± 0.90	16.38	14.44± 0.99	14.31± 0.91	0.90	7.93± 0.47	9.52± 0.61	20.05
February	0.37± 0.04	0.28± 0.05	24.32	14.79± 1.09	13.40± 0.94	13.88	14.34± 0.94	13.98± 0.88	2.58	8.49± 0.49	9.74± 0.57	14.73
March	0.31± 0.03	0.24± 0.04	22.58	14.88± 1.11	13.58± 0.99	8.74	14.28± 1.02	15.23± 1.12	6.65	11.95± 0.53	12.25± 0.69	2.51
April	0.28± 0.03	0.21± 0.06	25.00	15.19± 1.20	13.55± 0.98	10.79	14.33± 1.01	14.51± 0.98	1.26	10.75± 0.57	13.06± 0.76	21.49
May	0.29± 0.04	0.20± 0.07	31.03	15.26± 1.22	13.98± 0.94	8.03	14.29± 1.02	14.66± 0.90	2.59	10.40± 0.58	13.63± 0.78	31.06
June	0.33± 0.05	0.25± 0.03	24.24	15.37± 1.04	13.78± 0.90	10.34	14.21± 0.96	15.68± 0.88	10.34	9.17± 0.49	11.86± 0.68	29.33
July	0.36± 0.07	0.26± 0.05	27.78	14.89± 1.09	13.50± 0.88	13.98	14.17± 0.90	15.38± 0.86	8.54	8.44± 0.44	11.37± 0.61	34.72
August	0.37± 0.06	0.29± 0.04	21.62	14.77± 1.06	12.40± 0.77	16.05	14.19± 0.92	14.92± 0.90	8.39	8.28± 0.58	10.14± 0.49	22.46
September	0.39± 0.05	0.33± 0.03	15.38	14.80± 1.08	12.83± 0.83	13.31	14.33± 0.88	15.38± 0.91	7.37	7.82± 0.47	8.86± 0.50	13.30
October	0.34± 0.04	0.31± 0.04	8.82	15.55± 1.12	13.40± 0.86	13.83	13.89± 0.80	15.31± 0.96	10.22	9.06± 0.59	9.48± 0.53	4.64
November	0.38± 0.07	0.30± 0.03	21.05	16.40± 1.17	13.89± 0.80	15.30	13.66± 0.77	15.63± 0.93	14.42	8.15± 0.52	9.74± 0.55	19.50

Table 3.6: Monthly mean values of some Chemical Parameters of Soil Collected from Urban Area during 2007-2008

Months	Parameters											
	Available Phosphorus (%)			Potassium mg/100 gm (%)			C:N			C:P		
	Control (Site-1)	Polluted (Site-2)	D%	Control (Site-1)	Polluted (Site-2)	D%	Control (Site-1)	Polluted (Site-2)	D%	Control (Site-1)	Polluted (Site-2)	D%
					2007-2008							
December	0.36± 0.07	0.27± 0.05	25.00	16.81± 1.09	14.12± 1.01	16.00	13.64± 1.01	15.45± 1.12	13.27	8.54± 0.49	10.80± 0.67	26.46
January	0.35± 0.05	0.25± 0.04	28.57	16.47± 1.05	14.47± 0.88	12.14	13.59± 0.96	15.02± 1.04	10.68	8.81± 0.53	11.60± 0.80	31.67
February	0.39± 0.09	0.28± 0.06	28.21	15.89± 1.01	13.88± 0.89	12.65	13.99± 1.04	14.54± 1.17	3.93	8.00± 0.61	10.23± 0.76	27.88
March	0.36± 0.06	0.25± 0.07	27.78	15.96± 0.95	13.93± 0.92	12.72	13.40± 1.02	14.41± 1.01	7.54	8.50± 0.68	10.81± 0.72	27.18
April	0.38± 0.08	0.27± 0.06	28.95	15.98± 0.98	13.96± 0.91	12.64	15.21± 0.98	14.66± 1.03	3.62	7.97± 0.66	10.48± 0.68	31.49

Table 3.7: Monthly mean values of some Chemical Parameters of Soil Collected from Industrial Area during 2005-2006

Months	Parameters											
	Organic Carbon (%)			Organic Matter (%)			Nitrogen (%)			pH		
	Control (Site-3)	Polluted (Site-4)	D%	Control (Site-3)	Polluted (Site-4)	D%	Control (Site-3)	Polluted (Site-4)	D%	Control (Site-1)	Polluted (Site-2)	D%
1	2	3	4	5	6	7	8	9	10	11	12	13
					2005-2006							
December	3.25± 0.09	2.92± 0.09	10.15	5.61± 0.15	5.03± 0.11	10.34	0.229± 0.09	0.199± 0.03	13.10	7.52± 0.23	7.20± 0.11	4.26
January	3.29± 0.13	2.88± 0.07	12.46	5.67± 0.17	4.97± 0.09	12.35	0.231 ±0.11	0.202± 0.07	12.54	7.57± 0.20	7.17± 0.13	5.28
February	3.27± 0.14	2.89± 0.05	11.62	5.63± 0.14	4.99± 0.09	11.37	0.237± 0.09	0.207± 0.05	12.66	7.53± 018	7.14± 0.15	5.18
March	3.22± 0.11	2.92± 0.08	8.07	5.55± 0.12	5.04± 0.12	9.19	0.234± 0.12	0.195± 0.06	16.67	7.47± 0.21	7.19± 0.17	3.75
April	3.32± 0.08	2.96± 0.09	10.84	5.72± 0.11	5.10± 0.10	10.84	0.233± 0.10	0.189± 0.03	15.25	7.41± 0.17	7.15± 0.09	3.51
May	3.37± 0.12	2.97± 0.06	11.88	5.81± 0.15	5.12± 0.06	11.88	0.231± 0.10	0.188± 0.05	18.61	7.38± 0.15	7.19± 0.08	2.57
June	3.31± 0.09	2.92± 0.04	11.78	5.70± 0.13	5.03± 0.09	11.75	0.229± 0.13	0.192± 0.07	16.16	7.39± 0.18	7.09± 0.12	4.06
July	3.27± 0.13	2.94± 0.08	10.09	5.64± 0.12	5.07± 0.07	10.11	0.234± 0.11	0.190± 0.06	18.80	7.42± 0.16	7.05± 0.10	4.99

1	2	3	4	5	6	7	8	9	10	11	12	13
August	3.28± 0.11	2.95± 0.09	10.06	5.65± 0.13	5.09± 0.08	9.91	0.239± 0.06	0.191± 0.08	20.08	7.46± 0.17	7.11± 0.13	4.69
September	3.32± 0.09	2.96± 0.08	10.84	5.73± 0.10	5.11± 0.07	10.82	0.242± 0.09	0.193± 0.06	20.25	7.49± 0.18	7.13± 0.11	4.81
October	3.36± 0.07	2.98± 0.09	11.31	5.79± 0.12	5.13± 0.08	11.40	0.243± 0.08	0.197± 0.09	18.93	7.53± 0.15	7.04± 0.13	6.51
November	3.38± 0.09	2.96± 0.08	12.43	5.83± 0.14	5.10± 0.09	12.52	0.251± 0.06	0.195± 0.08	22.31	7.57± 0.19	7.01± 0.12	7.40

Table 3.8: Monthly mean values of some chemical parameters of soil collected from industrial area during 2006-2007

Months	Parameters											
	Organic Carbon (%)			Organic Matter (%)			Nitrogen (%)			pH		
	Control (Site-3)	Polluted (Site-4)	D%	Control (Site-3)	Polluted (Site-4)	D%	Control (Site-3)	Polluted (Site-4)	D%	Control (Site-1)	Polluted (Site-2)	D%
					2005-2006							
December	3.29± 0.15	2.95± 0.13	10.33	5.67± 0.17	5.09± 0.12	5.09	0.233± 0.08	0.204± 0.06	12.45	7.55± 0.25	7.22± 0.19	4.37
January	3.21± 0.17	2.87± 0.09	10.59	5.53± 0.16	4.95± 0.11	4.95	0.234± 0.06	0.205± 0.04	12.39	7.56± 0.29	7.19± 0.16	4.89
February	3.26± 0.11	2.88± 0.07	11.66	5.62± 0.11	4.97± 0.10	4.97	0.238± 0.04	0.209± 0.05	12.18	7.56± 0.26	7.16± 0.13	5.29
March	3.22± 0.13	2.93± 0.06	9.00	5.55± 0.15	5.05± 0.13	5.05	0.239± 0.07	0.197± 0.07	17.65	7.49± 0.21	7.22± 0.16	3.60
April	3.33± 0.16	2.95± 0.08	11.41	5.74± 0.11	5.09± 0.12	5.09	0.235± 0.05	0.193± 0.06	17.87	7.44± 0.23	7.17± 0.18	3.63
May	3.39± 0.14	2.98± 0.11	12.09	5.84± 0.13	5.14± 0.07	5.14	0.234± 0.08	0.189± 0.04	19.23	7.43± 0.27	7.24± 0.12	2.56
June	3.33± 0.17	2.93± 0.12	12.01	5.74± 0.11	5.05± 0.10	5.05	0.227± 0.06	0.191± 0.03	15.86	7.41± 0.29	7.11± 0.18	4.05
July	3.29± 0.13	2.95± 0.11	10.33	5.67± 0.12	5.09± 0.09	5.09	0.239± 0.07	0.195± 0.03	18.41	7.45± 0.21	7.08± 0.16	4.97
August	3.31± 0.12	2.96± 0.08	10.57	5.71± 0.13	5.10± 0.09	5.10	0.235± 0.08	0.197± 0.05	16.17	7.49± 0.17	7.14± 0.14	4.67
September	3.32± 0.14	2.98± 0.09	10.24	5.72± 0.14	5.14± 0.08	5.14	0.244± 0.06	0.191± 0.06	21.72	7.51± 0.19	7.16± 0.15	4.66
October	3.35± 0.11	2.96± 0.11	8.66	5.78± 0.15	5.10± 0.09	5.10	0.246± 0.07	0.194± 0.04	21.14	7.53± 0.21	7.09± 0.13	5.84
November	3.38± 0.13	2.94± 0.07	13.02	5.83± 0.16	5.07± 0.09	5.07	0.253± 0.05	0.196± 0.06	22.53	7.59± 0.18	7.05± 0.12	7.11

Table 3.9: Monthly mean values of some Chemical Parameters of Soil Collected from Industrial Area during 2007-2008

Months	Parameters											
	Organic Carbon (%)			Organic Matter (%)			Nitrogen (%)			pH		
	Control (Site-3)	Polluted (Site-4)	D%	Control (Site-3)	Polluted (Site-4)	D%	Control (Site-3)	Polluted (Site-4)	D%	Control (Site-3)	Polluted (Site-4)	D%
	2007-2008											
December	3.39± 0.14	2.96± 0.11	12.68	5.84± 0.13	5.10± 0.10	12.67	0.227± 0.07	0.194± 0.05	14.54	7.60± 0.16	7.04± 0.10	7.37
January	3.38± 0.16	2.97± 0.13	12.13	5.82± 0.17	5.12± 0.08	12.03	0.232± 0.09	0.197± 0.04	15.09	7.61± 0.15	7.09± 0.12	6.83
February	3.35± 0.12	2.96± 0.11	11.64	5.77± 0.15	5.10± 0.07	11.61	0.237± 0.09	0.199± 0.06	16.03	7.58± 0.11	7.08± 0.14	6.60
March	3.30± 0.13	2.92± 0.12	11.52	5.69± 0.12	5.03± 0.09	11.59	0.233± 0.07	0.196± 0.05	15.88	7.60± 0.13	7.10± 0.18	6.58
April	3.27± 0.15	2.90± 0.11	11.31	5.64± 0.13	4.99± 0.11	10.85	0.229± 0.08	0.192± 0.04	16.16	7.57± 0.16	7.07± 0.13	6.61

Table 3.10: Monthly mean Values of some Chemical Parameters of Soil Collected from Industrial Area during 2005-2006

Months	Parameters											
	Available Phosphorus (%)			Potassium mg/100 gm (%)			C:N			C:P		
	Control (Site-3)	Polluted (Site-4)	D%	Control (Site-3)	Polluted (Site-4)	D%	Control (Site-3)	Polluted (Site-4)	D%	Control (Site-3)	Polluted (Site-4)	D%
1	2	3	4	5	6	7	8	9	10	11	12	13
	2005-2006											
December	0.31± 0.09	0.27± 0.06	12.90	16.69 1.21	13.89± 1.08	16.78	14.21± 1.08	14.66± 1.01	3.17	10.50± 0.53	10.80± 0.43	2.86
January	0.33± 0.07	0.25± 0.05	24.24	17.14± 1.29	14.18± 1.11	17.27	14.23± 1.01	14.27± 0.98	0.28	9.96± 0.48	11.53± 0.50	15.76
February	0.36± 0.08	0.28± 0.09	22.22	17.58± 1.25	14.29± 1.07	18.71	13.78± 0.98	13.98± 0.97	1.45	9.07± 0.41	10.34± 0.58	14.00
March	0.30± 0.08	0.22± 0.07	26.67	17.92± 1.30	14.53± 1.12	18.92	13.76± 0.96	14.99± 1.08	8.94	10.73± 0.43	13.29± 0.55	23.86
April	0.27± 0.06	0.21± 0.08	22.22	18.13± 1.33	14.98± 1.10	17.37	14.24± 1.07	15.66± 1.12	9.97	12.29± 0.39	14.09± 0.47	14.65
May	0.31± 0.09	0.22± 0.07	25.80	18.00± 1.30	14.81± 1.04	17.72	14.56± 1.09	15.79± 1.20	8.44	10.87± 0.47	12.91± 0.53	18.77
June	0.33± 0.07	0.25± 0.03	24.24	17.89± 1.27	14.90± 1.01	16.71	14.44± 1.06	15.19± 1.03	5.19	10.02± 0.45	11.67± 0.56	16.47
July	0.30± 0.05	0.23± 0.03	26.67	18.72± 1.31	15.17± 1.07	18.96	13.98± 1.01	15.47± 1.09	10.66	10.90± 0.48	12.78± 0.55	17.25

1	2	3	4	5	6	7	8	9	10	11	12	13
August	0.26± 0.04	0.19± 0.02	24.14	19.57± 1.35	16.47± 1.09	15.84	13.71± 1.04	15.46± 1.07	12.76	12.60± 0.58	15.54± 0.61	23.33
September	0.29± 0.06	0.21± 0.06	27.59	19.41± 1.33	16.50± 1.13	20.14	13.73± 1.03	15.36± 1.03	11.87	11.46± 0.56	.14.11± 0.63	23.12
October	0.28± 0.05	0.23± 0.06	17.86	19.47± 1.30	16.67± 1.15	15.68	13.82± 1.06	15.10± 1.02	9.26	11.99± 0.55	12.93± 0.61	7.84
November	0.24± 0.06	0.22± 0.08	8.33	18.79± 1.33	15.58± 1.09	17.08	13.47± 1.01	15.17± 1.01	12.62	14.08± 0.53	14.09± 0.62	0.07

Table 3.11: Monthly mean values of some Chemical Parameters of Soil Collected from Industrial area during 2006-2007

Months	Parameters											
	Available Phosphorus (%)			Potassium mg/100 gm (%)			C:N			C:P		
	Control (Site-3)	Polluted (Site-4)	D%	Control (Site-3)	Polluted (Site-4)	D%	Control (Site-3)	Polluted (Site-4)	D%	Control (Site-3)	Polluted (Site-4)	D%
				2006-2007								
December	0.29± 0.08	0.20± 0.06	31.03	18.41± 1.14	15.41± 1.01	16.03	13.38± 0.83	15.16± 0.95	13.30	11.54± 0.69	14.56± 0.61	26.17
January	0.35± 0.09	0.27± 0.07	22.86	18.58± 1.17	15.32± 0.98	17.55	13.57± 0.87	15.26± 0.98	12.45	9.58± 0.58	10.74± 0.55	12.11
February	0.37± 0.05	0.25± 0.04	32.43	17.40± 1.12	14.79± 0.97	15.00	13.73± 0.81	15.33± 0.91	11.65	8.98± 0.63	11.53± 0.58	28.40
March	0.34± 0.07	0.29± 0.05	14.71	17.58± 1.01	14.82± 0.91	15.70	13.81± 0.84	15.29± 0.86	10.75	9.71± 0.67	9.86± 0.63	1.54
April	0.30± 0.06	0.28± 0.06	6.67	18.70± 1.06	14.50± 0.93	22.46	14.20± 0.88	14.80± 0.93	4.05	10.88± 0.69	10.15± 0.60	6.71
May	0.38± 0.07	0.29± 0.07	23.68	19.70± 1.12	13.59± 0.89	31.02	14.25± 0.80	15.60± 0.98	9.47	8.70± 0.64	10.22± 0.59	17.47
June	0.33± 0.08	0.27± 0.05	18.18	19.50± 1.18	13.88± 0.91	28.82	14.74± 0.77	15.30± 0.86	3.80	10.14± 0.81	10.93± 0.89	7.79
July	0.35± 0.05	0.28± 0.06	20.00	19.12± 1.17	13.19± 0.93	31.01	14.10± 0.79	14.81± 0.78	5.03	9.26± 0.73	10.42± 0.83	12.53
August	0.36± 0.05	0.24± 0.04	33.33	18.88± 1.14	13.28± 0.90	29.66	14.01± 0.72	15.18± 0.79	8.35	9.07± 0.70	12.20± 0.77	34.51
September	0.31± 0.04	0.21± 0.03	32.26	18.72± 1.13	14.22± 0.88	24.04	13.76± 0.71	15.08± 0.77	9.59	10.61± 0.77	14.00± 0.85	31.95
October	0.29± 0.06	0.20± 0.03	31.03	17.90± 1.16	14.80± 0.85	17.32	14.14± 0.78	15.59± 0.79	10.25	11.46± 0.79	14.73± 0.81	28.53
November	0.25± 0.06	0.22± 0.04	12.00	17.39± 1.17	14.88± 0.87	14.43	14.72± 0.81	15.87± 0.83	7.81	13.48± 0.83	13.42± 0.88	0.45

Table 3.12: Monthly mean values of some Chemical Parameters of Soil Collected from Industrial area during 2007-2008

Months	Parameters											
	Available Phosphorus (%)			Potassium mg/100 gm (%)			C:N			C:P		
	Control (Site-3)	Polluted (Site-4)	D%	Control (Site-3)	Polluted (Site-4)	D%	Control (Site-3)	Polluted (Site-4)	D%	Control (Site-3)	Polluted (Site-4)	D%
				2007-2008								
December	0.30± 0.06	0.23± 0.04	23.33	16.89± 1.12	15.59± 1.06	7.70	14.92± 1.11	15.25± 1.19	2.21	11.29± 0.56	12.86± 0.63	13.91
January	0.33± 0.08	0.25± 0.05	24.24	17.12± 1.17	15.67± 1.09	8.47	14.55± 1.08	15.07± 1.21	3.57	10.23± 0.59	11.88± 0.67	16.13
February	0.32± 0.06	0.27± 0.05	15.63	17.29± 1.18	15.89± 1.01	8.10	14.12± 1.07	14.87± 1.17	5.31	10.46± 0.58	10.96± 0.63	4.78
March	0.34± 0.07	0.30± 0.07	11.76	17.33± 1.20	15.92± 1.03	8.14	14.80± 1.09	14.90± 1.18	0.68	9.71± 0.63	9.73± 0.66	0.21
April	0.37± 0.09	0.32± 0.06	13.51	17.30± 1.21	15.90± 1.04	8.09	14.28± 1.12	15.10± 1.22	5.74	8.84± 0.57	9.06± 0.62	2.49

REFERENCES

Adriano, D.C., Chlopecka, A. and Kaplan, K.I. (1998). Role of soil chemistry in soil remediation and ecosystem conservation. Soil Sci. Soc. Am. Spec. Public. Madison,WI. pp. 361-386.

Belachew Taye and Abera Yifru (2010). Assessment of Soil Fertility Status with Depth in Wheat Growing Highlands of Southeast Ethiopia. *World Journal of Agricultural Sciences*, 6 (5), 525-531.

Henao, J. and Baanante, C. (1999). Estimating Rates of Nutrient Depletion in Soils of Agricultural Lands of Africa; IFDC: Muscle Shoals.

Msanya, B.M., Otsuka, H., Araki, S. and Fujitake, N. (2007). Characterization of volcanic ash soils in Southwestern Tanzania: Morphology, physicochemical properties, and classification. *African study monographs*, 34, 39-55.

Pieri, C., (1989). Fertilite´ Des Terres De Savanes; Ministe're De La Cooperation et CIRAD-IRAT: Paris.

Smaling, E.M.A., 1993. An Agro-ecological Framework for Integrated Nutrient Management with Special Reference to Kenya; Agricultural University: Wageningen, pp: 250.

Tomoyuki Makino, Yongming Luo, Longhua Wu, Yasuhiro Sakurai, Yuji Maejima, Ikuko Akahane and Tomohito Arao. Heavy Metal Pollution of Soil and Risk Alleviation Methods Based on Soil Chemistry. *Pedologist (2010) 38-49.*

4

Soil Quality of Himalayan River Basins of Ganga and Song River near Haridwar, India

—Vinay Kumar Daksh, India

Introduction

The Ganga is a holy river of India. Many Indians mainly Hindus worship it like a Goddess. Ganga is also known as Bhagarithi Ganga. Ganga is one of the four mighty rivers of world with its tributaries, and it is a symbol of purity. In India 14 major river system share about 83% of the drainage basin i.e Indian rivers carry about 1,64,5000 m.cm. of water annually (Rao, 1975). There are more than 50 big cities situated along 12,500 km long bank of river Ganga. Glaciers in the Himalayan region melt and the water passes through heavy and porous agent of erosion and transportation carrying some very important soil along with it Ganga along with Brahmaputra account for 3% the total amount of dissolved load to the oceans (Sarin *et al*, 1989).

The present work is aimed towards developing base line data for soil quality of the Song and Ganga river bed and to understand the weathering and geo-chemical processes active in Himalayan river basin.

Soil is one of the most significant ecological factors, which is derived from the transformation of surface rocks. It is noting but soil on which plants depend for their nutrients, water and mineral supply and anchorage. It constitutes an important medium where in numerous animals live. In fact, soil of nation is its most valuable material heritage. Life on earth depends directly on the living soil and the aquatic eco-system of rivers. Without fertile soil and the microbial fauna that inhabit it, food would not grow, dead things would not decay and nutrients would not be recycled. Yet the earth's soil are being stripped away, rendered sterile and contaminated with toxic chemicals at a rate that can not be sustained.

Composition of Soil

The soil consists of four major components, i.e., mineral matter, organic matter, soil air and soil water. All these components can not be separated with much satisfaction because they are present very intimately mixed with each other. The mineral matter forms the bulk of soil solids and a very small amount of the soil solids is occupied by organic matter.

Volumetric composition of mineral (inorganic) soil is.

1. Mineral Matter 45 percent
2. Organic Matter 5 percent
3. Soil Water 25 percent
4. Soil Air 25 percent

Mineral Matter in the Soil

The size and composition of mineral matter in soils are variable because of nature of parent rock from which it has been derived. Some minerals are as large as the smaller rock fragments. Others, such as colloidal clay particles, are so small that they cannot be seen without the help of an electron microscope. Soil is generally composed of very fine broken rock fragments and minerals either dominated by inorganic constituents or dominated by distinct minerals like quartz and feldspars. Quartz and some other primary minerals such as biotite, muscovite etc. have persisted with little change in composition from the original rock. In general , the primary minerals, such as quartz, biotite, muscovite etc. dominate the coarser fraction of soil . Secondary minerals such as silicate clays and hydrous oxide clay or Fe, Al etc. are prominent in the fine minerals, especially in clays. This indicates that properties of the soil are much affected by the mineral particle size.

Almost all soils contain gravel, coarse sand, fine sand, silt and clay, while the final texture and the property of a soil sample is decided by the type of particles which predominate.

The elements are geo-chemically distributed and on the basis of their bonding characteristics, they have been classified in the following 5 main groups.

(*a*) **Lithophile elements**–Those elements which are readily ionised oxyanions. Viz. O, Si , Ti , Fe, Mn, Al, H, Li, Na, K, Rb, Cs, Be, Mg, Ca, Sr, Ba, B, Ga, Ge, Sn, Sc, Y, F, Cl, Br, I, C, Th, P,V, Nb, Ta, Cr, W, A, U, Zr, Mo, Cu, Zn, Pb, Ti, As, Sb, Bi, S, Se, Te, Ni Co and rare earths.

(*b*) **Chalcophile elements**: Those elements which tend to form covalent bonds with sulphide. Examples are S, Se, Te, Fe, Ni, Co, Cu, Zn, Pb, Mo, Ag, Sb, Sn, Cd, In, Ti, As, Bi, Re, Mn, Ga and Ge.

(*c*) **Siderophile elements :** Those elements which are capable of forming metabolic bonds readily. Examples are Fe, Co, Ru, Rh, Td, Ir, Os and Au.

(*d*) **Atomosphile elements:** Those elements which tend to remain in at atmospheric gases, Examples are N, O, He, Ne, Ar, Kr, Xe.

(*e*) **Biophile elements:** Those elements which tend to be associated with living organisms. Are C, H, O, N, P, S, Cl, I, B, Ca, Mg, K, Na, Mn, Fe,Zn Cu, Ag, Mo, Co, Se, Ti, Sn, As and V.

Soil Respiration

The soil respiration is due to roots and other biota. Some of the biota (micro-organism) are actually a part of the root system, hence respiration, because of roots-and other biota can not be distinguished. Soil respiration is probably due to the combined root micro-organism component. The meso-fauna and macro-fauna contribute very little to respiration, although they are important in other respects as they affect the chemical activity of micro-flora.

Process of Soil Formation

Soil formation is started by weathering or disintegration of parent rocks by some physical, chemical or biological agents. As a result of weathering, soil rocks are broken down in small particles, called regoliths, which under the influence of various other pedogenic processes get converted into mature soil.

Thus, **weathering** is an inevitable natural process of breakdown and transformation of rocks and minerals into unconsolidated residues (regolith), lying on the surface of the earth, with varying depths, In other words, the process of transformation of solid rocks into soils is called weathering. Weathering processes are of two types:

(*a*) **Physical weathering**, brought about by the mechanical action of various weathering agents such as temperature, water, wind and biological agencies. This type of weathering is called **disintegration.**

(*b*) **Chemical weathering,** also known as **decomposition**, is the breakdown of rocks by chemical processes like oxidation, reduction, carbonation, hydrolysis etc. Beside these, the **biological weathering** is responsible for both decomposition as well as disintegration of rocks and minerals that are carried out by different biological or living agents like fungi, bacteria, actinomycetes, plants man and animal etc.

Factors Affecting Soil Formation

Joffe (1981) classified the whole sequence of soil formation as follows:

(1) Active Factors: Active factors involved in the soil formation are mainly rainfall, temperature, wind humidity and evaporation.

(2) Passive Factors: These are parent material and topography which influences the aeration, texture and chemical characteristics of the soil.

(3) Biospheric Factors: Living organisms are very important in soil development as they speed up and modify the physico- chemical processes in the soil.

Review of Literature

The organic carbon content was determined by rapid titration method of Walkley and Black, (1934). Sharma *et al.* (1944) worked on flood plain soil of soan river velly and show that the value of pH is ranged between (7-8.3). Piper, (1944) from Adelaide University, Australia worked on soil and plant analysis. He developed the method to analysis total nitrogen organic carbon total soluble salt and cl. Harper, (1945) gave a new method for nitrate determination by calorimetrically. Soil drying prior of flooding enhances mineralization of organic nitrogen. Shioiri *et al.* (1948). Tinsley, (1950) reported organic carbon in soil by dichromate mixture. The inter national pipette method was followed for the estimation of the soil samples. Piper, (1950) and Eschna, (1955) reported the volumetric determination of sulphate in aqueous soil extract sulphate may also be determined by turbidimetric method. As already pointed out, a period of submergence increased the available iron and manganese under flooded condition particularly of a soil that had been under arable farming before found that approximately 6 times as much manganese was extracted from the soil after 30 days of submergence as under air dried condition Rao, (1956).

The most commonly employed methods of determining phosphorous in soil was first introduced by (Cone, 1957) he also gave new calorimetric method of determinate of phosphorous in soil.The observed decrease may be due to the depression of the thickness of the diffuse double layer at higher concentration of soluble salts in the soil Russell,(1961).In most of the soils from shallow, medium and deep ravines, the contents were less than 10 ppm these soils fall in the category of phosphorus deficient soils Datta *et al.* (1963).Submergence tended to shift the soil pH values to near neutral point and, the specific conductance normally increases on submergence of soils. The increase recorded in the present investigation was very low. That submergence lead to more availability of soil phosphorus. The possibility of displacement of cations into soil solution during the period of incubation (Ponnamperuma, 1964).

Total phosphorus was determined by fusion with sodium carbonate available phosphorous by Olsen method available potash by excretion with morgan regent of ravines of yamuna by (Muhr *et al.* 1965).Tamhane and Datta,(1965) have reported similar relationship between soil aggregation and soil constituents in calluvial soil and semi and alluvial soil of Delhi. Ponnamperuma *et al.* (1966) observed that the high zonic strength of soil solution and relation to the value of factor can not necessary. Chhonkar *et al* (1967) worked on phosphate solubilization by fungi associated within legume root nodules.

Sethi and Rao, (1968) worked on solubilization of tri-calcium phosphate and calcium phosphate by soil fungi. Hess, (1970) observed that continuous is the most important and influential factors in production of crop after studying the relation ship between rain fall and crop yields.The role of microbes in soil productivity was studied by Gray *et al.* (1971).Mass balance & Ion-pair stability relation ship in soil were described by Adam,(1971). Ponnamperuma, (1972) observed that on submergences, a number of physical and chemical changes take place in soil which influences the exchange equilibria of an zone of interest.

The cation exchange capacity and exchangeable cations of soil were determined by Jackson, (1973) Grittin and Jurinak, (1973). The high zonic strength soil solution is just related the values of the factor. Morgan *et al.* (1974) reported that the low pH condition in wet land acid soils create condition conductive for Iron and beneficial for plant growth. The absorbed iron, manganese and phosphorus generally increased with period of submergence while potassium decreased after 3 weeks of submergence (Rao and Venkateswarlu, 1974).

Onikura *et al.* (1975) reported the ammonium production in wet land soils was related to total nitrogen content.Gupta *et al.* (1975) reported several microbiological properties certain soils of Himachal Pradesh. Lopez, (1975) reported that in the flooded soil the relation ship between mineralizable nitrogen and soils properties indicate that mineralizable nitrogen is related to organic matter and total nitrogen exchange capacity and clay content. The influences of moisture regime is critical for minaralization of soil nitrogen because the pattern of mineral nitrogen release is effected by soil drying (Shiga and Ventrura, 1976).

Yadav, (1978) studied the effect of soil type, climatic conditions and the rate of application on the persistence of B.H.C. The adsorption increased, abruptly beyond a critical pH range where hydrolysed form of MOH^+ becomes a significant fraction of the concentration of the aqueous metal ion (Jones and Jarvis, 1981). The standard analytical techniques for soil analysis is used by (Page, 1982, kulte, 1986). The threshold pH values were influenced by differences in texture and cation exchange capacity of soils (Sanders and Adams, 1987).

Pasricha, (1987) a close relation ship observed between actual zon strength and specific conduction of equilibrium in submerged soil. Song *et al.* (1988) reported that potassium bearing minerals as influenced by oxalic & citric acid in soil.The information available for soils in Krishna, Godavari and Sarada river. (Subbiah and Manickam, 1986 and 1990). The available nutrients were mostly lost by soil loss and runoff. Contents of the nutrients were minimum in side sample, followed by top samples and maximum in bottom samples with the exception of potassium, the soil are deficient in all the nutrients studied (Chaudhary and Das, 1990).

Sidhu and Bhangu, (1993) observed that water soluble and exchangeable

K in surface and profile samples of selected benchmark soils of Punjab was higher in acidic soils of south western region. The available nutrients bulk density, porosity, water stable aggregates and moisture retention capacity were much better under leucaena based cropping system in indo-gangatic plain. (Hazra, 1994). Sodic soils are deficent in Ca, N, Zn and marginal in Fe. (Swarup, 1995).While studying Cu adsorption in some soils and clays from Bulgaria, observed that the role of organic matter was more important than clay fraction.(Atanassova, 1995).

During the study of variability of soil chemical properties in to the sonel dunal soils, niger they observed the coefficient of variation and number requirement were calculated and semi variograms were constructed in the macro scale the (CVS for exchanged mg 74-114%) were highest exchangeable Ca (31-77%) and available phosphorus (25-55%) also had high CVS on both soils. Attanssova, (1995) reported that the role of organic matter was much more important then the clay fraction in-all types of soil.

Kumar, (1996) nutrient status of soan river valley soils of lower Shivaliks. Mazra *et al.* (1996) reported a simple correlation and multiple regression analysis between amount of Zn disrobed and soil properties and showed significant relationships. Sharma *et al.* (1998) reported that application of leucaena mulch improved moisture status of surface soil of indo-gangetic plains. Raychaudhri, (1998) reported managing soding soil for sustained crop production in Indo-Gangetic plains. Hundal *et al.* (1998) reported that that soil potassium is affect by temperature and back ground anions.

The relationship between the soil water characteristics at 0.03 and 1.5 Mpa tensions and physicochemical characteristics was studied in 108 horizon-wise soil samples collected from 22 representative pedons in Krishna, Godavari and Sarda river command area of Andhra Pradesh. The water retention was lower in surface horizons over sub-surface horizons. The caption exchange capacity, clay, silt and exchangeable Mg and Na had significant positive relationship with the available water content and with the water retained at 0.03 and 1.5 M.pa, while the sand had shown negative correlation with all the three water parameters start (Prasad *et al.* 1998). Gowrisonkar *et al.* (1998) reported Zn fractionation in the soil of Amravati river.A field experiment carried out at Research Farm of Soil Conservation and Water Management, C.S. Azad University of Agriculture and Technology, Kanpur, indicated soil field capacity 20.2%, bulk density 1.4Mg m^{-3}, water holding capacity 29.67% porosity 45.3%, pH 8.0, EC 0.45 dS m^{-1}, organic carbon 0.31%, total N029%, available $P_2O_5$13.42 kg ha^{-1} and available K_2O 156 kg ha^{-1}.(Kanaujia *et al.* 2000).

Vadivelu, (2001) Studied on the pH of flooded soils ranged were between (7-7.5). The Ghaggar flood plain was Physic graphically delineated using tone, texture pattern and such other Image character stick (Giri and

Shyampure, 2001). Pal and Rao, (2001) reported that soil of Indo-Gangetic plain,Bhramputra alluvion and black soils contain biotite and muscovite. Spark, (2001) reported that K becomes fixed because of the binding forces between K and clay surfaces one greater than hydration forces between individuals. K Ions. In soil.

Yasvidner singh *et al.* (2001) reported that effect of soil moisture in a sandy loam soil. Benipal and Pasricha, (2002) investigation no exchangeable K release in facile tating its uptak form 12 alluvial soils of three different agro ecozones of north western Indo-Gangetic plains.

Material and Methods

The material and methods include the following:

(A) Description of sampling sites.

(B) Collection of samples.

(C) Physical parameters.

(D) Chemical parameters.

Description of sampling sites:

During the study samples were collected two sites.

Site-1: Ganga River

Site-2: Song River

Site-1: Ganga River: This site is situated in the Hardwar near the Chandi Devi. Three samples were collected from this site.

(*a*) Ganga River Bank

(*b*) Ganga River Middle

(*c*) Ganga River Middle

Site-2: Songe River: This sites is situated in the Doiwala in Dehradun. Three samples were collected from this site.

(*a*) Song River Bank

(*b*) Song River Middle

(*c*) Song River Middle

Collection of Samples

Soil samples were collected every week during the period February to June (2004). Samples were collected for analytical purpose. A sample has been collected separately from each area which showed some difference in soil colour, texture and others parameters.

During collection of samples, stony cities were avoided; sampling was done after the dry of sample of soil. The surface material is removed by the help of scrubber. Approximately 500gm soil sample were collected from a depin of 15 cm for each site. These soil sample were taken and placed in a polythene bag. The stones and organic matter, like roots and pieces of leaf were removed from the samples. The following is the list of physico chemical parameters for this study.

Physical Parameters

(1) Water Absorbing Capacity

It significant that the tendency of soil of absorbing water depends upon that how much water is absorbed or retained by given amount of soil.

Procedure

Take a keen box and fill soil in it and after than it keen box take in the water for 24 hour for saturation. Now weight of keen box + water = a and after it is taken in oven at 105° C for 24 hour. And weight it = b

Calculation

Water Absorbing Capacity (%) = $a - b/a \times 100$

(2) Bulk Density

The bulk density of soil is defined as the dry weight of a unit volume of it & it is expressed as mg/cm^3 for medium to fine textured soil and from 1.2 to 1.65 mg/cm^3 for coarse textured soil but it is slightly higher in case of alkaline saline soils.

The bulk density is inversely related to pore space of soil.

Procedure

Dry the soil sample in an oven at 105°C until a constant weight is attained. Transfer a little dried soil to a measuring cylinder and not the volume. Record the weight of this volume of soil of an balance.

Calculation

$$\text{Bulk density mg/cm}^3 = \frac{\text{Weight of Soil (mg)}}{\text{Volume of Water (cm}^3\text{)}}$$

(3) Moisture Content

These samples were collected rapidly in the moisture boxes and after weighing allowed to dry in electric oven 105°C for 48 hours. After proper drying sample were weighed again. With the help of recorded value (Excluding wt. of moisture box), content of moisture was determined by using the formula:—

$$\text{Moisture (\%) Content} = \frac{\text{Fresh moisture weight of soil \& oven dry weight of soil}}{\text{Oven dry weight of soil}} \times 100$$

Chemical Parameters

(1) Hydrogen Ion Concentration (pH):

pH of the soil is the measure of the hydrogen Zone activity. It depends extremely on relative amounts of the absorbed hydrogen and metallic Zones.

P^H of the soil suspension highly depends on the soil water ratio and increase with dilution. It is measured on a long scale and equal to negative log 10 of hydrogen Zone concentration.

$pH = - \log [H^+]$

$pH = - \log 10 [1/H^+]$

A neutral soil has a pH of 7.0 while a pH less than 7.0 renders it acidic and pH more than 7.0 alkaline.

Apparatus and Regents

(*a*) THE pH METER: pH was estimated at the sampling site by help of pH strip and than confirmed by pH meter.

(*b*) Potassium hydrogen phthalate buffer: Dissolve 10.2 gm of potassium hydrogen phthalate in water to prepare 1000 ml buffer.

(*c*) Phosphate buffer: Dissolve 3.40 gm of KH_2PO_4 and 4.45 gm of $Na_2HPO_4.2H_2O$ in water to prepare 1000 ml of buffer.

Borax buffer: Dissolve 3.81 gm of $Na_2\ B_4O_7.10\ H_2O$ in water to prepare 1000 ml of buffer.

Procedure

pH is to be determined in 1:2.5 soil suspension. Take 20 gm of soil and 50ml distilled water to it. Stir for about on hour at regular intervals and then filter then pH is determined using pH strip and electrometrically using glass electrode pH meter.

Expression of result: Result are expressed directly in pH units associated with the specific dilution suspension.

(2) Electrical Conductivity: E.C. gives a clear idea of soluble salts present in soil. E.C. is measure of the current carrying capacity.

Conductivity values depend on the dilution of soil suspension.

Apparatus: Conductivity meter, thermometer, glassware to prepare soil suspension conductors depend on the area of the metallic electrodes and distance between them. The factor used to convert the observed conductance into conductivity is called as the cell constant is the ratio of the specific conductance and observed conductance and can be calculated by finding out the conductance of different cone of KCl solution.

Procedure

1:2.5 soil suspension by taking 20 gm of soil in 50ml distilled water shake it for one hour.

Measure the conductivity of the soil suspension with conductivity meter by directly dipping the all into the suspension.

Take temperature of the soil suspension and take result at 25°C.

Calculation

Conductivity = observed conductance X Cell constant X Temp. (at 25°C)

(3) Total Nitrogen [Kjeldahl Method]

Apparatus and Reagent–

1. 0.1N H_2SO_4 (Cons. H_2SO_4 2.8 mg/L)
2. 40 % NaOH (about 2 kg in 5 liter water)
3. 0.1 N NaOH (4 gm. A.R. grade NaOH/L)
4. 0.1 N oxalic acid.
5. Methyl red indicator 0.5% (0.5 gm ®100ml alcohal)
6. Phenolphthalein indicator
7. Mixture of sodium sulphate ($Na2SO_4$ + $FeSO_4$ + $CuSO_4$) (500 + 100 + 50 gm) (5 : 1 : 0.5)

Standardized of chemical (NaOH and H_2 SO_4):

Procedure (For standardized) (N/10 NaOH):

N/10 oxalic acid in burette

10 ml N/10 NaOH in 150 ml conical flask.

Add 15-20 ml D.W and 1-2 drop methyl red indicator- titration – colour less.

Procedure (For standardized) (N/10 H_2SO_4) .

N/10 H_2SO_4 burette.

N/10 NaOH 10 ml in 150 ml conical flask.

Add 1-2 drop phenolphthalein pink colour will be appear.

Procedure:

1. Take 10 gm soil sample (oven dry) in 500 ml kjeldahl flask.
2. Add 5 gm salt mixture and 35 ml con. $H_2SO_{4/}$sample.
3. Digestion about 2 hour-brown and white colour of soil sample. Completely digested (after cool).

Distillation process

1. Washing 3 times (300 to 350 ml digest material).
2. Add 150-200ml 40% NaOH/sample.
3. Add 10 ml N/10 H_2SO_4 in 500 ml conical flask.
4. Add 150-200 ml D.W. and 1-2 drops methyl red indicator in conical flask.
5. Heating on distillation plant 25-30 minutes.
6. Check the ammonia by the help litmus paper if red litmus becomes blue (Digestion incomplete)

Titration

N/10 NaOH in burette (titration) end point colour will be changed pink to colourless.

Formula:

$V_1 = A - B$

$R = C - V_1$

Total Nitrogen (%) = $R \times F$

A = End point reading in burrate

B = Starting point reading in burrate

R = Valance reading

F = Factor (0.14)

(4) Available Phosphorous:

Extracting Reagent:

0.5 molar sodium bicarbonate, (pH 8.5) prepare by dissolving 42 gm. $NaHCO_3$ in distilled water to give one litter of the solution the pH is adjusted to 8.5 with 10% NaOH.

Extraction:

1. Take 2 gm soil in 100 ml conical flask and add charcoal (Phosphorous Free) and add 50 ml (Extracting reagant).
2. Blank is to run with out soil shake is on platform shaker for 30 minutes and filtered immediately by what man no. 42.

Reagent:

1. 12 gm of ammonium molybedate is dissolved in 250 ml. of D.W. In 100 ml of D.W. a solution of 0.291 gm of antimony potassium titrate in prepared separately.
2. Both these solution are added to 1000 ml of approx. 5N H_2SO_4 (140ml H_2SO_4 in 1 litter)and mixed thoroughly. Made to two litters with distilled water)
3. 1% para-nitrophenol indicator (1gm dissolved in 100 ml) volume make up in distilled water.
4. Ascorbic acid solution: Dissolved (1.056 gm of ascorbic acid in 200 ml of reagent (*i*) mixed well this should be prepared as when required. (Ascorbic acid 0.528 gm- 100ml reagent—(*i*) sample required.

Procedure

Take 10 ml filtrate in 50 ml volumetric flask and acidified with 1 : 4 ratio H_2SO_{4-} adjusted (pH 5). This can be done by adding 1-2 drops of para-nitrophenol indicator yellow colour will appear when dissolving this by adding 1:4 $H_{-2-}SO\text{-}_{4-}$ drop by drop. On adjustment of pH. It is approx diluted to 20 ml of add 4 ml (reagent ii) the volume is made to 25 ml and shake well. After waiting for 10 minutes blue colour will appear by the help of colorimeter at 690 nm. reading.

Calculation:

$$\text{A.V.P. (ppm)} = \frac{\text{Volume of Olsen solution}}{\text{Weight of Soil}} \times \frac{(\text{Volume of extract} + \text{Volume of D.W.})}{\text{Volume of extract}} \times \frac{R}{F}$$

$$= \frac{40}{2} \times \frac{(10+40)}{10} \times \frac{R}{F} = 100 \times \frac{R}{F}$$

100 = Dilution

R = Reading

F = Factor

Standard Curve

100 ppm stock solution of phosphorus dissolved KH_2PO_4 (0.439 gm is dissolved in ½ liter of distilled water. 25 ml of 7 N. H_2SO_{-4} (approx.) is add and made to 1 liter with distilled water from this a 2 ppm (phosphorus) solution is made (50 time dilution).

For preparation of standard curve different concentration of phosphorus (1, 2, 3, 4, 5 and 10 ml of 2 ppm solution) is taken in 25 ml of 0.5 $NaHCO_3$ extracting reagent is add and colour is developed with the above procedure.

Standard Curve of available Phosphorus

100 ppm stock solution by (KH_2PO_4) working solution 2 ppm

ppm	ml in pipette	Volume	Reading-Blank	Final Reading
0.00	50	0.00	37 (B.R)	
0.04	50	1ml	52-37=15	15/0.04=375
0.06	50	1.5	60-37=23	23/0.06=383
0.08	50	2	67-37=30	30/0.08=375
0.10	50	2.5	78-37=41	41/0.10=410
0.12	50	3	88-37=51	51/0.12=425
0.16	50	4	109-37=72	72/0.16=450
0.24	50	6	131-37=94	94/0.24=392
				Total = 2810

Factor = 2810/7 = 401.4

(5) Available Potassium

Instruments: Flame Photometer, direct reading type and glass electrode pH meter.

Regents

Neutral normal ammonium acetate: Solution of 2N acetic acid and 2 N ammonium hydroxide are prepared (By titration with standard alkali and acid) and equal volumes of the two are mixed in a large beaker and on colling the pH addyut 7.0 with acitic acid or ammonia.

Potassium chloride solution: A stock solution of 1000mg K/ml is made by dissolving 1.908 of A.R. grade potassium chloride (dried at 60°C for 1hour) in distilled water and making up the volume 1 litter.

Procedure:

1. 5g of soil is taken with 25 ml of neutral normal ammonium acetate (pH 7) for 5 minutes shake and filtered immediately through a dry filter paper.
2. First few ml of the filtrate may be rejected potassium concentration in the extract is determined in the flame photo meter after and calibration of instrument.
3. Prepare one blank sample:

Stander curve of potassium: From the stock solution, measured extract on diluted in 100 ppm stock solution with the ammonium acetate solution to give 2 to 10 of K. After attaching the appropriate filter and adjusting the gas and air pressure (as per direction given in the operation manual) the flame photometer reading is set at Zero for the blank. (ammonium acetate) and at 100 ppm.

The curve is obtained by plotting the readings against the different concentration (0, 2, 4, 6, 8, 10 ppm) of potassium any fluctuation in gas and air pressure does not allow steady reading the meter and must be taken care of.

Preparation of 100 ppm stock solution of potassium

ppm	Vol	ml (in pipette)	Reading
0	50ml	0	0
2	50ml	1	20
4	50ml	2	40
6	50ml	3	60
8	50ml	4	80
10	50ml	5	100

Calculation:

$$\text{A.V.K. (ppm)} = \frac{\text{Volume of N ammonium acetate}}{\text{Weight of soil}} \times \frac{\text{(Extract + D.W.)}}{\text{Extract}} \times \frac{\text{R}}{\text{F}}$$

$$= \frac{25}{5} \times \frac{10+30}{10} \times \frac{R}{F(10)}$$

AV.K (ppm) = R X 2

(6) Organic Carbon (Walkley and Black method)

Principle

The organic matter present in the soil is digested with excess of potassium dichromate and sulphuric acid, and the residual unutilized dichromate is then titrated with ferrous ammonium sulphate.

The elementary carbon present as graphite, charcoal, etc, is not attacked in this method and only organic carbon is determined.

Reagents

1. **Potassium dichromate solution 1N:** Dissolve 49.04 g of $K_2Cr_2O_7$ in distilled water to prepare 1 litre of solutions.
2. Sulphuric acid
3. Phosphoric acid
4. **Ferrous ammonium sulphate 0.4 N:** Dissolve 156.86 g Fe $(NH_4)_2$ (SO_4) in distilled water, adding 14 ml conc.
5. H_2SO_4 to prepare 1 litre of solution.
6. **Diphenylamine indicator:** Dissolve with care 0.5gm diphenylamine in a mixture of 20 ml distilled water and 100 ml conc. Sulphuric acid.

Procedure .

1. Take oven dried or freeze dried soil sample and pass through a 0.5 mm non ferrous screen.
2. Weight a suitable quantity of soil not exceeding 10 g (containing about 10-25 mg carbon) and transfer to a dried 500 ml conical flask.
3. Add 10 ml 1 N $K_2Cr_2O_7$ solution and 20 ml conc. H_2SO_4 and mix by gentle swirling.
4. Keep the flask to react the mixture for about 30 minutes.
5. After the reaction is over, dilute the contents with 200 ml of distilled water and add 10 ml phosphoric acid followed by 1 ml of diphenylamine indicator.
6. Titrate the sample with 0.4 N ferrous ammonium suplhate; at the end point colour changes to brilliant green.
7. Run a blank with same quantity of the chemical but without soil.

Calculation:

(*a*) $\%C = \frac{3.951}{g}\left(1 - \frac{T}{S}\right)$

(*b*) % Organic Carbon = %C × 1.724

Where: g = Weight of sample in gm.

S = ml ferrous solution with blank titration.

T = ml ferrous solution with sample titration.

The factor 1.724 is based on the assumption that carbon is only 58% of the organic carbon.

(7 & 8) Carbonates and Bicarbonates

Like water, total alkalinity, soluble carbonates and bicarbonates can be determined by the direct titration of the soil solution with a strong acid HCl or (H_2SO_4) using methyl orange and phenolphthalein as indicators.

Reagents

All the reagents needed for determination of total alkalinity, carbonates and bicarbonates in water.

Procedure

1. Prepare 1:5 sail solution as described in determination of soil chloride.
2. Determine total alkalinity, carbonates and bicarbonates in 100 ml of soil solution.

Calculation:

$$(a)\ \text{Carbonate \%} = \frac{V_1 \times N \text{ of } HCl \times 1000 \times 60}{\text{ml soil solution} \times 2000} = V_1 \times 0.03$$

$$(b)\ \text{Bicarbonate \%} = \frac{(V_2 - V_1) \times N \text{ of } HCl \times 1000 \times 61}{0.0305}$$

$$= (V_2 - V_1) \times \text{ml soil solution} \times 2000$$

Where V_1 = Volume of HCl used for phenolphthalein end point.

V_2 = Additional volume of HCl used from phenolphthalein end point to methyl orange end point.

To convert the values in mg/100 g for carbonates and bicarbonates, multiply the results in % by 1000.

(9) Copper: (Lindsay and Norvell 1969, 1978) Instrument—(AAS)

Reagents:

DTPA (Die-ethylene-tri-amine penta acetic acid) .005m solution.

TEA (Tri-ethanol amine). 1 m (A R)

Preparation of DTPA

The extracting reagent is prepared by taking of DTPA and 1.470 g $Cacl_2 \cdot 2H_2O$ in beaker. To this 20 to 25 ml of double distilled water is added and 13.3 ml of TEA followed by 100 ml of double distilled water. This is transferred to 1 liter volumetric flask with 3-4 washing and the volume made up to mark with water. The pH of the solution is adjusted to 7.3 with dil HCl.

Procedure

Take 10 gm of soil in 100 ml conical flask, 20 ml of DTPA regent is added and shaken for 2 hours. The extract is filtered (what man No- 40/42) Cu estimated with the help of AAS.

Standard curve for copper

A stock solution of 1000 ppm Cu is obtained by dissolving exactly one gram of the pure (A.R) metal (wire) in 50 ml of dilute (1:1) HNO_3 and finally diluting to 1000 ml with double glens distilled water from working solutions (0.25, 0.5, 1.5, 2.0, 2.5) and 3 ppm are prepared by dilution in 100 ml volumetric flask.

Results

The soil chemistry influences the distribution of organisms. For example earthworms prefer soil rich in humus, whether the soil is acidic or alkaline makes little difference to them. Land snails are found in the soil, which is rich in calcium salts that are required for their shells. The composition of the soils concern the geochemistry of that portion of the mantle of the earth currently exposed to the atmosphere and have under gone change by the influence of biotic factors.

The results obtained with mean values (±SE) for various Physico-chemical parameters of the soil samples viz moisture content, water absorbing capacity, bulk density, pH, electrical conductivity, bicarbonates, carbonates, available phosphorus, potassium, organic carbon, total nitrogen and copper from two sites are summarized in (Table 4.1) and have been depicted diagrammatically (Fig. 4.1 to 4.11). All the observation and estimation were made during the month of February to June 2004.

Table 4.1: Physical Properties of Collected Soil Samples

Parameters	Site I (Ganga River)			Site-II (Song River)		
	Bank	Middle	Middle	Bank	Middle	Middle
Water absorbing capacity (%)	44.24	22.12	22.99	32.38	24.48	21.96
Bulk density (mg/cm³)	1.16	1.2	1.26	1.141	1.22	1.23
Moisture Content (%)	21.14	13.12	14.39	18.27	14.77	13.42

Table 4.2: Chemical Properties of Collected Soil Samples

Parameters	Site-I (Ganga River)			Site-II (Song River)		
	Bank	Middle	Middle	Bank	Middle	Middle
pH (1:2.5)	7.83	8.47	8.59	7.97	8.5	8.34
Electrical conductivity (dSm-1)	0.406	0.116	0.093	0.203	0.126	0.11
Total Nitrogen (%)	0.0294	0.0154	0.0098	0.056	0.028	0.0418
Available phosphorous (ppm)	6.234	5.985	6.982	11.221	4.987	7.231
Available potassium (ppm)	58	32	32	48	34	32
Organic carbon (%)	0.1838	0.0188	0.0255	0.3863	0.0555	0.0614

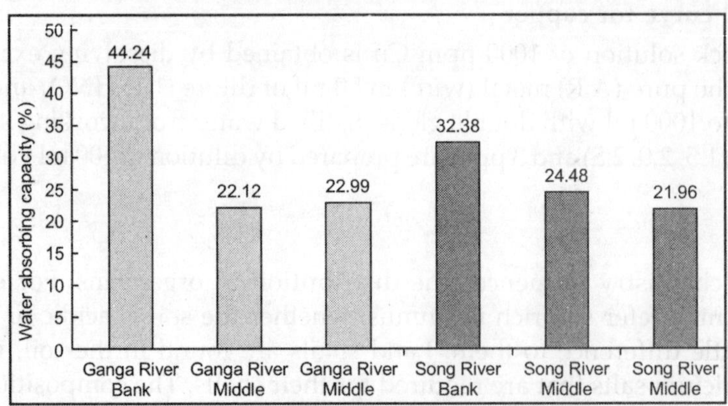

Fig. 4.1: Graph showing mean values of water absorbing capacity of soil at site I & II

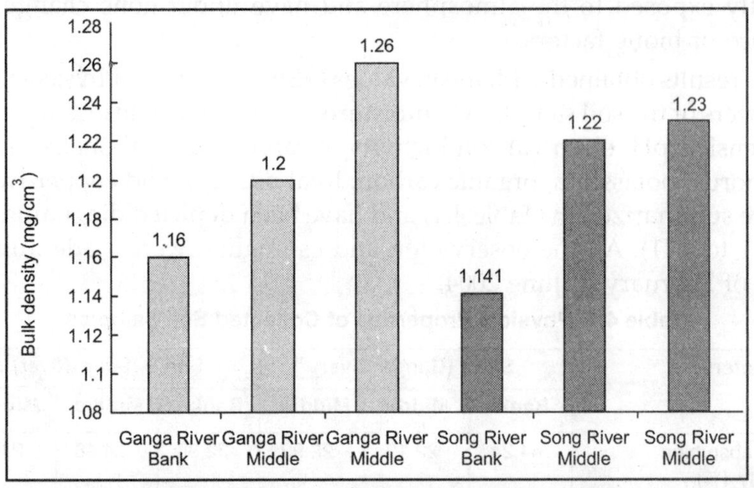

Fig. 4.2: Graph showing mean values of bulk density of soil at site I & II

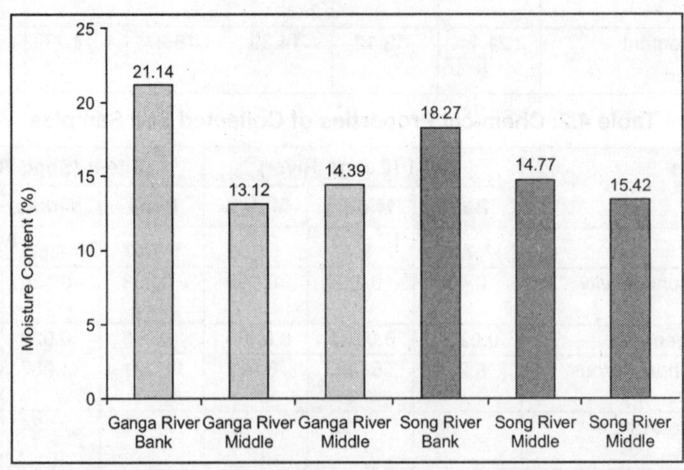

Fig. 4.3: Graph showing mean values of moisture content of soil at site I & II

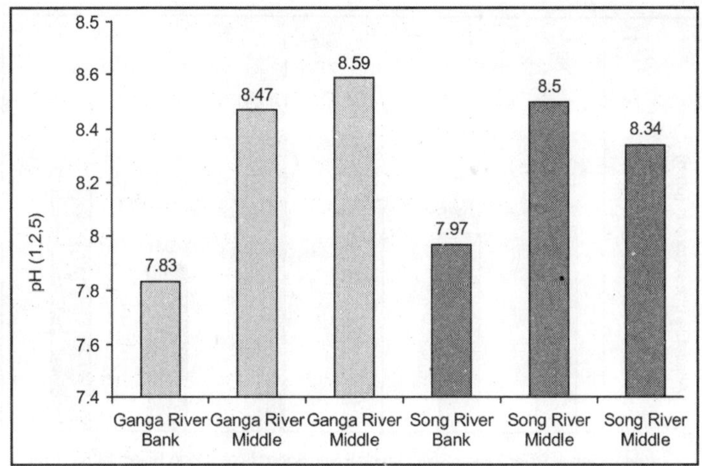

Fig. 4.4: Graph showing mean values of pH of soil at site I & II

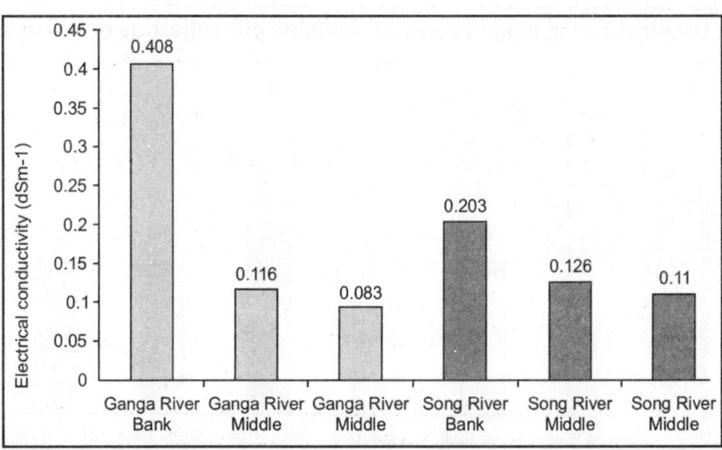

Fig. 4.5: Graph showing mean values of electrical conductivity of soil at site I & II

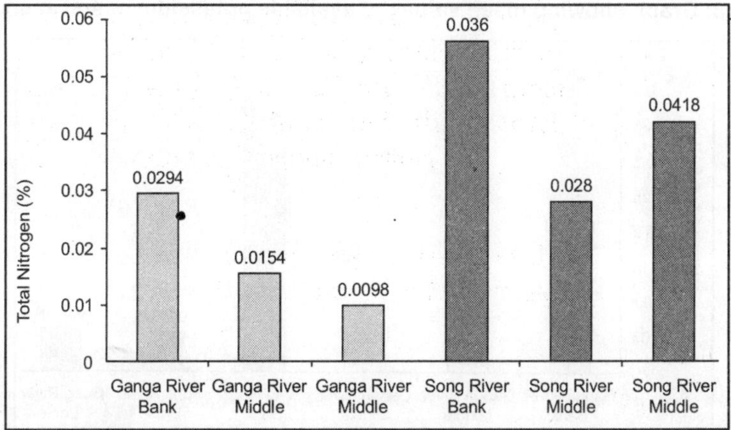

Fig. 4.6: Graph showing mean values of total nitrogen of soil at site I & II

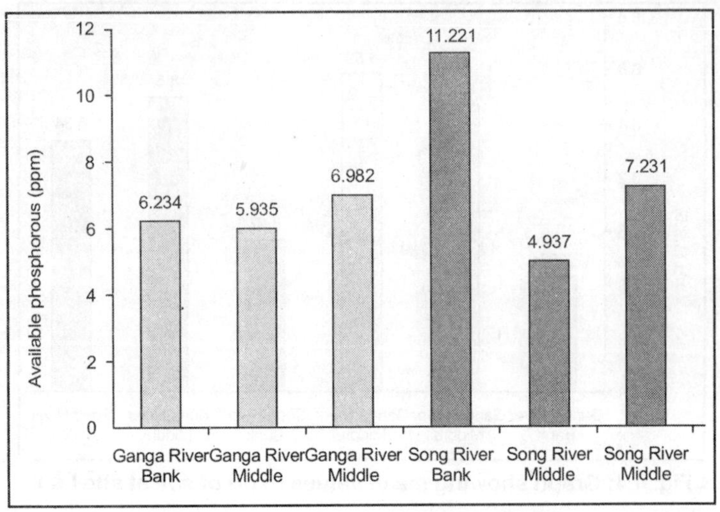

Fig. 4.7: Graph showing mean values of available phosphorous of soil at site I & II

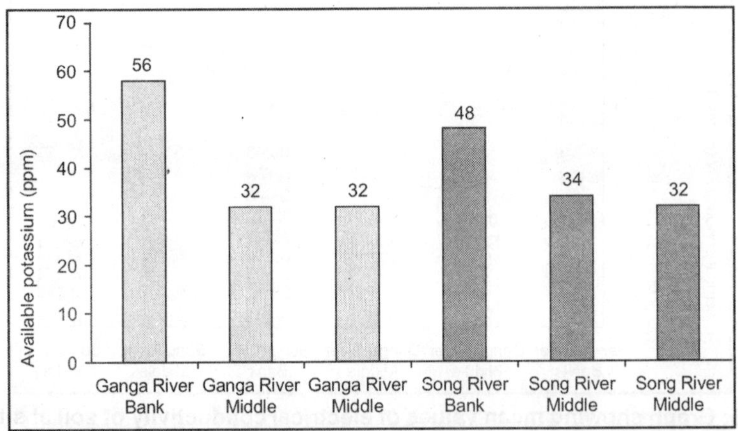

Fig. 4.8: Graph showing mean values of available potassium of soil at site I & II

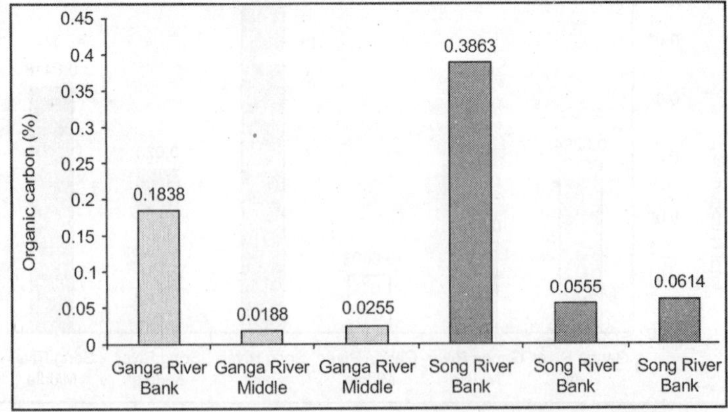

Fig. 4.9: Graph showing mean values of organic carbon of soil at site I & II

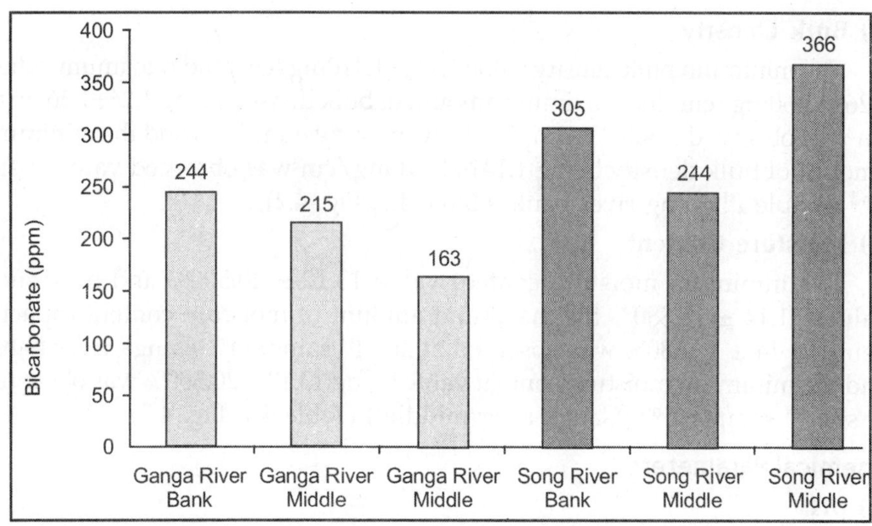

Fig. 4.10: Graph showing mean values of bicarbonate of soil at site I & II

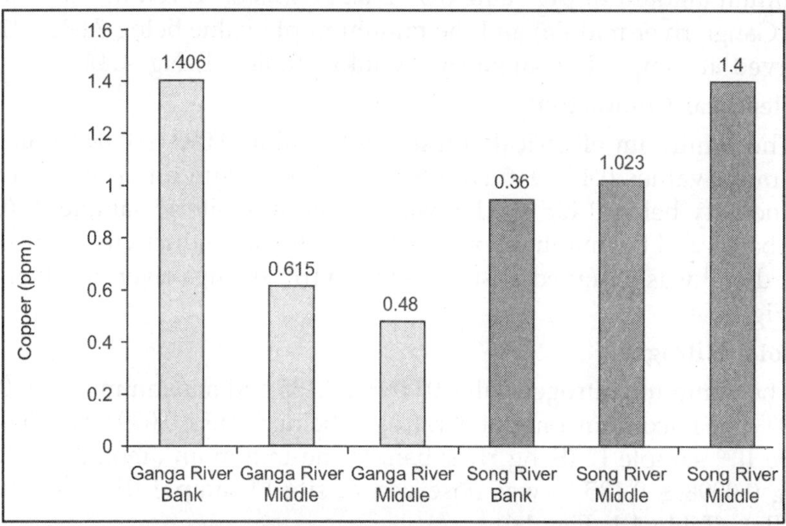

Fig. 4.11: Graph showing mean values of copper of soil at site I & II

Physical Parameters

(1) Water Absorbing Capacity

The minimum water absorbing capacity value 21.96 ±2.480% and maximum values 44.24 ± 8.340% the maximum amount of water absorbing capacity being 44.24 ± 8.340% was observed at site Ist sample Ist (Ganga river bank) near Chandi Devi, Hardwar. The minimum amount of water absorbing capacity being 21.96 ± 2.480% was observed at site second sample IIIrd (Song river middle), Doiwala, Derhadun. (Table 4.1, Fig. 4.1).

(2) Bulk Density

The minimum bulk density value 1.141±1.410mg/cm^3 and maximum values 1.26±1.360mg/cm^3.the maximum amount of bulk density being 1.26±1.360mg/cm^{3}was observed at site Ist sample IIIrd (Ganga river middle) and the minimum amount of bulk density being 1.141±1.410mg/cm^{3}was observed value at site IInd sample Ist (Song river bank) (Table 4.1, Fig. 4.2).

(3) Moisture Content

The minimum moisture content value 13.12 ± 20.500% and maximum values 21.14 ± 15.880% the maximum amount of moisture content capacity being 21.14 ± 15.880% was observed at site Ist sample Ist (Ganga river bank) and the minimum moisture content value being 13.12 ± 20.500% was observed at site Ist sample IInd (Ganga river middle) (Table 4.1, Fig. 4.3).

Chemical Parameters

(1) pH

The minimum pH value 7.83±0.219 and maximum values 8.59 ± 0.219 the maximum amount of pH being 8.59 ± 0.219 was observed at site Ist sample IIIrd (Ganga river middle) and the minimum pH value being 7.83±0.219 was observed at sample Ist (Ganga river bank). (Table 4.1, Fig. 4.4).

(2) Electrical Conductivity

The minimum electrical conductivity value 0.093 ± 0.064 dSm^{-1} and maximum values 0.406 ± 0.116 dSm^{-1} the maximum amount of electrical conductivity being 0.406 ± 0.116 was observed at site Ist sample Ist (Ganga river bank) and the minimum amount of electrical conductivity being 0.093 ± 0.064 dSm^{-1} was observed at site Ist sample IIIrd (Ganga river middle). (Table 4.1, Fig. 4.5).

(3) Total Nitrogen

The minimum nitrogen value 0.0098 ± 0.135 and maximum values 0.056 ± 0.039%. the maximum amount of nitrogen being 0.056 ± 0.039% was observed at site IInd sample Ist (Song river bank). The minimum amount of nitrogen being 0.0098 ± 0.135 % was observed at site Ist sample IIIrd (Ganga river middle). (Table 4.1, Fig. 4.6).

(4) Available phosphorous

The minimum phosphorous value 4.987 ± 1.610ppm and maximum values 11.221± 1.970 ppm. The maximum amount of phosphorous being 11.221± 1.970 ppm was observed at site IInd sample Ist (Song river bank) and the minimum amount of phosphorous being 4.987 ± 1.610ppm was observed at site IInd sample IInd (Song river middle). (Table 4.1, Fig. 4.7).

(5) Available potassium

The minimum potassium value 32 ± 4.960 and maximum value 58±10.400ppm. The maximum amount of potassium being 58±10.400ppm was observed at site Ist sample Ist (Ganga river bank) and the minimum amount of potassium being 32 ± 4.960 and 32±5.033 ppm was observed at site Ist (sample IInd & IIIrd) and site IInd (sample IIIrd). (Table 4.1, Fig. 4.8).

(6) Organic carbon

The minimum organic carbon value 0.0188 ± 0.064% and maximum values 0.3863± 0.076%. The maximum amount of organic carbon being 0.3863± 0.076% was observed at site IInd sample Ist (Song river bank) and the minimum amount of organic carbon being 0.0188 ± 0.064% was observed at site Ist sample IInd (Ganga river middle). (Table 4.1, Fig. 4.9).

(7) Carbonate

The amount of carbonate was nil in all of samples. (Table 4.1).

(8) Bicarbonate

The minimum bicarbonate value 163 ± 25.400ppm and maximum values 366 ± 123ppm. The maximum amount of bicarbonate being 366 ± 123ppm. was observed at site IInd sample IIIrd (Song river middle). and the minimum value of bicarbonate being 163± 25.400ppm was observed at site Ist sample IIIrd (Ganga river middle). (Table 4.1, Fig. 4.10).

(9) Copper

The minimum **copper** value 1.40 ± 1.130ppm and maximum values 1.406 ± 0.631ppm.The maximum amount of copper being 1.406 ± 0.631ppm was observed at site Ist sample Ist (Ganga river bank) and the minimum and the copper being 1.40 ± 1.130ppm was observed at site Ist sample IIIrd (Ganga river middle). (Table 4.1, Fig. 4.11).

The result of present investigation showed that in site Ist (Ganga river) some of the important parameters viz-moisture content, water absorbing capacity, bulk density, potassium electrical conductivity , pH etc. were high as compared to site IInd (Song river).

Discussion

The eternal truth that soil and water are the two significant capitals of mankind and the natural forests are the mothers of river and the factories for manufacturing soil. The soil provides homes and ideal environment conditions for living beings.

Soil is a natural body, bio-chemically weathered and synthesized product of nature. In other words, pedology considers soil as a natural entity, a biologically weathered and synthesized product of nature. Pedologists study soils, which includes the study of origin of the soil, its classification and its description.

Soil is considered to be a natural habitat for plants and other living organisms and justifies soil studies primarily on that basis. In other words, Edaphology consider the soil as a natural habitat for plant.

Life on earth depends directly on the living soil and the aquatic eco-system of rivers. Without fertile soil and the microbial fauna that inhabit it, food would not grow, dead things would not decay and nutrients would not be recycled. Yet the earth's soil are being stripped away , rendered sterile and contaminated with toxic chemicals at a rate that can not be sustained.

A typical soil contains a large number and varieties of elements, trace elements, inorganic and organic compounds. The oxygen, silicon, aluminum, calcium, magnesium, sodium, potassium and iron etc are the elements which are present in the soil. The trace elements present in the soil include cobalt, boron, iodine, cadmium, arsenic, zinc and barium etc. The inorganic compounds present are chlorides, sulphates and oxides, while the organic compounds derived from the dead remains of plants and animals and animal excreta are present in various stages of decomposition.

The organic matter in the soil comes from the remains of plants and animals. As new organic matter is formed in he soil, a part of the old organic matter is mineralized. The original source of the soil organic matter is plant tissues. Under natural conditions the tops and roots of trees, grasses and other plants supply large quantities of organic residues. Thus, higher plant tissues are the primary source of organic matter. Animals are usually regarded as secondary sources of organic matter. Various organic manures such as farmyard manure, compost, green manure etc, that are added to the soil from time to time, further add to the store of soil organic matter.

Various physico-chemical parameters like moisture content, water absorbing capacity, bulk density, pH, electrical conductivity, bicarbonates, carbonates, available phosphorus, organic carbon, total nitrogen, and copper play a significant role in determining the fertility/nutrition of soil (Piper, 1944, Trivedy and Goel, 1984).

During present study the physico-chemical parameters of river soil at Site–Ist Sample- Ist (Ganga River Bank):

Water absorbing capacity (44.24 %), bulk density (1.16 mg /cm3), moisture content (21.14 %). pH (1: 25), (7.83), E.C. (0.406 dSm^{-1}), total nitrogen(0.0294 %), available phosphorous, (6.234 ppm) available potassium (58 ppm), organic carbon (0.1838 %), carbonate (NIL), bicarbonate (244 ppm), and copper (1.406 ppm).

At Site – Ist Sample- IInd (Ganga River Middle)

Water absorbing capacity (22.12%), bulk density (1.20 mg/cm^3), moisture content (13.12%)., pH (1:25), (8.47), E.C. (0.116 dSm^{-1}), total nitrogen (0.0154%), available phosphorous, (5.985 ppm), available potassium (32 ppm), organic carbon (0.01875%), carbonate (NIL), bicarbonate (215 ppm), and copper (0.615 ppm), (Table 4.1)

At Site – Ist Sample-IIIrd (Ganga River Middle)

Water absorbing capacity (22.99%), bulk density (1.26 mg/cm^3), moisture content (14.39%), pH (1:25), (8.59), E.C. (0.093 dSm^{-1}), total nitrogen (0.0098%), available phosphorous, (6.982 ppm), available potassium (32 ppm), organic carbon (0.0255%), carbonate (NIL), bicarbonate – (163 ppm), and copper (0.480 ppm). (Table 4.1)

At Site- IInd Sample-Ist (Song River Bank)

Water absorbing capacity (32.38%), bulk density (1.141 mg/cm^3), moisture content (18.27%), pH (1:25), (7.97) E.C. (0.203 dSm^{-1}), total nitrogen (0.056%), available phosphorous, (11.221 ppm), available potassium (48 ppm), organic carbon (0.3863%), carbonate (NIL), bicarbonate (305 ppm), and copper (0.950 ppm). (Table 4.1)

At Site- IInd Sample- IInd (Song River Middle)

Water absorbing capacity (24.48%), bulk density (1.22 mg/cm^3), moisture content (14.77%)., pH (1:25), (8.5) E.C. (0.126 dSm^{-1}), total nitrogen (0.028%), available phosphorous (4.987 ppm), available potassium (34 ppm), organic carbon (0.0555%), carbonate (NIL), bicarbonate (244 ppm), and copper (1.023 ppm). (Table 4.1)

At Site-IInd Sample-IIIrd (Song River Middle)

Water absorbing capacity (21.96%), bulk density (1.23 mg/cm^3), moisture content (13.42 gm), pH (1:25), (8.34), E.C. (0.110 dSm^{-1}), total nitrogen (0.0418%), available phosphorous, (7.231 ppm), available potassium (32 ppm), organic carbon (0.06144%). carbonate (NIL), bicarbonate (366 ppm) and copper (1.40 ppm), (Table 4.1).

The soil pH is generally regarded as a very important soil property since it tends to correlate with other properties such as the degree of base saturation. The reaction of the soil normally range form pH 3.0-9.0 but occasionally values outsides these limits are encountered. pH tends to be related to rainfall. As rainfall increases the pH falls as a result of the depletion of basic cations. It is a good measure of the intensity of acidity and alkalinity of soil suspension and provides a good identification of the soil chemical nature. The pH of different soil samples showed slightly basic nature. The pH of site Ist sample IIIrd (Ganga river middle) were higher than the another. Almost same observation have been reported by G.N. Singh, H.P. Agarwal and M. Singh, (1991) in their topic clay mineralogy of alluvial soils in different physio-graphic position and J.S.P. Yadav, (2000) in their topic Northern Punjab plain Ganga, Yamuna doab and Rajhsthan upland, hot dry semi arid ecosubrigion.

Conductivity is measured of the current capacity, thus gives a clear idea of the soluble salts present in the soil. Conductivity values depend on the dilution of the soil suspension. The electrical conductivity of site Ist sample Ist (Ganga river bank) was higher than other Sites, therefore the percentage of soluble salts was also high in this site. Almost same observation have been reported by M.Badrinarayon rao and J. Venkater warlu, (1974). In their topic the physico-chemical changes of newly flooded soils and Laxmi Narayan and V.Raj Gopal, (2000). In their topic comparison of different methods for evolution of available nitrogen.

The bicarbonates of the soil is affected by a number of eco-biological factors. The alkalinity of soil is an anionic phenomenon, which is mainly due to carbonates, bicarbonates, hdydroxyl, phosphate, silicate etc. The value of carbonate were nil in all samples. Supported by Sarkar and A.K. Sahoo, (2000). In their topics Scripts of Indo-Gangatic plain of bihar and their suitability for some crops.

The copper concentration of soil can be determined in soil solution. It is also affected by a number of eco-biological factors. Value of copper in site Ist (sample Ist) and site IInd (sample IInd) were approximately same. Almost same observation have been repotted by Sarkar and A.K. Sahoo, (2000). In their topics scripts of Indo-Gangatic plain of Bihar and their suitability for some crops.

The phosphate level of different soil samples showed remarkable character. The phosphate concentration in soil is governed by heterogeneous equilibria in which phosphorus takes part. The phosphorus absorbed by the plants comes from the soil solution in which it exits as the inorganic orthophosphate ion, Hydrogen Phosphate and Phosphate. The relative abundance of these ions is largely dependent on the soil pH. The phosphorus of site IInd sample Ist (Song river bank) was higher then other samples. Al almost same observation have been supported by H.P.Chaudhary and S.K.Das, (1990) in their topic nutrient status in relation to intensity of Erosion in ravines of Yamuna and M.Badrinarayon rao and J. Venkater warlu, (1974). In their topic the physico-chemical changes of newly flooded soils.

The organic carbon of the soil is affected by a number of eco-biological factors. Organic carbon constituents the principal carbonaceous and nitrogenous constituents of soil micro-organisms. The sources of organic matter in the soil include crop residues, animal manures, cover crops, green manures and organic fertilizers etc. It has been observed that, if the soil has the organic carbon percentage above 0.75%, then the organic matter content is high in soil of the organic agricultural land, Khanna and Yadav, (1979). According to the Joffe, (1981) the organic matter percentage in sandy soil was between 1.0-1.5 and sandy loam 1.8-1.3 Organic matter of the source of plant nutrients which are liberated in available forms during materialization. The organic carbon in site IInd sample Ist (Song river bank) higher than the other sample. Almost all value is supported by D.D. Dubey and O.P. Sharma, (1990). In their topic salt affected soil in flood plain area of Gujrat and Laxmi Narayan and V.Raj Gopal, (2000). In their topic comparison of different methods for evolution of available nitrogen and Sarkar and A.K. Sahoo, (2000). In their topics Scripts of Indo-Gangatic plain of Bihar and their suitability for some crops.

Soil rarely contain enough nitrogen for maximum plant growth. In soil it is mostly present in the organic form together with small quantity of ammonium and nitrate forms, roots of plants take up nitrogen in the form nitrate and ammonium in the available form. The nitrogen of site Ist sample Ist (Ganga river bank) was higher than other samples almost all value is supported by K.D,Sah. Sahoo, S.K. Gupta and S.K, BanerJee, (1990). In their topic seasonal variation of nutrient concentration in tidal water interstitial water and mangrove muds of sunder bans.

The cations sodium and potassium are found in all soil sample. The cations concentrations showed high variation. The concentration of potassium is almost below than the concentration in soil samples the higher value of potassium in site Ist sample Ist (Ganga river bank) was higher than other samples supported by H.P.Chaudhary and S.K. Das, (1990) in their topic nutrient status in relation to intensity of erosion in ravines of Yamuna.

It has been observed that soil character is the most important factor with regard to selection of crops of development of Orchard or bringing a plot of land under agricultural, aquaculture, horticultural use Joshi *et al.* (1988).

Summary

The present investigation was aimed to a preliminary study of the physico-chemical parameters of soil of Song and Ganga river beds. Form the two sites six sample were collected form Song and Ganga rivers soil.

Sampling was done during the month of the February (2004) to June (2004). The composite samples were used for the determination of some physico-chemical parameters.

The important parameters selected for soil study of these sites were water absorbing capacity, bulk density, moisture content, pH, electrical conductivity, total nitrogen, available phosphorus, available potassium, organic carbon, carbonate, bicarbonate and copper.

During present study the values of physico-chemical parameters site Ist and site IInd showed normal characteristics of soil. The salient features of the present investigation are summarized here below.

Physical Parameters

Water absorbing capacity

The minimum water absorbing capacity value 21.96 ± 2.480% (Song river middle) and maximum values 44.24 ± 8.340% (Ganga river bank).

Bulk Density

The minimum bulk density value 1.141 ± 1.410 mg/cm^3 (Song river bank) and maximum values 1.26 ± 1.360mg/cm^3 (Ganga river middle).

Moisture Content

The minimum moisture content value 13.12 ± 20.500% (Ganga river middle) and maximum values 21.14 ± 15.880% (Ganga river bank).

Chemical Parameters

pH

The minimum pH value 8.5 ± 0.138 (Song river middle) and maximum values 8.59 ± 0.219 (Ganga river middle).

Electrical Conductivity

The minimum electrical conductivity value 0.093 ± 0.064 dSm^{-1} (Ganga river middle) and maximum values 0.406± 0.116 dSm^{-1} (Ganga river bank).

Total Nitrogen

The minimum nitrogen value 0.0098 ± 0.135 (Ganga river middle) and maximum values 0.056 ± 0.039% (Song river bank).

Available Phosphorous

The minimum phosphorous value 4.987 ± 1.610 ppm (Song river middle) and maximum values 11.221± 1.970 ppm (Song river bank).

Available Potassium

The minimum potassium value 32 ± 3.460 ppm (Song river middle) and maximum values 58 ± 10.400 ppm(Song river bank).

Organic carbon

The minimum organic carbon value 0.0188 ± 0.064% (Ganga river middle) and maximum values 0.3863± 0.076%(Song river bank).

Carbonate

NIL

Bicarbonate

The minimum bicarbonate value 163 ± 25.400 ppm (Ganga river middle) and maximum values 366 ± 123ppm(Song river middle).

Copper

The minimum **copper** value 1.40 ± 1.130 ppm (Song river middle) and maximum values 1.406 ± 0.631ppm (Ganga river bank).

The result of present investigation showed that in site Ist (Ganga river) some of the important parameters viz-moisture contents, water absorbing capacity, bulk density, potassium electrical conductivity, pH etc. were high as compared to site IInd (Song river). While in site IInd (Song river) Bicarbonates, Organic Carbon, Available Phosphorus and Nitrogen were high as compared to Site Ist. (Ganga river). The value of carbonate was nil in both of site.

REFERENCES

Adams, F. (1971). Ionic concentrations and activates in soil solutions, *soil Sci, Am. Proc. 35: 420-426.*

Attansova, I.D. (1995). *Env. Pollu. 87, 17.*

Benipal, D.S. and Pasricha, N.S. (2002). Non-exchangeable K release and supplying power of Indo-Gangetic alluvial soils, *Geoderma 108:197-206.*

Benipal, D.S. Pasricha, N.S. Rachhpal Singh. (2002). Potassium release to proton saturated resin and its diffusion characteristics in alluvial soils of Northern India. *(Communicated).*

Bhangu, S.S. and Sidhu, P.S. (1993). Potassium mineralogy of five bench mark soils of Central Punjab. *J. Pot. Res.. 9: 105-112.*

Brummer, G.W. & Herms. (1983). In: effects of accumulation of air pollutant in forest Ecosystem *(B. Ulrich & J. Pankorah Ed) P 23 D Reidel Publishing company.*

Chaudhary, H.P and Das, S.K. (1990). Nutrient status in relation to intensity of Erosion in ravines of Yamuna *J. of Indian. Soc. of Soil vol-38 , PP 126-129(1990).*

Chhorkar, PK, and subborv, N.S. (1967). Phosphate solubulization by fungi associated with legume root Nodules can. *J. Microbical 13: 749-753.*

Conde, F.L. and Prat L. (1957). New colorimetric determination of phosphorous in soil. *J.soil Science. 16: 1-18.*

D.K. and Srinivasa Rao, Ch. (2001). Potassium mineralogy and its effect on K. availability. In Proceedings of International Symposium on importance of potassium in Nutrient Management for Sustainable Crop Production in India. (N.S. Pasricha and S.K. Bansla, eds). *Dec 2001, New Delhi, India.*

Davis-Horsner, (1995). During the study of variability of soil chemical properties into the sand dunal soils niger- *J.Soil. Sci. 159, No-5, 321-323.*

Dubey, D.D and Sharma, O.P. (1990). Salt affected soil in flood plain area of Gujrat *J. of Indian. Soc. of Soil vol-38 , PP 122-125.*

Ellis, BG.& Knezek, B.D. (1972). In: micronutrient agriculture. *(J.J.Mortvedt P.M. Glordano & Wilium Lindsay) P 57 soil science American wiskonsin U.S.A.*

Eschna, T. (1955). Volumetric determination of sulphate in aqueous soil extract *Pemifa Ann Afron 11: 66-75.*

G.N. Singh, H.P.Agarwal and M. Singh (1991). Clay mineralogy of alluvial soils in different physio graphic position. *J. of Indian. Soc. of Soil vol-39, PP 160-163.*

Gowrisankar, D and MruGuppon (1998). Zinc fractiation studies in one soil of Amravaty river command area of Tamil Nadu. *J. of Indian Soc. Of Soil science Vol 46 No-1 PP 140-142.*

Gray, T.R.G williom, S.T. (1971). Microbial productivity in soil. *Microbs and biological productivity: 255-286, E.D.S. D.E Hughes and A.H. Rose combrige university press London.*

Griffin, R.A. and Jurinak, J.J. (1973). Estimation of activity coefficient form electrical conductivity of natural aquatic systems and soil extracts. *Soil Sci. 116: 26-30.*

Gupta, R.D. and Sharma G.S. (1980). Distribution of micro organism in relation to Physico chemical properties of Jammu & Kashmir. *J.Ind. Soc. Soil sci. 12: 259-262.*

Hazra, G.C and Biswapati Mandal (1996). Desorption of Absorbed zinc in soil in relation to soil properties. *J. of . Indian. Soc. Of soil. Sci. vol- 44- No-233-237.*

Hazzra, C.R. (1994). Soil and water conservation aspects of agro forestry on natural resource regeneration and plant production *J. Soil water conservation India 38: 69-89.*

Hess, P.R. (1970). A test book of soil chemical analysis. *Jhon murray Ltd. London.*

Horper. (1945). Nitrate determination calorimetrically with nitro phenol disulphonic acid *J.soil science: 59, 42-47.*

Hundal, L.S. and Pasricha, N.S. (1998). Adsorption- desorption kinetics of potassium as influenced by temperature and background anions. *Geoderma, 83, 215-225.*

Hussain, A. Chughati, F.A. and Zabir, M. (1988). Leucaena Leucocephala prunings as a source of nitrogen for wheat Leucaena *Research report 9:84-85.*

Jackson, M.L. (1973). Soil chemical analysis. *IBH Publishing company Bombay.*

Joffe, Jones, I.H.P & Jarvis, S.C. (1981). In the chemistry of soil process (D.J. Green land & M.B Hyr Ed) *P 593, Jhon willey & sons Limited.*

Krishna, N.D.R. Giri, J.D. and Shyampura, R.H. (2001). Characterization of soil of part Ghaggar River basin in Rajhsthan with Endoreic Drainage. *J. of the Ind. Soc. Of soil science Vol – 49, No-2 PP 316-324.*

Kulte, A. (1986). Methods of soil analysis part-I Physical and mineralogical methods 2nd ed. Agronomy monograph No. a, published by American Soc. Of. Agronomy and soil science . *Society of America Inc. Madison Wisconsin U.S.A.*

Laxmi Narayan and Raj Gopal, V. (2000). Comparison of different methods for Evolution of available Nitrogen. *J. of Indian. Soc. of Soil analysis vol-48 No-4, PP 797-802.*

Lopez, A.B. and Galvez, N.L (1958). The mineralization of the organic matter of some phillipine soil under submerged condition. *Phillipine Agric 42, 281-90.*

Mittal, S.P and Grewal, S.S. Agnihotri (1992). Substitution of nitrogen requirement of maize through leaf biomass of Leucaena Leucocephala. *Agronomics and Economics consideration Agro forestry System 19, 207-210.*

Morgan, J.T. and Patric, W.H. Jr. (1974). Selected metabolic process in a submerged soil at controlled pH values. *Tran 10th Int. Cong. R. soil sc. Vol-11 PP- 264-279.*

Mulder, E.G lie, T.A. and Walden, drop J.W (1969) biology and soil productivity . *In soil biology Rev of Rss. Unesco paris 168-208.*

Onikura, Y. Yoshino, T. and Maeda. (1975). Mineralization patterns of soil nitrogen during the growth of rice plant. *J. Sci. soil manure. Japan 46, 255-9.*

Page, AL. (1982). Methods of soil analysis part-I physical and mineralogical methods 2nd ed. *Agronomy monograph No. a, published by American Soc. Of. Agronomy and soil science. Society of America Inc. Madison Wisconsin U.S.A.*

Pasricha, N.S. (1985). Potassium Q/1 relationships as influenced by calcium and magnesium treated as separate Ionic species and by soil submergence. *J. agric. set. camb.104; 577-581.*

Piper, C.S. (1950). Soil and plant analysis. *Univ. of Adelaide Australia.*

Piper,C.S.(1944). Soil and plant analysis. Adelaide the Univ. of Australia 368.

Ponnamperuma, F.H (1964). Mineral nutrition of the rice plant IRRI manila 295.

Ponnamperuma, F.N. (1972). The chemistry of submerged soils. *Adv. In Agron. 24; 29-96.*

Ponnamperuma, F.N. Tianco, E.M. and Loy, T.A. (1966). Ionic strength of solutions of flooded soils and other natural aqueous solutions form specific conductance. *Soil Sci. 102: 408-413.*

Rama Krishna Prasad, P. Subbia, G.V. Saffy Narayan H.V and Rao, Srinivas. (1998). Water relation characteristics of predominant soil types in command area of Krishna, Godovari and Sarda River of Andhra Pradesh. *J. of. Ind. Soc.Soil Sci. Vol 46 No PP. 171-176 (1998).*

Rao, M. Badrinarayon and Venkater warlu, J. (1974). The physico-chemical changes of newly flooded soils. *Journal. Indian. Soc. Soil sci. vol-22 PP-13-18, (1974)*

Ray chaudhary, S.P. (1998). Managing soding soils for sustained crop production in Indo-gangatic plains. *J. of Indian. Soc. of Soil vol-46, No-4, PP 534-550(1998).*

Russell, E.W. (1961). Soil condition & plant growth. *9th edition longmans green and Co.Ltd London.*

S. P. Sharma, PD Sharma, S.P. Singh. R.S. Minahs. (1944). Characterization of soan river velly soils in lower shiwaliks of Himachal Pradesh II. Piedmont and flood plain soils. *J. of Indian. Soc. Of . Soil. Sci. Vol-42, No-1, PP 105-110 (1944).*

Sah, K.D and Sahoo. Gupta, S.K and BanerJee, S.K (1990). Seasonal variation of nutrient concentration in tidal water, Inter stitial water and mangrove muds of sunder bans. *J. of Indian. Soc. of Soil vol-48 , PP 148-151(1990).*

Sanders, J.R. & Adams. (1987). *Environmental Pollution 43-219.*

Sarin, M.M., Krishnaswamy, S.K., Trivedi, J.R. and Sharma, K.K. (1992). Major ion chemistry of the Ganga source waters: weathering in high altitude Himalaya. In: *Proc, Indian acad. Sci. (Earth Planet Sci.)* 1, 89-98.

Sarkar, and Sahoo, A.K. (2000). Scripts of IndoGangatic plain of bihar and their suitability for some crops. *J. of Indian. Soc. of Soil vol-48 No-3, PP 562-566(2000).*

Sethi, R.P. and Subba, Rao N.S. (1968). Solubilization of tri-calcium phosphate by soil fungi. *J. gen. Apl. Micro vial 14: 329-331.*

Sharma, N.K. Singh, P.N. Tyagi PC. and Mohan, S.C. (1998). Effect of leucaena mulch on soil water use and wheat yields. *Agri water management 35, 191-200.*

Sharma, Pradeep Sharma,P.D. (1996). Micro-nutrients status of different land forms of soan river vally soil of Lower Shiwaliks. *J.of Indian. Soc. Of. Soil. Sci. Vol-44, No-2, PP- 330-331.*

Shiga, H. and Ventura, W. (1976). Nitrogen supplying obility of paddy soils under field condition in the phillippinies. *Soil. Sci. plant nutri (Tokyo) 22, 287-299.*

Shioiri. (1948). Effect of air drying of paddy soil (in Japanese) *J. Sci. soil manure japan 15, 331-334*

Sidhu, P.S, Bhangu, S.S., and Jassal, H.S. (1993). Mineralogy of potassium in some benchmark mineral soils of Punjab. *J. Potassium. Res. 9: 206-217.*

Singh, S.K. Das, Shyampura, K.R.L. and. Singh, R.S. (1996). Forms of potassium in relation to soil moisture regime *J.of. I. Soc. of. soil science. Vol-44, No-2 PP- 229-233 (1996).*

Song, S.K. and Huang, P.M. (1988). Dynamics of potassium release form potassium bearing minerals as influenced by oxalic and citric acids. *Soil Sci. Soc. Am. J. 52:383-390.*

Sparks, D.L. (2001). Dynamics of K in soil and their role in management of K nutrition. In proceedings of international sysposium on Importance of Potassium in Nutrient Management for Sustainable Crop Production in India. (N.S. Pasricha and S.K. Bansal, eds). *Dec. 2001, New Delhi, India.*

Sparks, D.L. and Huang, P.M. (1985). Physical chemistry of soil potassium, p 201-276. In R.D. Munson (ed.) Potassium in Agriculture . *Am Soc. Agron., Madison, WI, USA.*

Sri Nivas Rao (1990). Water retention characteristics of some of Andhra Pradesh soil. *In tropical agriculture 41 & 335.*

Swarup, A. (1995). *Fert news 40 (11), 39.*

Tamanhe, R.V. & Datta, N.R. (1965). Water stable aggregates in renges soil. *J. Indi. Soc. Soil. Science (13, 205)*

Tinsley, J. (1950). Determination of organic carbon in soil by dichromate mixture. *Univ. of London England 161-178.*

Vadivelu, S. Baruah, U. Sarkar, D. and Butte, P.S. (2001). Delineation and characterization of flood deposited sediments. *J.of. the . Indian. Soc.of soil Science. Vol-49, No-3 PP- 521-524 (2001).*

Walkey, A. Black, I.A. (1934). Soil *& plant analysis soil science (37, 29).*

Yadav, J.S.P- Northern Punjab Plain Ganga, Yamuna doab and Rajhsthan upland, hotdry semi arid ecosub region. *(Natural Resource Management for Agricultural Production in India Feb 14-18 (2000). Written by M. velay tham and T. Bhattacharya.*

Yadav, P.R. Srivastava, B.P and Kavadia, V.S. (1978). Effect of soil type climatic condition Indian *J. Env. 40:26-38.*

Yasvinder singh, J.P.S. Grewal, Bijay singh and C.S. Khind, (2001). Effect of soil moisture on nitrification in a sandy loam soil. *J. of Indian. Soc. Of soil . scie. Vol-49 No.2 PP. 342-344 (2001).*

5

Assessment of Heavy Metals in Agricultural Soil

—*Pawan Kumar 'Bharti', India*

ABSTRACT

In the last three decades, the rapid growth of industrialization and urbanization has created negative impacts on the environment. The industrial wastes containing organic pollutants and heavy metals in their effluents have been polluted surface and ground water. In India, the industrial effluents have contributed a major source of pollution. Textile effluent when discharged into the pond and through pond they percolated to the ground water. Thus, contaminated ground water has deteriorated immensely the drinking utilities, post agriculture irrigation and impacts on soil systems and crop productivity.

The aim of this study is to emphasized on the transfer of heavy metals and extent of heavy metal contamination of soil due to irrigation with contaminated ground water affected by textile industrial effluents, on agricultural land. Metal transfer factors from effluent to ground water, from ground water to irrigated agricultural soil and from soil to vegetation are described in a simplified method in water, soil and vegetation.

Key words: *Heavy metals, textile industry, agriculture soil, accumulation, transfer factor.*

Introduction

The textile effluents have consisting high concentrations of heavy metals, organic and inorganic pollutants and toxic colours, which may alter the surface water quality of the region. Toxic pollutants may percolate down via soil profile and reach in ground water, which ultimately cause the health hazards among human being and livestock after consumption as daily drinking requirements. The waste water without any treatment may cause adverse effect on the health of human, domestic animals, wildlife and environment (Sharma *et al.*, 1999). Thus, contaminated ground water has deteriorated immensely the drinking utilities, post agriculture irrigation and impacts on soil systems and crop productivity.

It is essential to know the status and functions of heavy metals discarding from textile industries in to surface, ground water, soil and crop plant vegetation for health safety of regional people, which may help in recent research in the field of soil and water pollution by industries and for advance alarming against pollution to public, NGOs and GOs. The present paper deals with the distribution and transfer of heavy metals between water and soil. Regarding human consumption and irrigation practices ground water may cause the human and livestock health hazards and reduce soil fertility and agricultural plant productivity.

Waste water of dye houses generally discharged openly into Binjhole pond water, thus polluted the surface water quality of the region (Malik *et al.*, 2006). After delaying for a long period of time the heavy metal contents may leach down in to ground water regime through soil profile very slowly. Because the ground water movement is very slow (CPCB, 2003), so metal contents remain in ground water for a long period even in toxic form. Thus metals reach in local ground water and deteriorated the ground water quality of neighborhood area. Metals reach in agricultural soil through repeated irrigation by contaminated ground water. Some concentrations of metals again percolate in to ground water and some of them delay in soil water. Soil particles bound a huge amount of heavy metals due to adsorptive nature, which remain in capillary water and easily available for plants.

Plants absorb the sufficient amount of water for their different requirements. Metals present in this available water arrive in plant tissues with water and accumulate in various parts of plant bodies (Malik *et al.*, 2004). These metal contents may affect the plants activities and generate some physiological changes in plants sometimes (Garg and Kaushik, 2006). In other cases, accumulated amount of heavy metals may reach in livestock and human beings after continuous uptake of these crop parts.

Agricultural soil requires sufficient irrigation for high production in agricultural fields. Irrigation water with poor quality can result in the alteration of physico-chemical characteristics of irrigated agricultural soil. Several minerals such as chloride, sulphate, bicarbonate, sodium, calcium and magnesium in irrigation water may change the soil quality with its continuous application on soil. These minerals contained in the irrigation water can build up the soil's trophic level and ultimately influence the agriculture productivity (Malik and Bharti, 2007).

Historical Resume

Different researchers from India and abroad have been discussed various aspects of heavy metals pollution of water and soil in term of characteristics of water bodies, affected agricultural soils and bottom sediments from time to time. This review includes some of important contribution made in the field of industrial pollution, with references to heavy metals parameters of ground water, surface water, characterization of textile industrial effluents, contaminated agricultural irrigated soil and bottom sediment soils by different authors of country and abroad.

Aggarwal and Mehrotra (1952) surveyed the soil and soil water affected by effluent in some selected regions of Uttar Pradesh. Richards (1954) evaluated the quality of saline and alkali soils and gave a technique for the improvement of these sick soil systems in the agricultural sector for good performance of agriculture productivity.

Kanwar (1961) assessed the quality of irrigation water as an index of suitability for irrigation purposes. Darra *et al.*, (1964) evaluated the water quality of irrigation water used in Rajasthan. Saksena *et al.*, (1966) evaluated the quality of ground waters for irrigation in Ahor developmental block, Jalore. Bhakuni and Bopardikar (1967) stated the method of recovery Zinc from the spinning bath waste of Viscos reyon factory by using ion exchange method and found it significant useful in metal removal process.

Williums (1972) described the characteristics and various properties of Metals. Katz (1975) highlighted the effect of heavy metals on some environmental components and biotic organisms of aquatic environment in New York. Dowedy and Larson (1975) reported the availability of some metals in various vegetable crops in a polluted region in the vicinity of an industrial area. Dulka and Risby (1976) stated ultra trace metals in some environmental and biological systems in the vicinity of textile industrial sector. Shivakumar *et al.*, (1977) made a geo-graphical approach for toxic trace element pollution in ground water around Patancheru and Bollaram Industrial area, A.P., India.

Martin and Cougherty (1982) stated the basic monitoring techniques for detection of heavy metals pollution through the biological agents. Ireland (1983) described the heavy metals uptake and their distribution in tissues of organisms. Numberg (1984) studied on the volumetric approach in trace metal chemistry of natural waters and atmospheric precipitation.

Nriagu and Pacyna (1988) carried out a study on the quantitative assessment of worldwide contamination of air, water and soil with trace metals. Mishra *et al.*, (1990) reported the occurrence of heavy metals in crop plants of Sanagar more than the permissible limits presence of which may cause the adverse effect on the plant/human health and may cause high mortality of fish population in affected aquatic environment.

Singh *et al.*, (1994) highlighted the degradation of water and soil quality of Parwanoo area with respect to heavy metals. Sharma and Patel (1996) determined copper in water of Raipur with the help of spectrophotometer. Prasad and Chandra (1997) studied well water quality status of Hyderabad and Khurshid and Shabeer (1997) observed water quality degradation due to heavy metal pollution.

Mohan *et al.*, (1998) observed heavy metals (Fe, Pb, Ca & Zn) in the ground water of Naini industrial area; Dist. Allahabad, U.P. Kashem and Singh (1999) had also found the decreasing concentration of Cu, Mn, Pb and Zn with increasing distance from disposal point. Stetzenbach *et al.*, (1999) evaluated the heavy metals in ground water and used multivariate statistical analysis.

Tyagi and Budhi (2000) postulated the degradation of ground water quality due to heavy metals in industrial area of India. Kumar *et al.*, (2001) studied on the impact of textile industry on ground water quality of Sanagar, Jaipur and found the high amount of chemicals (e.g. sulphuric acid and acetic acid) and dyes (e.g. chrome and metal dyes) suspended solids and toxic metals in the waste which may enter in the groundwater and deteriorate its quality.

Siddiqui and Pathania (2002) made some studies on heavy metals in surface and ground water of Jalandhar and Ludhiana districts of Punjab state. Shrivastava *et al.*, (2003) collected soil samples from surface of the soil from different agriculture fields in the Khandesh region and Tapi River sediment samples were also collected from five different stations which were 7-8 km away from each other and detected the concentrations of heavy metals have been determined by ICP-AES.

Khan *et al.*, (2003) harvested some *Solanum melongena* plant in a laboratory experiment using five different levels of textile waste water and observed the contamination of heavy metals as 1.417 mg/g of Zn, 1.003 mg/g of Cu, 0.378 mg/g of Ni, 0.378 mg/g of Cd, 0.773 mg/g of Cr, 1.139 mg/g of Pb and 0.427 mg/g of Co in the soil of pots treated with highest ratio of distilled water and waste water. Yadav and Sumanlata (2003) indicated the heavy metal pollution in ground water in Bahadurgarh block of districts Jhajjar, Haryana.

Malik *et al.*, (2004) evaluated the accumulation of heavy metals in crop plants through irrigation of contaminated ground water in Panipat region and emphasized on bioremediation processes for combat ground water pollution. Chao *et al.*, (2005) reported the heavy metal contaminated site in Taiwan and described the status and distribution of heavy metals in environment.

It is necessary to reduce the levels of toxic metals from industrial effluents before discharging into surface waters. The general methods of treating wastewater-containing metals are coagulation, ion exchange, reverse osmosis and adsorption. Adsorption is a highly effective physico-chemical treatment for removing heavy metals for effluents. Due to high cost of activated carbon, efforts are being directed towards finding low cost adsorbents. Recently much interest has been shown for removal of heavy metals using a large number of low cost materials. Coal fly ash, the solid waste of power plants is one of the cheapest and non-conventional adsorbents (De, 2005).

Zheng *et al.*, (2006) assessed the heavy metals pollution of agricultural soil in Guanzhong district of China. Lokeshwari and Chandrappa (2006) evaluated the impact of heavy metals contamination of a Lake on soil and cultivated vegetation near Bangalore and found the presence of some heavy metals in rice and vegetables, beyond the limit of Indian Standards and calculated metal transfer factors from soil to vegetation are found significant for Zn, Cu, Pb and Cd. Hedge *et al.*, (2006) revealed the provenance of heavy minerals with special reference to ilmenite of the Honnevar beach in central west coast of India and observed some trace heavy elements like Co, Cr, V and Ni in the sandy soil of the beach. Singh (2006) indicated the contamination of ground water of Ganges-Brahmaputra river basin in north east India and found the ground water unfit for direct human consumption and noticed the rice and vegetable fields irrigated by ground water received a large amount of arsenic through shallow tube wells in the affected areas of north 24 *Parganas* and Murshidabad, West Bangal.

Malik *et al.*, (2007) assessed the migration of heavy metals in the ground water regime of Panipat industrial area on the behalf of different spatial variations the heavy metals were found in maximum quantities at point source of pollution. Malik and Bharti (2007) studied on soil quality of irrigated agricultural fields in a textile industrial area of Panipat city. Va´zquez, *et al.*, (2007) monitored the heavy metal pollution in San Antonio Bay, Rý´o Negro, Argentina. Obiri (2007) determined the heavy metals in water from boreholes in Dumasi in the Wassa West District of Western Region of Republic of Ghana. Huang *et al.*, (2007) indicated the speciation and mobility of heavy metals in mud in coastal reclamation areas in Shenzhen in China. Walker *et al.*, (2007) identified the influence of heavy metals and mineral nutrient supply on *Bituminaria bituminosa*.

Golia *et al.*, (2007) measured the accumulation of metals on tobacco leaves (primings) grown in an agricultural area in relation to soil. Mico *et al.*, (2007) described the comparison of two digestion methods for the analysis of heavy metals by flame atomic absorption spectroscopy. Padmavathiamma and Li (2007) explained the phytoremediation technology through the hyper-accumulation metals in plants and different aspects of phytoremediation technology and the biological mechanisms underlying phytoremediation.

Study Area

In Panipat city, Dye houses are situated on Jatal road in industrial area, these are quite famous for handloom business. Textile dying industries in

Panipat region consume large quantities of water and discharge it into a common effluent drain, which ends up in to a large pond situated near Binjhole village. Since last five or six years, it was noticed that ground water quality is degrading day by day of the regions and local people think that the dye waste water is the major source of heavy metal pollution in area.

But these heavy metals are travelling from wastewater to ground water and ground water to soil system and from soil system to agricultural crop tissues. In this paper, the route of heavy metals in soil and water is highlighted with proper illustrations and flow diagrams.

Methodology

Metals that are naturally introduced into the waterbody come primarily from such sources as rock weathering, soil erosion, or the dissolution of water-soluble salts. Naturally occurring metals move through aquatic environments independently of human activities, usually without any detrimental effects. Humans consume metallic elements through both water and food. Some metals such as sodium, potassium, magnesium, calcium, and iron are found in living tissue and are essential to human life-biological anomalies arise when they are depleted or removed. Probably less well known is that currently no less than six other heavy metals including molybdenum, manganese, cobalt, copper, and zinc, have been linked to human growth, development, achievement, and reproduction (Vahrenkamp, 1979; Friberg *et al.*, 1979). Even these metals, however, can become toxic or aesthetically undesirable when their concentrations are too great. Several heavy metals, like cadmium, lead, and mercury, are highly toxic at relatively low concentrations, can accumulate in body tissues over long periods of time, and are nonessential for human health.

The toxic heavy metals entering the ecosystem may lead to geo-accumulation, bioaccumulation and biomagnifications. Heavy metals like Fe, Cu, Zn, Ni and other trace elements are important for proper functioning of biological systems and their deficiency or excess could lead to a number of disorders. Food chain contamination by heavy metals has become a burning issue in recent years because of their potential accumulation in biosystems through contaminated water, soil and air. Therefore, a better understanding of heavy metal sources, their accumulation in the soil and the effect of their presence in water and soil on plant systems seem to be particularly important issues of present-day research on risk assessments (Lokeshwari and Chandrappa, 2006).

Path of heavy metals in various trophic levels may be different due to the nature of heavy metals and quality of host abiotic components. Transfer rate may be evaluated by the calculation of concentrations of heavy metals between two different trophic levels.

Transfer factor between plants and soil may be calculated for each metal according to the following formula:

TF = *Ps* (μg g–1 dry wt)/*St*(μg g–1 dry wt),

Where, *Ps* is the plant metal content originating from the soil and *St* is the total metal content in the soil (Lokeshwari and Chandrappa, 2006). Thus transfer factor (coefficient) may evaluate also among every two trophic levels and between any two levels.

Analysis of Metals

Collected, preserved, diluted water samples were prepared for the evaluation of metal concentrations with the help of AAS 4129. In the case of soil samples, a suspension (1:5) should be prepared in the distilled water; rest processes are like surface water and ground water samples.

Metals enter in the surface, ground water and soil/sediments through the disposing of toxic textile effluents of dye houses. For every metal a standard was required and concentration may be detected by AAS. Diluted and completely digested samples were required for metal detection by AAS 4129. Metal elements were determined with the help of Atomic absorption spectrophotometer (Model AAS 4129). Alan Walsh first developed the technique of atomic absorption spectrophotometry in 1955, and since then it has emerged as a powerful tool in quantitative analysis of more than 70 metals. The major advantages of the method are that it is free from any kind of interferences and very small concentrations are possible to be measured (De, 2002). The AAS is based on the principle that atoms of elements, which normally remain in ground state under flame condition, absorb energy when subjected to radiation of specific wavelength. The absorption of radiation is proportional to the concentration of atoms of the element. The absorption of radiation by the atoms is independent of the wavelength of absorption and temperature of the atoms. These to feature provide AAS a distinct advantage over flame spectroscopy.

Copper (Cu)

Copper in the natural waters also results in higher concentration due to pollution. It is used with sulphate as a pesticides and also separately as an algicide. Although, it passes as such through the body but there is evidence of accumulation of trace quantities in liver. The limits of it in the standards are not due to its toxic effects but are due to its taste producing capacity.

Preparation of 1000 Cu (μg/ml) standard: Dissolve 1 gm of Cu in 50 ml of 6N of HNO_3 and dilute to 1 L to give 1000 μg/ml Cu.

Cadmium (Cd)

Cadmium is fairy dense silver white malleable and most toxic metal, which melts at 320.9°C. Cadmium is used for dye and paint pigment production, batteries, ceramic industries, wooden industries and plastic production. The Cd found in a sample of Ca is likely in a inorganic form and may be relatively less toxic to plants and animals, while same amount of Cd when present in zinc or phosphates may be highly toxic to plants and animals, especially when there is calcium deficiency in soil or livestock rations.

Preparation of 1000 Cd (µg/ml) standard: Dissolve 1 gm of Cd Metal in 20 ml of 5N HCl containing 0.5 ml of concentrated HNO_3 and dilute to 1 L to give 1000 µg/ml Cd.

Iron (Fe)

Iron is one of the most abundant elements of the rocks and soil, ranking fourth by weight. All kinds of waters including ground water have appreciable quantities of iron. Iron has more solubility at acidic pH, therefore large quantities of iron are leached out from the soils by acidic waters. In the alkaline medium iron remain comparatively low in soluble phase.

Preparation of 1000 Fe (µg/ml) standard, dissolve 1.000 g of iron wire in 50 ml of (1+1) HNO_3 and dilute to 1 liter with de-ionized water to give 1000 µg/ml Fe.

Manganese (Mn)

Although not a toxic metal; Mn imparts objectionable and tenacious stains to laundry plumbing fixtures and clothing. It occurs in domestic waste water, industrial effluents, acid mine drainage and receiving strums and therby enters water bodies. Mn is relatively non-toxic to animals, but toxic to plants at higher levels.

Preparation of 1000 Mn (µg/ml) standard: Dissolve 1 gm of Mn in 50 ml of 6N of HNO_3 and dilute to 1 L to give 1000 µg/ml Mn.

Nickel (Ni)

At high concentrations, nickel has toxic properties. Aquatic organisms have varying sensitivities to nickel salts depending on the water's pH, hardness, alkalinity and type of nickel compound under consideration. Nickel as a metal is a carcinogen.

Preparation of 1000 Ni (µg/ml) standard: Dissolve 1 gm of Ni metal in 50 ml of 6N of HNO_3 and dilute to 1 L to give 1000 µg/ml Ni.

Lead (Pb)

It is a dense soft metal and is quite resistant to corrosion. It has melting point of 327°C. Major source of lead is PbS (Galena). Lead is used for pipes, solders, electrodes, batteries, newsprint, and pigments in paints. Lead is also used in insecticides, beverages, ointments and synthetic dyes. The chemical form of lead determines its solubility in water and biological fluids, the extent of its fixation on soil and type of chemical reactions occurring in atmospheric, aquatic as well as soil environment.

Preparation of 1000 Pb (μg/ml) standard: Dissolve 1 gm of Pb metal in 20 ml of 6N of HNO_3 and dilute to 1 L to give 1000 μg/ml Pb.

Zinc (Zn)

Zinc is present in high concentrations in the wastes from pharmaceuticals, paint, galvanizing, cosmetics, dyes and pigments, etc., and their discharge increases its concentration in appreciable amounts in the waters. Zinc is very essential micronutrient in human beings and only at very high concentration it may cause some toxic effects. Zinc salts produce an undesirable taste to the water and causes water to appear milky and on boiling, a greasy surface scum may also form in the water (Mani *et. al.*, 2005).

Preparation of 1000 Zn (μg/ml) standard! Dissolve 1 gm of Zn metal in 40 ml of 5N HCl and dilute to 1 L to give 1000 μg/ml Zn.

Standards and Calibration

Whenever, possible metals and metals oxides are to be preferred in the preparation of standards. This enables the analyst to dissolve them that samples and standards will contain identical elements and hence minimizes any chemical or physical interference effects.

Only concentrated standards (above 1000 μg/ml) should be held in storage. Working standards should be diluted from standards stock solutions only when needed. At low concentrations (less than 10 μg/ml) solutions have been found to deteriorate quite quickly because of the absorption on the walls of the container. Similar standard addition solutions can be prepared containing all of the required elements. This will avoid multiple splitting of the sample for individual elements and reduce the amount of time spent in preparing standards.

Before weighting, standards materials should be treated to ensure that they are in a standard state.

Metals: Wash with acetone and ether to remove any oil layers. Remove any oxide coating by abrasion with emery cloth or by acid pickling and drying.

Oxides: Dry at 110°C for two hours. If necessary, heat to evaluated temperatures to remove bound water.

Compounds: Equilibration at constant water content, or drying at 110 °C for two hours to remove any water.

Standards of known concentrations were prepared and evaluated the concentration of metal in water/ soil digested sample. Every metal has some specific properties and atomic weight, so for every metal different condition of standard and calibration was applied for every metal (ECIL methods manual, 2004).

Observations

Experimental site:

Heavy metals in agriculture soil-

Cadmium (ppm):

The cadmium concentration in agricultural soil was recorded maximum 3.4 ± 0.7 in summer 2006 and minimum 0.70 ± 0.60 in monsoon 2005 ranged between 0.1 to 4.0 ppm. The highest value of cadmium in agricultural soil was found 4.0 ppm during June 2006 and lowest 0.1 ppm in August 2005.

Copper (ppm):

The concentration of copper in agricultural soil was recorded maximum 36.3 ± 7.4 in summer 2005 and minimum 13.4 ± 6.0 in winter 2005-06 ranged between 5.0 to 42.5 ppm. The highest value of copper in agricultural soil was found 42.5 ppm during June 2006 and lowest 5.0 ppm in December 2005.

Iron (ppm):

The concentration of iron in agricultural soil was recorded maximum 82.8 ± 18.1 in summer 2006 and minimum 26.8 ± 10.8 in monsoon 2005 ranged between 14.40 to 100.5 ppm. The highest value of iron in agricultural soil was found 100.5 ppm during May 2006 and lowest 14.40 ppm in October 2005.

Manganese (ppm):

The concentration of manganese in agricultural soil was recorded maximum 13.6 ± 1.4 in summer 2005 and minimum 5.8 ± 1.7 in winter 2006-07 ranged between 2.0 to 15.0 ppm. The highest value of manganese in agricultural soil was found 15.0 ppm during June 2005 and lowest 2.0 ppm in December 2005.

Nickel (ppm):

The concentration of nickel in agricultural soil was recorded maximum 10.5 ± 0.8 in summer 2005 and minimum 5.3 ± 1.1 in winter 2006-07 ranged between 3.8 to 12.1 ppm. The highest value of nickel in agricultural soil was found 12.1 ppm during May 2006 and lowest 3.8 ppm in December 2006.

Lead (ppm):

The concentration of lead in agricultural soil was recorded maximum 62.4 ± 10.9 in summer 2005 and minimum 25.1 ± 6.7 in winter 2006-07 ranged between 16.0 to 73.5 ppm. The highest value of lead in agricultural soil was found 73.5 ppm during June 2006 and lowest 16.0 ppm in November 2005.

Zinc (ppm):

The concentration of zinc in agricultural soil was recorded maximum 19.4 ± 4.7 in monsoon 2006 and minimum 7.7 ± 2.8 in winter 2005-06 ranged between 4.3 to 23.5 ppm. The highest value of zinc in agricultural soil was found 23.5 ppm during July 2006 and lowest 4.3 ppm in January 2006.

Control Site

Heavy metals

Cadmium (ppm):

The cadmium concentration in soil on control site was recorded maximum 2.23 ± 0.31 in summer 2005 and minimum 0.225 ± 0.21 in winter 2006-07 ranged between 0.00 to 2.80 ppm. The highest value of cadmium in agricultural soil was found 2.80 ppm during June 2006 and lowest 0.00 ppm in September 2006.

Copper (ppm):

The concentration of copper in soil on control site was recorded maximum 27.4 ± 5.7 in summer 2005 and minimum 10.0 ± 4.1 in winter 2005-06 ranged between 3.5 to 32.0 ppm. The highest value of copper in agricultural soil was found 32.0 ppm during May 2005 and lowest 3.5 ppm in December 2006.

Iron (ppm):

The concentration of iron in soil on control site was recorded maximum 68.6 ± 17.5 in summer 2005 and minimum 18.4 ± 9.0 in winter 2006-07 ranged between 6.90 to 84.50 ppm. The highest value of iron in agricultural soil was found 84.50 ppm during April 2005 and lowest 6.90 ppm in October 2005.

Manganese (ppm):

The concentration of manganese in soil on control site was recorded maximum 11.5 ± 1.1 in summer 2005 and minimum 4.8 ± 1.5 in winter 2006-07 ranged between 3.2 to 12.5 ppm. The highest value of manganese in agricultural soil was found 12.5 ppm during June 2005 and lowest 3.2 ppm in December 2006.

Nickel (ppm):

The concentration of nickel in soil on control site was recorded maximum 8.43 ± 1.2 in summer 2005 and minimum 2.6 ± 1.87 in winter 2006-07 ranged between 0.00 to 9.20 ppm. The highest value of nickel in agricultural soil was found 9.20 ppm during June 2006 and lowest 0.00 ppm in November 2006.

Lead (ppm):

The concentration of lead in soil on control site was recorded maximum 42.3 ± 3.1 in summer 2005 and minimum 18.25 ± 5.9 in winter 2006-07 ranged between 11.3 to 46.8 ppm. The highest value of lead in agricultural soil was found 46.8 ppm during June 2006 and lowest 11.3 ppm in November 2005.

Zinc (ppm):

The concentration of zinc in soil on control site was recorded maximum 16.5 ± 3.3 in monsoon 2006 and minimum 7.3 ± 0.8 in summer 2007 ranged between 5.1 to 19.1 ppm. The highest value of zinc in agricultural soil was found 19.1 ppm during July 2006 and lowest 5.1 ppm in January 2006.

Correlation Coefficient

For cadmium correlation was found maximum 0.8421 and 0.7499 with water holding capacity and sodium respectively. Correlation for copper was found maximum 0.9134 and 0.9454 with temperature and Electric conductivity respectively. Correlation for iron was found maximum 0.8736 and 0.8436 with water holding capacity and sodium respectively. Correlation for manganese was found maximum 0.8162 and 0.9076 with temperature and Electric conductivity respectively. Correlation for nickel was found maximum 0.7798 and 0.8286 with water holding capacity and Electric conductivity respectively. Correlation for lead was found maximum 0.8483 and 0.8596 with water holding capacity and Electric conductivity respectively. Correlation for zinc was found maximum 0.8513 and 0.7586 with temperature and Electric conductivity respectively.

For cadmium correlation was found maximum 0.8706 and 0.7532 with water holding capacity and Electric conductivity respectively. Correlation for copper was found maximum 0.9142 and 0.8290 with temperature and chloride respectively. Correlation for iron was found maximum 0.8397 and 0.8795 with water holding capacity and sodium respectively. Correlation for manganese was found maximum 0.8814 and 0.7925 with temperature and chloride respectively. Correlation for nickel was found maximum 0.7267 and 0.6699 with temperature and water holding capacity respectively. Correlation for lead was found maximum 0.8608 and 0.8055 with water holding capacity and Electric conductivity respectively. Correlation for zinc was found maximum 0.8704 and 0.7613 with temperature and chloride respectively.

For cadmium correlation was found maximum 0.7611 and 0.6466 with cadmium and lead respectively. Correlation for copper was found maximum 0.9733 and 0.9121 with iron and nickel respectively. Correlation for iron was found maximum 0.8074 and 0.8628 with manganese and lead respectively. Correlation for manganese was found maximum 0.9279 and 0.9548 with nickel and zinc respectively. Correlation for nickel was found maximum 0.9458 and 0.9475 with manganese and nickel respectively. Correlation for lead was found maximum 0.9482 and 0.9664 with copper and manganese respectively. Correlation for zinc was found maximum 0.8065 and 0.5301 with iron and nickel respectively.

For cadmium correlation was found maximum 0.7650 and 0.7646 with copper and manganese respectively. Correlation for copper was found maximum 0.2703 and 0.2542 with cadmium and iron respectively. Correlation for iron was found maximum 0.2989 with cadmium. Correlation for manganese was found maximum 0.7224 and 0.5619 with cadmium and iron respectively. Correlation for nickel was found maximum 0.8617 and 0.8799 with cadmium and iron respectively. Correlation for lead was found maximum 0.8432 and 0.7390 with copper and manganese respectively. Correlation for zinc was found maximum 0.7216 and 0.8553 with manganese and lead respectively.

Metals Accumulation Factor

Metal accumulation factor for cadmium was found maximum 8.56 in winter 2006-07 and minimum 0.91 in monsoon 2005. For copper metal accumulation factor was found maximum 3.15 in summer 2005 and minimum 1.31 in monsoon 2005. Metal accumulation factor for iron was maximum 1.49 in winter 2006-07 and minimum 1.12 in summer 2005. For manganese metal accumulation factor was maximum 1.31 in summer 2007 and minimum 1.11 in monsoon 2005. Metal accumulation factor for nickel was found maximum 2.05 in winter 2006-07 and minimum 1.17 in monsoon 2005. For lead metal accumulation factor was found maximum 1.48 in summer 2005 and minimum 1.28 in monsoon 2005. Metal accumulation factor for zinc was maximum 1.20 in monsoon 2005 and minimum 1.02 in winter 2006-07.

Discussion

An increasing number of ground water wells were found to be contaminated by chemical waste from point sources and also widespread known point source pollution from fertilizers was threatening the water resources in extensive areas (Lagas *et al.*, 1989 and Meier and Mull, 1989).

Waste waters from textile industries have the high amount of the heavy metals entering them most hazardous for soil plant and other organisms including human beings (Sial *et al.*, 2006). Many effects of Cd action results from interactions of various micro and macro elements as it antagonizes to Cu, Zn and Fe and also interferes with Ca absorption. Cadmium found in a sample of Ca is likely in an inorganic form and may be relatively less toxic to flora and fauna, while same amount of Cd when present in zinc or phosphates may be highly toxic to plants and animals, especially in calcium deficiency in soil. The use of contaminated water into irrigation may be increase the cadmium status in agricultural soil (Mani *et al.*, 2005).

Cadmium concentrations in textile industrial effluent (0.005-0.052 ppm), pond water (0.001-0.012 ppm) and agricultural soil (0.7-3.4 ppm) turn down in rainy season due to the dilution factor, while in the ground water system its impact seems after monsoon and cadmium concentration reduces. Cadmium slightly fluctuated and remains mostly constant in pond sediment (4.0-5.7 ppm) and drain sediment (4.2-5.8 ppm). Transfer factor for cadmium (0.12-1.5) from textile industrial effluent to ground water was recorded high in winter months (after monsoon). In geo-accumulation index cadmium (3.77-3.81) laid in between 3 to 4 mean strongly polluted by cadmium. Metal accumulation factor for ground water (57.1-250.0) was found mostly very high or infinite for cadmium, because in most samples of control sites cadmium was absent.

Transfer factor of cadmium from ground water to agricultural soil on control site was found infinite, because cadmium was almost absent in ground water and agricultural soil at control site. So, any correlation between ground water and agricultural soil was not noticed. Cadmium transfer is due to some other non-point sources of cadmium pollution. Figure-5.4.6 showing the transfer factor of cadmium from ground water to agricultural soil clearly indicated the transfer level of metal. During the last decade, the industrial use of Cd has increased and can create both acute and chronic cases of clinically identifiable toxicity in humans. In human, absorption of dietary Cd is limited up to 15 % and that of inhaled Cd is high 40 % and not absorbed from skin (Mani *et al.*, 2005). When the animal kept on contaminated feed along with the industrial polluted environment for long time, they suffer from its toxicity symptoms which may be sub clinical or clinical. The retention time of Cd is quite high, half life being 40 years. Cadmium is produced as inevitable by-product of zinc (or occasionally lead) refining (lenntech.com). Cd was found slightly high in ground water for drinking purposes, because it should not be more than 0.003 mg/l for health views, while it should be less than 1 µg/l generally in drinking water (WHO, 2006). Helena (1999), Umar and Ahmad (2000), Kumar *et al.*,(2001) and Yadav *et al.*,(2002) observed the high Cd concentrations in industrial area like the present study of ground water, while Krebs *et al.*, (1999), Singh *et al.*,(1994) and Fakayode and Oniyawa (2002) in soil and Bordas and Bourg (1998), Vazquez *et al.*, (2007) and Korfali and Davies (2004) in sediment.

During the last decade, the industrial use of Cd has increased and can create both acute and chronic cases of clinically identifiable toxicity in humans. In human, absorption of dietary Cd is limited up to 15 % and that of inhaled Cd is high 40 % and not absorbed from skin (Mani *et al.*, 2005). When the animal kept on contaminated feed along with the industrial polluted environment for long time, they suffer from its toxicity symptoms which may be sub clinical or clinical. The retention time of Cd is quite high, half life being 40 years. Cadmium is produced as inevitable by-product of zinc (or occasionally lead) refining (lenntech.com). Cd was found slightly high in ground water for drinking purposes, because it should not be more than 0.003 mg/l for health views, while it should be less than 1 µg/l generally in drinking water (WHO, 2006). Helena (1999), Umar and Ahmad (2000), Kumar *et al.*,(2001) and Yadav *et al.*,(2002) observed the high Cd concentrations in industrial area like the present study of ground water, while Krebs *et al.*, (1999), Singh *et al.*,(1994) and Fakayode and Oniyawa (2002) in soil and Bordas and Bourg (1998), Vazquez *et al.*, (2007) and Korfali and Davies (2004) in sediment.

Concentrations of copper in textile industrial effluent are due to the residues of some dyes especially used for blue or green colours. Copper concentrations in textile industrial effluent (0.16-0.44 ppm) were found parallel or sometimes higher than iron. Most of the part of copper content reach in pond water (0.25-0.43 ppm) and rest settle down on drain sediment (45.8-54.8 ppm). Copper in pond sediment (38.6-52.4 ppm) also settled down after some time. Transfer factor of copper from pond water to ground water (0.97-1.17) and ground water to agricultural soil (0.45-0.82) was found higher than other microelement except cadmium. In geo-accumulation index copper was not recorded in polluted condition. Metal accumulation factor for copper was recorded high in winter season (3.28) for ground water; while in agricultural soil high metal accumulation factor was found in summer months (1.20).

Copper is sometimes found in insufficient quantity in soil (Miller and Turk, 2002) but it may be added in to soil system by some anthropogenic activities. Copper may accumulate in living organisms and their various body parts (Kudesia, 1992). High amount if heavy metals like cu and Zn may harm to living organism of existing ecosystem (Aslam *et al.*, 2004).

However, Cu concentration was not detected high in ground water samples as described by WHO (2006) in drinking water i.e. 2.0 mg/l. The Cu concentrations level in study area have compared with those observed by Yusus and Sonibare (2004), Aslam *et al.*, (2004), Helena (1999), Umar and Ahmad (2000), Kumar *et al.*,(2001) and Yadav *et al.*,(2002) in ground water; Krebs *et al.*, (1999), Singh *et al.*,(1994) and Fakayode and Oniyawa (2002) in soil and Bordas and Bourg (1998), Nasr *et al.*,(2006), Vazquez *et al.*, (2007) and Korfali and Davies (2004) in sediments. Ather and Vohra (1985) reported that heavy metal enters in water system by various ways in natural resources like erosion, weathering, volcanic activities and anthropogenic activities that include direct emissions of heavy metal by different industries.

Iron is one of the most abundant elements of the rocks and soil, ranking fourth by weight. All kinds of waters including ground water have appreciable quantities of iron. Iron has more solubility at acidic pH, therefore large quantities of iron are leached out from the soils by acidic waters. In the alkaline medium iron remain comparatively low in soluble phase. Excess calcium can reduced the activity of iron in soil and soil aeration may influence the availability of iron to plants (Miller and Turk, 2002).

In ground waters most of the iron remains in ferrous state due to general lack of oxygen. In alkaline conditions in ground waters, the iron is mostly ferrous bicarbonate, which is a colourless substance. When the ground water with higher concentrations of iron is tapped, it quickly oxidizes to ferric state in the form of insoluble ferric hydroxide, a brown substance. If appreciable quantities of ferrous bicarbonates are present in ground water, and they come in contact with oxygen at surface, the hydroxides are formed, CO_2 is released and hence it increases the pH, facilitating the oxidation processes (Minhas and Gupta, 1992). Generally, movement of iron compounds take place downward through the soil profile and reach in to ground water table (Miller and Turk, 2002). However, iron was not found in high concentration in textile industrial effluents (0.24-0.54 ppm), but the high concentrations of iron were observed in effluent drain sediment (5656.0-8467.7 ppm) due to the continuous settlement and abundantly natural occurrence in earth crust materials. Iron in shallow ground water samples (1.5-3.8 ppm) was found higher to textile effluents, while iron in deep ground water (0.48-1.05 ppm) and control ground water (0.363-0.868 mg/l) was not detected in high concentrations. Iron was present in high quantity in pond sediment (3803.5-6013.4 ppm) and effluent drain sediment (5656.0-8467.7 ppm). Iron concentration in agricultural soil was analyzed comparatively higher than other metals.

Iron's transfer factors were found very high from textile industrial effluent to ground water (5.93-9.64), from textile industrial effluent to pond water up to 25.00, while iron was transferred from pond water to ground water with highest 0.40 coefficient. However, transfer factor of iron was noticed low in comparison to other metals from shallow ground water to agricultural soil. Metal enrichment factor in all seasons and in all sediment samples was calculated 1000.0 due to the comparative parameter for other metals for determination metals enrichment factor. In geo-accumulation index for drain sediment and pond sediment iron was not indexed at very high rank, it was found very low because the natural occurrence of iron in earth crust shale was very high, so iron was not a pollution causing agent in industrial area during the present study. Metal accumulation factor of iron was found from 2-4 for ground water in Panipat region. Iron was detected in ground water with 2-4 times high quantities in comparison to control site's ground water. Iron in textile industrial effluent and pond water was found very high, while in ground water samples it was also found very high for drinking purposes (WHO, 2006) Helena (1999), Yusus and Sonibare (2004), Umar and Ahmad (2000), Kumar *et al.,*(2001) and Yadav *et al.,*(2002) observed the similar trends of iron concentrations in ground water and Singh *et al.,*(1994) in agricultural soil of industrial area.

Manganese was found as a second abundant element in the effluent drain and pond sediment after iron. However, manganese was comparatively low in textile industrial effluent (0.11-0.31 ppm) and very low in ground water samples (0.28-0.55 ppm). In ground water samples manganese remains below 1.0 during the study even in shallow aquifer. In agricultural soil, manganese was comparatively low in concentrations (5.8-13.6 ppm) regarding other metals. Manganese was third most enriched element in ground water samples. Mn was found slightly high at experimental sites in the case of soil samples. Manganese has positive relationship with all the physico-chemical parameters of ground water as correlated with temperature (0.6892), total solids (0.8508) electric conductivity (0.8544), total alkalinity (0.7074) except dissolved oxygen.

Transfer factor of Mn from textile industrial effluent to pond water was noticed from 1to 4 almost in all seasons, while below 1 in winter season.

Transfer factor was calculated near 1 in all seasons from pond water to ground water. Transfer factor from ground water to agricultural soil was noticed very low at experimental sites as well as at control site. Enrichment factor of Mn was found around 100-200, highest after Fe in drain sediment, while enrichment factor was noticed higher in pond sediment. The value of Mn in geo-accumulation index was noticed always below 1 with negative rank even highest value in drain sediment as well as pond sediment due to the high natural shale value of Mn in earth crust. Metal accumulation factor of Mn in ground water was high and ranged between 2 to 4, while in soil environment it was found below 2 always. Mn was found slightly high in ground water for drinking purposes, because it should not be more than 0.5 mg/l for health views in drinking water (WHO, 2006).

Mathess (1974) reported that fresh ground water constitutes 0.00-0.007 ppm cadmium, WHO (1984) recommended Cd concentration should not exceed maximum of 0.01 ppm in raw drinking water supply, 0.5 ppm in irrigation water. USEPA (1990) recommended maximum permissible Cd concentration as 0.04 and 0.02 ppm to protect aquatic life including fish. Hart (1982) reported a concentration range of Pb 0.0003-0.03 ppm in natural fresh water, while Frostner and Wittman (1979) the likely level as 0.002 ppm. Siddiqui and Pathania (2002) reported that the high value of Pb, Cr and other trace metals in ground water in Jalandhar and Ludiana industrial area.

Manganese, Iron and potassium may deficient in alkaline soil (Miller and Turk, 2002), while manganese and iron is soluble in acidic soil (Brady, 1995). Manganese usually is present in sufficient quantity in most soils and need not be added for plant growth (Miller and Turk, 2002). Yusus and Sonibare (2004), Umar and Ahmad (2000), Kumar *et al.,*(2001) and Yadav *et al.,*(2002) gave a report of Mn status in ground water, Fakayode and Oniyawa (2002) in soil system and Nasr *et al.,*(2006) in sediments of aquatic system affected by industrial pollution.

Nickel is one of the second trace elements of the present study after cadmium. As it is very toxic to plants and animals in low concentrations and has a tendency to accumulate in body parts. However Ni was presented in very minor concentrations in textile industrial effluent (0.007-0.067 ppm), and pond water (0.047-0.13 ppm), it was found comparatively high due to the regular input. Ni concentrations in pond were noticed higher during the summer season due to the loss of water by vaporization from pond system. About similar conditions were observed in ground water samples. In deep ground water, Ni was almost absent like cadmium. In agricultural soil all metals were found higher than ground water so, nickel was also found high (5.3-10.5 ppm). Ni was found very high like other metals due to the settling of metals on bottom beds in pond sediment (49.0-63.7 ppm) and drain sediment (58.0-75.0 ppm). Nickel has no positive correlations with any physico-chemical parameter of soil and water except total alkalinity, Calcium, electric conductivity and water holding capacity. Highest transfer factor of Ni from textile industrial effluent to pond water and ground water (14.14) was found in monsoon seasons. However, transfer factor from pond water to ground water (0.83-1.29) was not found effective comparative to transfer factor of other metals from ground water to agricultural soil at control site. Like cadmium, Ni was sometimes found infinitive in winter seasons.

Enrichment factor of Ni (7.35-11.7) was not effective in comparison to iron in drain sediment, but in pond sediment (8.38-14.85) it was slightly high due to the high retention time of wastewater in pond. The observations of present study reveals that Ni never reflected the pollution load in drain or pond sediment through the geo-accumulation index because it was found always below than 1. Metal accumulation factor in agricultural soil was recorded around 1-2, while in ground water it was found slightly high or sometimes infinitive. Ni was found high in ground water for drinking purposes, because it should not be more than 0.07 mg/l for health views, while it should be less than 0.02 mg/l generally in drinking water (WHO, 2006). Nickel may accumulate in aquatic life but its presence is not magnified along food chains (lenntech.com). So, there is not so big fear of nickel toxicity to higher animals including human beings, but agricultural plant health will be affected in contaminated agricultural soil. This trend of Ni concentrations in present study have been supported on the basis of recommendation of Kumar *et al.,* (2001) and Yadav *et al.,*(2002) in ground water, Kasem and Singh (1999), Singh *et al.,*(1994) and Fakayode and Oniyawa (2002) in soil and Nasr *et al.,* (2006) in sediment. Jayabaskeran and Sree Ramulu (1996) observed a great heavy metal movement in sewage irrigating light textured soil than in heavy textured soil. It may be pointed out that the builds up of heavy metal like Cr, Pb, Ni warrant toward continuous monitoring and suitable measures are needed before these become toxic.

Lead was found highest in textile industrial effluent, but it accumulated in drain sediment in comparatively less quantity. Lead mostly remained in effluent (0.25-0.50 ppm) and fluctuated in pond (0.5-1.8 ppm). Rest quantity of lead settled down on bed sediment of drain and pond, so, the lead concentration was found low in pond sediment (44.0-69.0 ppm) and high in drain sediment (47.2-70.0 ppm). Lead was the second most abundant metal species after iron. Lead was found in high concentrations in shallow ground water (0.85-1.84 ppm) in comparison to deep ground water (0.28-0.41 ppm). Pb was also second most enriched element after iron in agricultural soil (25.1-62.4 ppm) due to the high distribution of these metals in earth crust. Lead is deposited mostly in bones and some soft tissues. High concentrations of lead may create toxicity in human (Kudesia, 1992).

Pb was found slightly high in ground water (0.85-1.84 ppm) for drinking purposes and also in pond water (0.50-1.8 ppm), because it should not be more than 0.01 mg/l for health views, while it should be less than 0.1 mg/l generally in drinking water (WHO, 2006). Helena (1999), Umar and Ahmad (2000), Kumar *et al.*,(2001) and Yadav *et al.*,(2002) were observed the same trend of occurrence of Pb concentrations in ground water, Fakayode and Oniyawa (2002), Krebs *et al.*, (1999) and Singh *et al.*,(1994) in soil environment and Bordas and Bourg (1998), Nasr *et al.*,(2006) and Vazquez *et al.*, (2007) in sediment.

However, zinc was not found so high in textile industrial effluent (0.11-0.34 ppm) in comparison to lead, but it was found in very high concentrations in drain sediment (143.5-260.0 ppm). Similarly, it was found in less quantity in pond water (0.11-0.2 ppm) and accumulated in very high quantity in bed sediment (116.2-240.0 ppm) of pond. Zinc concentration was fluctuated in pond sediment (116.2-240.0 ppm) season to season, while in drain sediment (143.5-260.0 ppm) the fluctuation of zinc concentrations was not observed in high concentration. Zinc concentration (0.13-0.22 ppm) was found at fifth position in ground water samples among the all seven metals, while zinc concentration was found at fourth position in agricultural soil (7.7-19.4 ppm) among all metals studied. However, the concentrations of zinc in agricultural soil was found manifold than ground water, pond water and textile industrial effluent due to the natural occurrence of zinc in soil profile. During the study, in all experimental soils zinc concentration was found slightly higher than those at control soil (7.3-16.5 ppm). Positive correlations were found between zinc and temperature (0.8704), electric conductivity (0.2569), Cl (0.7613), pH (0.4955) in agricultural soil. Positive relationship was noticed between heavy metals of ground water with Zn. Transfer factor of zinc from textile industrial effluent to pond water was not found more than 1. However, transfer factor of Zn was found more than 1 from pond water to ground water during almost all seasons.

Transfer factor of Zn from ground water to agricultural soil was found slightly higher than 1 at experimental sites, while it was also found higher even more than 2 at control site. Enrichment factor of zinc in drain sediment was ranked at third position, while it was noticed slightly high in pond sediment due to the long retention time. In geo-accumulation index, the value of zinc was found more than 1.0 in all seasons, and ranked below 1 in geo-accumulation index in drain sediment.

Metal accumulation factor of Zn was calculated between 2 to 3 in ground water samples, while metal accumulation factor was found near 1 in the case of agricultural soil and always remain below 2. Zn was found low in ground water and in pond water for drinking purposes, because it should not be more than 3.0 mg/l for health views, while it should be less than 5.0 mg/l generally in drinking water (WHO, 2006).

Zinc is sometimes found in insufficient quantity in soil (Miller and Turk, 2002). Zinc salts are relatively non-toxic, but high concentrations may cause health problems like vomiting, renal damage, etc. (Kudesia, 1992). High amount of Zn may harm to living organism of that ecosystem (Aslam *et al.*, 2004). Helena (1999), Umar and Ahmad (2000), Kumar *et al.*,(2001), Yadav *et al.*,(2002), Yusus and Sonibare (2004) and Aslam *et al.*, (2004) reported the same fluctuations of Zn concentrations in ground water, Singh *et al.*,(1994), Krebs *et al.*, (1999) and Fakayode and Oniyawa (2002) in soil and Bordas and Bourg (1998), Nasr *et al.*,(2006), Vazquez *et al.*, (2007) and Korfali and Davies (2004) in sediment.

Heavy metals added to the soil in the field strongly absorbed by first component of upper part of undisturbed soil horizons. Subsequent redistribution to lower soil layers probably takes a very long time due to slow adsorption and heavy metals in upper layer tend to increase with time (Alumaa *et al.*, 2001). The trace heavy metal ions activities, depends on the solubility in the soil and often a much better indicator of heavy metal in soil solution reflected the soil metal fraction, that is most directly available for plants uptake, absorption by soil biota or leaching to ground water (McBride *etal.*, 1997; Cances *et al.*, 2003 and Lofts *et al.*, 2004).

Minor or secondary elements such as magnesium, manganese, calcium, zinc, copper, boron, iron, and perhaps others are essential but except in certain specific cases either they are injurious to crop and soil in large quantity. If any element is lacking in soil or it is present in improper proportions normal plant growth will not occur (Miller and Turk, 2002). It is urgently required that industries should continuously monitor textile effluent and take necessary actions to properly treat waste water prior their disposal to water bodies and save already depleting natural water resources (Aslam *et al.*, 2004).

Transfer of Heavy Metals

In the recent years there has been a growing concern with environmental protection. This can be achieved either by decreasing the afflux of pollutants to the environment or by their removal from contaminated media. The former is a feasible choice only for pollutants of anthropogenic origin, whereas, the latter is unavoidable for those of natural origin (Gomez-Serrano *et al.*, 1998). The presence of heavy metals in the aquatic environment has been of great concern to scientists and engineers because of their increased discharge, toxic nature, and other adverse effects on receiving waters (Singh, 2006).

In heavy metals analysis, the total concentrations of the metals are often determined (Okonwo et al., 1999, 2001; Castro Dentros *et al.*, 2003). However, total concentration of trace metals provides no information concerning the fate of the metal in the terms of its interaction with sediments, its mobility, bioavailability, or resultant toxicity (Christie, 1995). It is now widely accepted that measuring total metal concentrations cannot fully assess the role of aquatic sediments as a sink or as a source of pollutants. In addition, determination of total elements does not given an accurate estimate of the likely environmental impact. Instead, it is desirable to have information on the potential availability of metals (whether toxic or essential) to biota under various environmental conditions. Since the mobility of heavy metals, as well as their bioavailability and related eco-toxicity to plants, critically depends upon chemical forms in which, a metal is present in the sediment, considerable interest exists in trace element speciation (Davidson *et al.*, 1994).

Heavy metals are introduced into aquatic system from various anthropogenic sources. Heavy metals constitute a special group of contaminants of aquatic systems and deserve special attention. Since metals are not removed by natural degradation processes, they may become enriched in sediments over time. Metal contamination of sediments is an issue of growing concerns worldwide (NRC, 1989). Both natural processes and anthropogenic activities are responsible for introducing metals in to the aquatic system (Nriagu, 1989). Many contaminants discharged into surface waters rapidly become associated with the particulate matter and incorporated in sediments. Metals in aquatic systems become part of the water-sediment system and their distribution is controlled by a dynamic set of physical-chemical interactions and equilibrium, largely governed by pH and type of legends and chelating agents, oxidation state of the mineral components and the redox conditions of the system. Metal contaminated sediments may release heavy metals back to the overlying water column and, thus, pose risk to aquatic life and ecosystems. Due to their particle reactivity, heavy metals tend to accumulate in sediment as a result may persist in the environment long after their primary sources have been removed (Forstner and Wittman, 1981).

Heavy metals travel from one level to another in the ecological system due to the accumulation in abiotic and biotic components. In the study area, basically anthropogenic source of heavy metals are the dye houses in textile industrial area. Heavy metals reach in effluent drain and also its bottom sediment and further into pond and bed sediment of pond near village Binjhole adjoining to textile industrial area of Panipat. Heavy metals percolate slowly from the bed sediment of Binjhole pond towards the ground water table and there may be a threat to deep aquifers also by leaching process of metals. As the ground water was mostly used in irrigation and drinking purposes in most rural parts of Haryana, which have affected the agricultural soil health after irrigation by contaminated ground water and ultimately influence on the agricultural productivity, vegetation health and grain quality also. The use of ground water for drinking purposes of human and cattle in contaminated conditions, a threat of various health hazards and diseases have occurred to public at present. Some of the diseases caused by toxic heavy metals have been lethal to living organisms.

Accumulation of Heavy Metals

The development and pollution are the two faces of the same coin having the forever positive relationship between each other. Due to the industrialization, a huge quantity of waste materials discarded outside from the industries, in which various toxic substances including heavy metals are present. These large quantities of discarded heavy metals have been created havoc in the environmental ecosystem and affected all biotic components of the surrounding water and agricultural system.

The accumulating processes of run off derived metals from the point and non-point pollution sources and their significant accumulation in the sediment of drain and pond with furthermore retention in agricultural soil has been observed by many investigators (Harper *et al.,* 1984; Nightangle, 1987 and Yusuf *et al.,* 1986). The extent of contamination due to heavy metal deposition in different industrial sites in relation to quite vulnerable metal toxicity among soil biota and plants have been investigated by Moon *et al.,* (1991) and recorded Cd, Cu, Pb, Zn level in the industrial drain and top soil of agricultural fields.

Heavy metals have a tendency to accumulate and store in a component or trophic levels. The storage of heavy metals has created harmful effects for biotic components. The heavy metals accumulated in sediment and percolated down in to ground water known as bio-accumulation of metal. From ground water, heavy metals may turn into two ways; one is though irrigation and second is through drinking by human beings. The accumulation of heavy metals through the food chain is called the biomagnifications. The concentrations of metal increased at every next trophic level, whereas metals can cause various harmful effects on irrigated agricultural soil, human beings and livestock by alteration in some biochemical reaction in body cells (De, 2002).

In the present study, heavy metals in pond water were observed slightly lower than textile industrial effluents, whereas the heavy metal concentrations in effluent drain were higher than pond sediment. Shallow ground water of about 40 ft depth was highly polluted in comparison to increasing depth of water table. Although the effect of spatial variation was also found in the study, when the heavy metals concentrations in ground water and soils at control site were presented comparatively in less or very less quantities. Some metals like cadmium and nickel were not detected in ground water at control site. After all, if the conditions will be same in textile industrial area then definitely there is a fear to contamination of ground water into horizontal direction also and this will affect the ground water of surroundings and deep aquifers with the time.

Table 5.1: Seasonal variation of heavy metals in Agricultural Irrigated Soil

Heavy metals	Unit	Summer 2005		Monsoon 2005		Winter 2005-06		Summer 2006		Monsoon 2006		Winter 2006-07		Summer 2007	
		Mean	SD	Mean	SD	Mean	SD	Mean	SD	Mean	SD	Mean	SD	Mean	SD
Cadmium (Cd)	ppm	3.333	0.611	0.667	0.551	1.780	0.444	3.350	0.686	1.200	1.153	1.925	0.350	2.650	0.212
Copper (Cu)	ppm	36.300	7.422	30.200	5.345	13.400	5.968	34.875	9.309	32.333	5.498	14.350	4.916	20.850	3.748
Iron (Fe)	ppm	76.667	16.805	26.767	10.772	28.800	13.221	82.825	18.097	30.400	12.375	27.450	10.051	62.100	13.859
Manganese (Mn)	ppm	13.567	1.401	10.233	2.380	5.900	2.799	13.075	1.910	11.033	1.960	5.775	1.676	10.450	1.768
Nickel (Ni)	ppm	10.467	0.757	7.633	1.137	5.780	1.244	10.525	1.812	8.067	1.504	5.325	1.056	9.050	1.061
Lead (Pb)	ppm	62.400	10.922	39.333	11.675	25.340	9.226	61.300	11.385	44.933	15.791	25.100	6.733	46.150	4.738
Zinc (Zn)	ppm	13.167	3.911	18.533	5.150	7.680	2.805	13.025	3.471	19.400	4.747	9.150	3.101	8.000	1.697

Table 5.2: Seasonal variation of heavy metals in soil at control site

Heavy metals	Unit	Summer 2005		Monsoon 2005		Winter 2005-06		Summer 2006		Monsoon 2006		Winter 2006-07		Summer 2007	
		Mean	SD	Mean	SD	Mean	SD	Mean	SD	Mean	SD	Mean	SD	Mean	SD
Cadmium (Cd)	ppm	2.233	0.306	0.733	0.473	0.460	0.351	2.000	0.770	1.233	0.451	0.225	0.206	1.400	0.141
Copper (Cu)	ppm	11.533	15.396	23.000	4.036	9.980	4.141	20.525	13.495	22.733	4.966	10.250	5.637	15.800	4.667
Iron (Fe)	ppm	68.633	17.539	19.000	11.207	20.940	12.563	66.450	15.315	21.133	11.208	18.400	9.038	48.250	9.263
Manganese (Mn)	ppm	11.500	1.114	9.200	1.833	4.962	2.028	10.775	1.791	9.533	2.159	4.800	1.490	7.950	1.202
Nickel (Ni)	ppm	8.433	1.172	6.533	1.026	3.380	1.846	8.050	1.313	6.767	1.026	2.600	1.867	6.300	0.283
Lead (Pb)	ppm	42.267	3.121	30.633	8.999	19.000	7.316	41.925	3.677	31.400	7.602	18.275	5.934	34.600	4.101
Zinc (Zn)	ppm	12.100	1.500	15.400	3.830	7.460	2.475	11.700	2.655	16.467	3.275	8.950	2.885	7.250	0.778

Table 5.3: Mean Values (±SD) of Heavy Metals in Soil at Control and Experiment Sites

Heavy metals	Unit	2005-06				2006-07			
		Control Site	SD	Experi-mental sites	SD	Control Site	SD	Experi-mental sites	SD
Cadmium (Cd)	ppm	1.033	0.819	1.950	1.098	1.183	0.893	2.292	1.099
Copper (Cu)	ppm	14.317	9.218	24.100	11.451	17.050	9.744	26.075	11.391
Iron (Fe)	ppm	35.267	25.354	43.150	25.433	36.975	24.866	49.417	29.212
Manganese (Mn)	ppm	7.984	3.215	9.283	3.850	8.158	3.086	9.908	3.601
Nickel (Ni)	ppm	5.675	2.527	7.608	2.161	5.767	2.731	8.133	2.611
Lead (Pb)	ppm	29.317	11.729	39.967	17.818	30.508	11.188	43.750	18.264
Zinc (Zn)	ppm	10.667	4.148	11.867	5.640	11.525	4.195	12.833	5.460

Table 5.4: Correlation between Heavy Metals and Physico-chemical Parameters of Agricultural Soil

Parameters	Temperature	WHC	Bulk density	Soil moisture	pH	EC	Cl	Na	K
Cadmium (Cd)	0.2211	0.8421	-0.5639	-0.8066	-0.2848	0.3965	0.3654	0.7499	0.6852
Copper (Cu)	0.9134	0.5300	-0.0815	0.0914	0.3754	0.9454	0.8479	0.0853	-0.1689
Iron (Fe)	0.3455	0.8736	-0.6445	-0.6449	-0.4051	0.4198	0.3249	0.8436	0.7116
Manganese (Mn)	0.8162	0.6657	-0.2403	-0.0712	0.2034	0.9076	0.7254	0.3169	0.0611
Nickel (Ni)	0.7218	0.7798	-0.3816	-0.2585	0.0187	0.8286	0.6603	0.4813	0.2623
Lead (Pb)	0.7091	0.8483	-0.4542	-0.2607	0.0462	0.8596	0.6972	0.4876	0.2369
Zinc (Zn)	0.8513	0.0750	0.3246	0.5031	0.6535	0.7586	0.7744	-0.4581	-0.6269

Table 5.5: Correlation between Heavy Metals of Agricultural Soil

	Cadmium (Cd)	Copper (Cu)	Iron (Fe)	Manganese (Mn)	Nickel (Ni)	Lead (Pb)	Zinc (Zn)
Cadmium (Cd)	1						
Copper (Cu)	0.3719	1					
Iron (Fe)	0.7981	0.5348	1				
Manganese (Mn)	0.4834	0.9502	0.6730	1			
Nickel (Ni)	0.6368	0.8904	0.8093	0.9581	1		
Lead (Pb)	0.6911	0.8811	0.7809	0.9274	0.9566	1	
Zinc (Zn)	-0.1615	0.7484	-0.0190	0.5876	0.4374	0.466065186	1

Table 5.6: Metal accumulation factor for the Agricultural Soil of Panipat Region

	Summer 2005	Monsoon 2005	Winter 2005-06	Summer 2006	Monsoon 2006	Winter 2006-07	Summer 2007
Cadmium (Cd)	1.49	0.91	3.87	1.68	0.97	8.56	1.89
Copper (Cu)	3.15	1.31	1.34	1.70	1.42	1.40	1.32
Iron (Fe)	1.12	1.41	1.38	1.25	1.44	1.49	1.29
Manganese (Mn)	1.18	1.11	1.19	1.21	1.16	1.20	1.31
Nickel (Ni)	1.24	1.17	1.71	1.31	1.19	2.05	1.44
Lead (Pb)	1.48	1.28	1.33	1.46	1.43	1.37	1.33
Zinc (Zn)	1.09	1.20	1.03	1.11	1.18	1.02	1.10

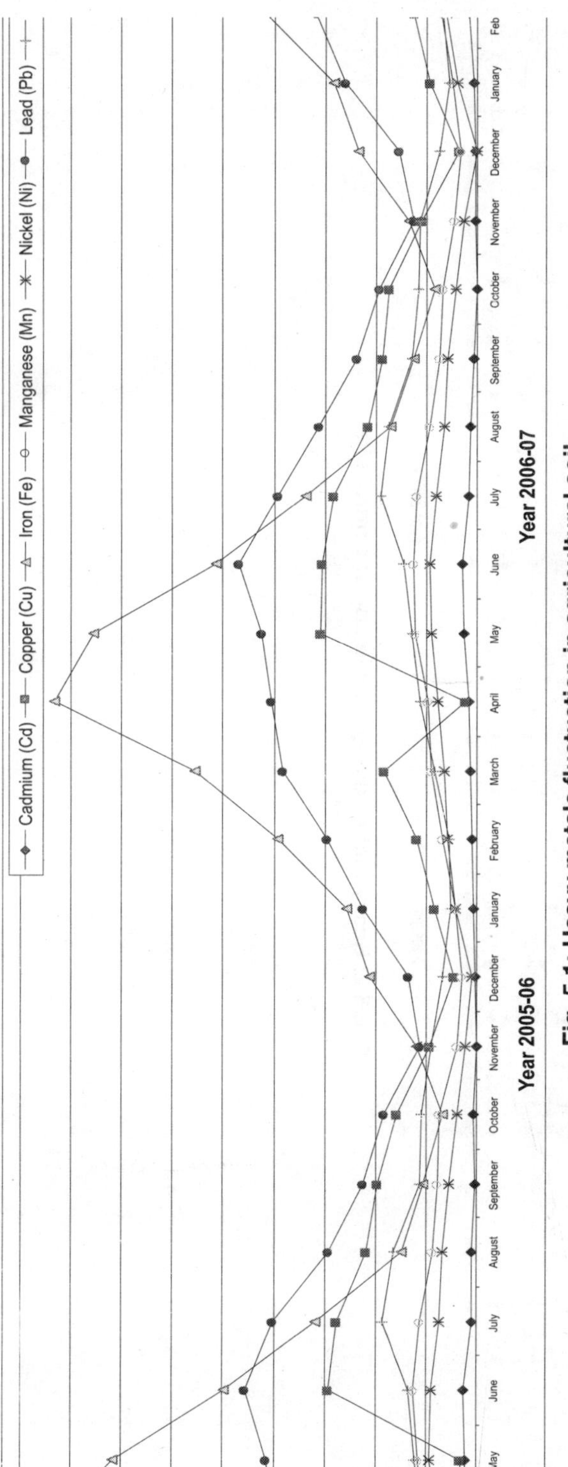

Fig. 5.1: Heavy metals fluctuation in agricultural soil

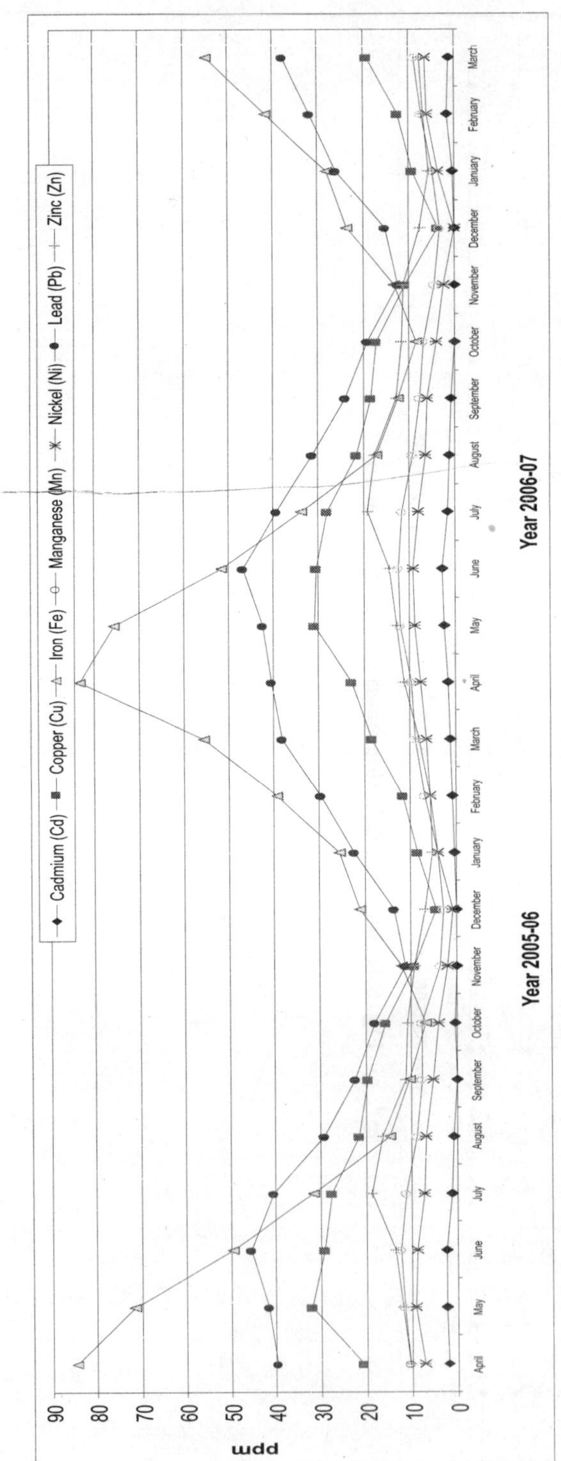

Fig. 5.2: Heavy metals fluctuation in soil at control site

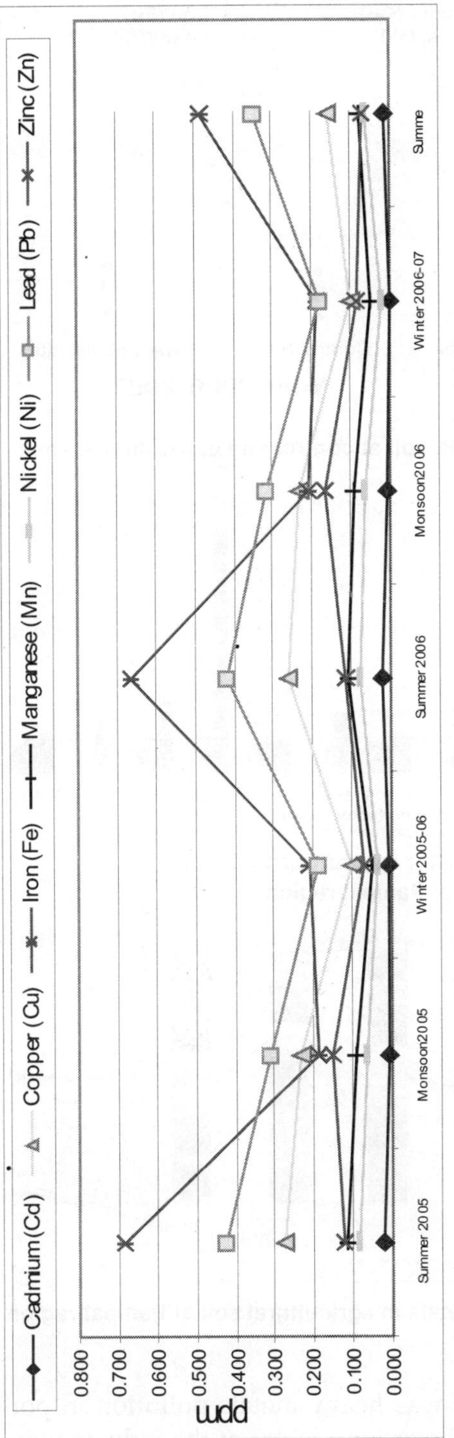

Fig. 5.3: Seasonal fluctuation of heavy metals in soil at control site

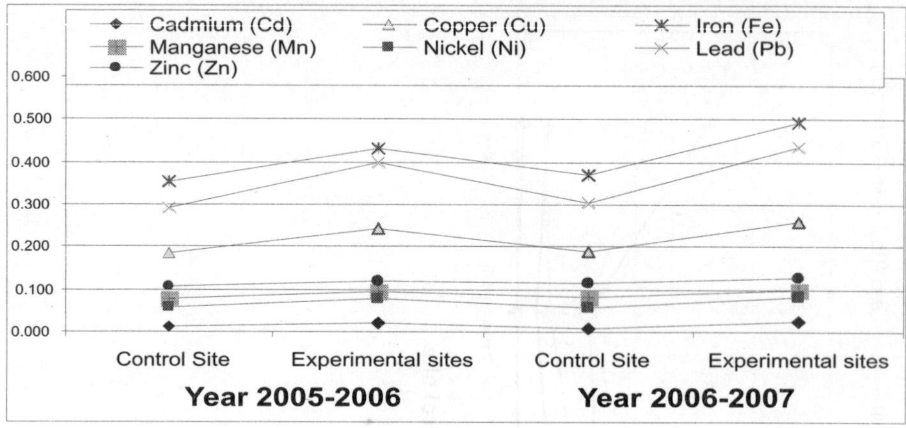

Fig. 5.4: Mean values of heavy metals in soil at control and experimental sites

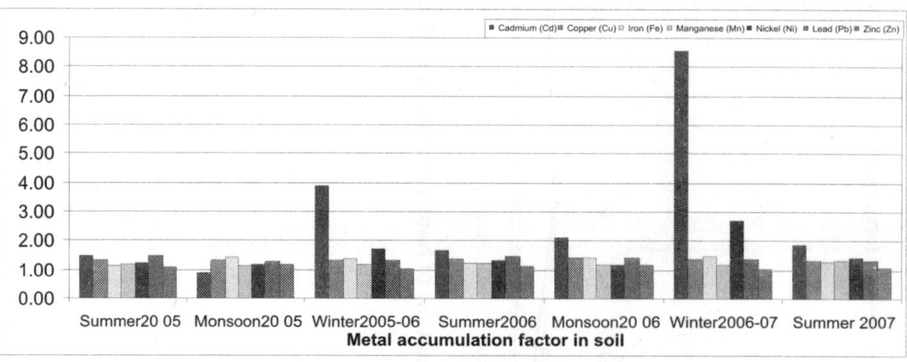

Fig. 5.5: Accumulation factor for various metals in agricultural soil of Panipat region

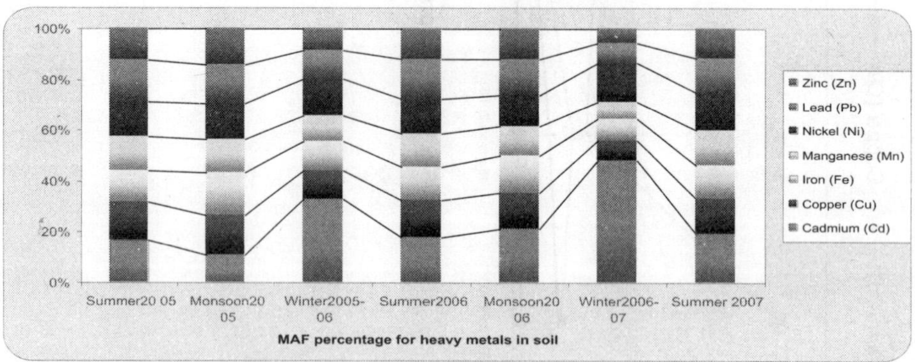

Fig. 5.6: Percentage MAF for various metals in agricultural soil of Panipat region

Conclusion

The present study reveals that there was heavy metals pollution in pond water and sediment, which affected the ground water of the industrial area of Panipat region. Beside this, the bottom sediment of common effluent drain stored the heavy metals in high quantities, which have no secure or pre-managed future. Thus, textile industrial effluents discharging from dye houses contaminated the surface water, drain sediment, pond sediment and ground water also. Furthermore, the impact of heavy metals reflected negative impacts on agricultural soil after irrigation by contaminated ground water. Heavy metals remained in upper part of soil horizons mostly but moved in to lower soil layers probably after a long time due to slow adsorption (Alumaa *et al.*, 2001). Heavy metals strongly absorbed by first component to which they make contact and plants uptake them. So there is a fear to accumulate the heavy metals in different body parts of vegetation. High quantity of heavy metals accumulated in organisms may be harmful for health of organisms and create various diseases, which may magnify through food web of the water and agricultural ecosystems.

Heavy metals from textile industries affected the shallow ground water quality in shallow badly, while deep ground water affected slightly. Vertically, heavy metals contamination decreased with the increasing depth of water table. In the case of horizontal distribution, the heavy metal concentrations decrease with increasing distance from pollution source. In the circle of 1 Km from pollution source almost heavy metals level was found higher than the outer wide circle in the industrial area. Heavy metals contamination was found to be low in soil at control site and also in outer circle of textile industrial area. However, the area of around 1 Km from textile industrial area was found highly affected by heavy metals in Panipat region. Textile industrial effluent or contaminated ground water has been altered the physico-chemical parameters of agricultural soil. It was indicated that the comparison of agricultural soil to control soil that some characteristics were influenced by contaminated irrigated ground water. Heavy metals in agricultural soil were found slightly higher than control soil. Due to the regular discharging of metals residues in the textile industrial area, threat have been appear on plant vegetation, livestock and human beings also of the region. So, some appropriate measures for the amendment and control of textile pollution should be adopted by industrialists, municipality, government, NGOs and local people also at various levels for the protection of environmental components.

An effluent treatment plant of appropriate capacity must be installed in the industrial area for the primary and biological treatment of for composite effluent from textile industries. Unlike most organic pollutants, heavy metals are generally refectory and cannot be degraded or readily detoxified biologically. Hence the safe and effective disposal of wastewater containing heavy metals is always a challenge to industrialists and environmentalists, since cost-effective treatment alternative are not available (Manahan, 1984). However, some researchers like Singh (2006) developed a low cost adsorbent of heavy metals from some cheap byproducts.

Restoration of affected agricultural soil is still an environmental aspect for Haryana state. Almost agricultural soils were noticed alkaline already, however, the soil in the industrial area of selected location was not so alkali, but its pH was more than 7. All the above observation and data indicated that the qualities of effluents sometimes do not meet the CPCB, BIS, MINAS and WHO specified norms. The effluents may also cause various health problems among the human being through contaminated ground water supply by municipal tube wells water scheme. In order to achieve the standards it is suggested to install the effluent treatment plants for the treatment of composite effluents of the textile industries.

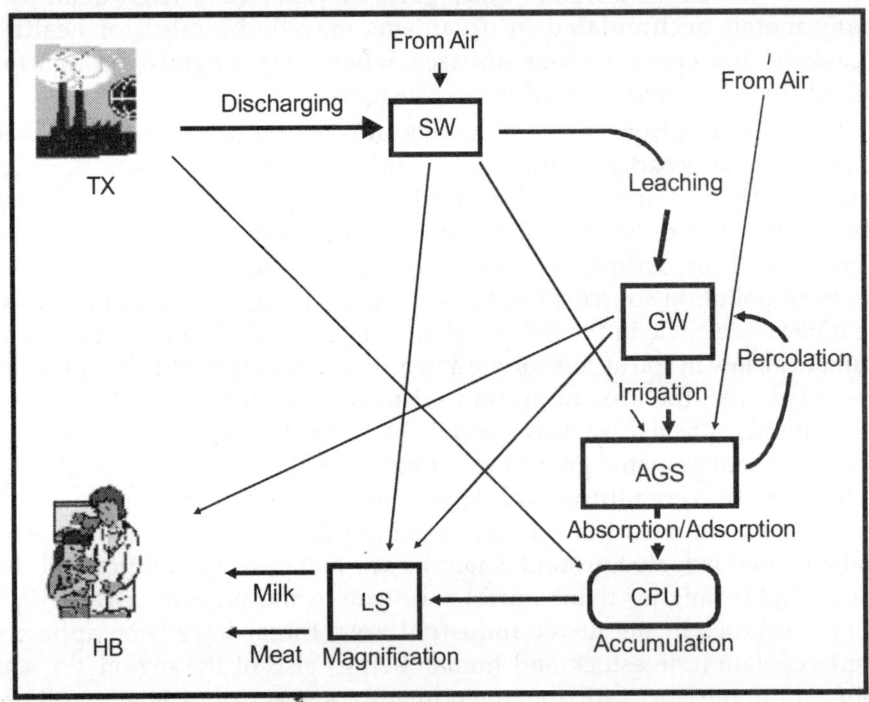

Fig. 5.7: Basic mechanism of heavy metal transfer between water and soil

Keeping all above in the mind, all the facts, formula and functions related to water, soil, plants and heavy metals, it is concluded that heavy metals travel among all the abiotic environmental components and ultimately reach in livestock and human beings. Available figure may also express the movement of heavy metals from textile industrial waste to surface water, from surface water to ground water, from ground water to agricultural soil, then in crop plants and at last to livestock and human beings. In nature, every element has a natural cycle in the environment but these heavy metals have not any appropriate recycle way in industrial environment, which may be harmful to all environmental living and non-living components.

REFERENCES

Aboulhassan, M.A.; Souabi, S.; Yaacoubi, A. and Baudu, M. (2005): Treatment of textile wastewater using a natural flocculants, *Environmental Technology*. 26: 705-711.

Abson, J.N.; Furness, C.D. and Howe, C. (1967): Development of the simicar resipirometer and its application to waste treatment, *Waste Poll. Control*, 66: 607.

Aggarwal, R.R. and Mehrotra, R.R. (1952): Soil survey and soil water in Uttar Pradesh, *Suptd. Printing and Stationery*, Aallahabad, pp: 361-372.

Ajmal, M. and Khan, A.U. (1985): Effects of a textile factory effluent on soil and crop plants, *J. Env. Poll.*, 37(2): 131-137.

Al-Degs, Y.; Khraisheh, M.A.M.; Allen, S.J. and Ahmed, M.N. (2000): Effect of carbon surface chemistry on the removal of reactive dyes from textile effluent, *Water Research*, 34(3): 927-935.

Alumaa, P.; Steinnes, E.; Kirso, U. and Petersell, V. (2001): Heavy metal sorption by different Estonian soil types at low equilibrium solution concentrations, *Proc. Estonian Acad. Sci. Chem.*, 50(2): 104–115.

Ameta Suresh C., Punjabi Pinki Bala, Kothari Shilpa, Sancheti Anjali (2003): Effect of untreated and photocatalytically treated dyeing industry effluent on growth and biochemical parameters of *Allium cepa* (Onion), *Poll. Res.*, 22(3): 389-392

Annadurai, G.; Juang, R.S. and Lee, D.J. (2002): Use of cellulose based wastes for adsorption of dyes from aqucous solutions, *J. Haz. Mat.*, B92: 263-274.

APHA (2005): Standard methods for the examination of water and waste water, *American Public Health Association,* 21st edition, 1015, Fifteenth Street, NW, pp: 1170.

Aslam, M.M.; Baig, M.A.; Hassan, I.; Qazi, I.A.; Malik, M. and Saeed, H. (2004): Textile wastewater characterization and reduction of its COD and BOD by oxidation, *Electron. J. Environ. Agri. Food Chem.*, 3(6): 804-811.

Ather, M. and Vohra, S.B. (1985): Heavy metals and environment, *New Age International Publisher Limited, Wiley Eastern Limited, New Delhi*, pp: 635.

Aurangabadkar, K.; Swaminathan, K.; Sandhya, S; Uma, T.S.; Jothikumar, N. and Paramasivam, R. (2001): Ground water quality around a municipality solid waste dumping site at Chennai, *IJEP*, 21(4): 323-327.

Bachmat, Y. (1994): Ground water as part of the water system. In: Ground water contamination and control, ed. V. Zoller. Marcel Dekker, Inc, New York, pp: 1-560.

Bae, W.; S.H. Lee; and G.B. Ko (2004): Evaluation of predominant reaction mechanisms for the Fenton process in textile dyeing waste. *Water Sc. and Tech.* 49 (4): 91-96.

Baruah N.K.; Kotoki, P.; Bhattacharya, K.G. and Borah, G.C. (1996): Metal speciation in Jhanjhi river sediments. *Sci. Total Environ.,* 193: 1-12.

Basu, A.K.; Rao, C.G.S.; Dhaneshwar, G; Mukharjee, M.K.A.; Kutty, D. Ray and Trivedi, R.C. (1973): Study on Hooghly estuaries pollution in the vicinity of tissue mill, *Proc. Symp. on Environ. Poll.*, pp: 24-26.

Beven, K. (2000): On the future of distributed modeling in hydrology, *Hydrological Processes*, 14: 3183-3184.

Bhakuni, T.S. and Bopardikar, M.V. (1967): Method of recovery Zinc from spinning bath waste of Viscos reyon factory by ion exchange process, *Env. Health*, 9(4): 327-338.

Bhargava, G.P.; Singhla, S.K. and Abrol, I.P. (1972): Characteristics of some typical saline sodic soils occurring in Karnal district Haryana state, Report No. 2, Division of soils and agronomy; *CSSRI, Karnal*, pp: 35.

Bhat, R. and Kulkarni, R. (2005): COD reduction of dye industry effluent, *J. Ind. Poll. Control*, 21 (1): 147-150.

Bordas, S, and Bourg, C.M. (1998): A critical evaluation of sample pretreatment of contaminated sediments to be investigated for the potential mobility of their heavy metal load, *Water, Air and Soil Pollution*, 103: 137-149.

Bousselmi, L.; Gelsson S.V. and H. Schroeder (2004): Textile wastewater treatment and reuse by solar catalysis: results from a pilot plant in Tunisia, *Water Sc. & Tech.*, 49(4): 331-337.

Brady, N.C. (1995): The nature and properties of soils, Prentice Hall of India Pvt. Ltd., New Delhi, pp: 621.

Cances, B.; Ponthieu, M.; Castrec-Rouelle, M.; Aubry, E. and Benedatty, M.F. (2003): Metal ion speciation in a soil and its solution: Experimental data and modal results, *Geoderma*, 113: 341-355.

Canter, L.W. (1987): Ground water quality protection, *Lewis publications*. Inc., Chelsea, MI, pp: 1-650.

Castro Dentros, T.S. Dentos Neto, A.A. Moura, M.C., P.A. Barros Neto, E$.I., Forte K.R., Leite, R.H.L. (2003): Heavy metals extraction by micromulsion, *Wat. Res.*, 37: 2709-2717.

Chao, Keh-Ping; Tsai, Ching-Tsan; Wang, John H.C.; Lin, Shaw-Tao and Chiang, Chow-Feng (2005) Health risk assessment of a heavy metal contaminated site in Taiwan. *Jr. Practice Periodical of Hazardous, Toxic, and Radioactive Waste Management,* pp: 167-171.

Christie, S.L. (1995): Speciation, In: Fitfield, F.W., Haines. P.J. (Eds). *Environmental Analytical Chemistry*, Chapman and Hall, UK, pp: 245-273.

Chung, K.T. (1983): The significance of azo-reduction in the mutagenesis and carcinogenesis of azo dyes, *Mutation Research*, 114: 269-279.

Considine, D.M. (1974): Chemical and process technology encyclopedia, *McGraw Hill Book Co.*, New York, pp: 655.

CPCB (2003): Ground Water, *Central Pollution Control Board, Parivesh Bhawan,* Delhi, pp: 56.

CPCB (2003): Parivesh: Ground water, *Central Pollution Control Board*, Delhi-32, July, pp: 40.

Darra, B.L.; Mehta, K.M. and Pareek, B.L. (1964): Quality of irrigation water in Rajasthan, *J. Indian Soc, Soil Sc.*, 12: 121-130.

Dash, S.K. and Sahoo, H.K. (1998): Quality assessment of groundwater in a part of Sundargarh district, *Indian J. Environmental Protection*, 19(4): 273-278.

Davidson, C.M., Thomas R.P., McVey, S.E., Perala, R., Littlejohn, D. and Ure, A.M. (1994): Evaluation of a sequential extraction procedure for the speciation of heavy metals in sediments. *Anal.Chim. Acta.,* 291: 277-286.

Dayama, O.P. (1987): Influence of dyeing and textile water pollution on nodulation and germination of gram, *J. Acta. Ecol.*, 9(1-2): 34-37.

De, A.K. (2002): Environmental Chemistry, *New Age International (P) Limited Publishers*, pp: 392.

De, A.K. (2005): Adsorption of cadmium and zinc on coal fly ash, *J. Ind. Poll. Control,*

21 (1): 27-30.

Desh, D. (1981): Activated sludge treatment of liquid waste- A review, *J. IAWPC Tech.*, Vol-VII, pp: 69-72.

Dhar, N.R.; Khoda, A.K.M.B.; Khan, A.H.; Bala, P. and Karim, M.F. (2005) A study of effect of acid activated saw dust on the removal of different dissolved tannery dyes (Acid dye) from aqueous solutions. *Journal of Environ. Sci. & Engg.* 47 (2): 103-108.

Doneen, L.D. (1954): Stalinization of soils of salts in irrigation waters, *Trans. Geophys. Union,* 35: 943-952.

Dowedy, R.H. and Larson, W.E. (1975): The availability of sludge borne metals in various vegetable crops, *J. Env. Qual.*, 4: 278-282.

Dulka, J.J. and Risby, T.H. (1976): Ultra trace metals in some environmental and biological systems, *Analytical Chemistry*, 48(8): 640-653.

Dutta, P.S. (1999): Ground water situation in Delhi- Red alert, Nuclear research laboratory, *IARI, New Delhi*, pp: 39.

Dutta, P.S. (2005): Ground water ethics for its sustainability, *Current Science*, 89 (5): 812-817.

Dwivedi, A.K.; Shashi and Singh, J. (2005): Water pollution and ground water recharging, *Current Science*, 91 (4): 407-408.

Eaton, F.M. (1950): Significance of carbonates in irrigation waters, *Soil Sc.*, 39: 123-133.

ECIL methods manual (2004) Methods Manual, Atomic Absorption Spectrophotometer, AAS 4129, *Electronic Corporation of India Limited*, Hyderabad-500062, pp: 85.

Eckenfelder, W.W. and Bornad, J.L. (1971): Treatment cost relationship for industrial waste, *Chemical Engg. Progress*, 67(9): 76.

Fakayode, S.O. and Onianwa, P.C. (2002): Heavy metal contamination of soil, and bioaccumulation in Guinea grass (*Panicum maximum*) around Ikeja industrial Estate, Lagos, Nigeria, *Environmental Geology*, 43: 145-150.

Fetter, C.W. (1994): Applied Hydrology, 3rd edition, Macmillan, New York.

Florence, T.M. (1982): The speciation of trace elements in waters, *Talanta*, 29: 345-369.

Forstner, U. (1985): chemical forms and reactivities of metals in sediments in chemical methods for assessing bioavailable metals in sludge and soils, In: Leschber, R., Davies, R.D. and Hermite, L.P. (Eds), *Elsevier, London*, pp: 1-30.

Forstner, U. and Wittman, G.T.W. (1981): Metal pollution in the aquatic environment, second ed. *Springer, Berlin*, pp: 486.

Forstner, U.; Ahlf, W.; Calmano, W.; Kersten, M. and Schoer, J. (1990): Assessment of metal mobility in sludge and soild wastes, In: Metal speciation in the environment (Eds.- Broeckaert, J.A.C; Gucer, S. and Adams, F.) Springer, Berlin, pp: 1-41.

Fransson, Åsa (2007): A case study to verify methods for estimating transmissivity distributions along boreholes, *Hydrogeology Journal*, 15: 307–313,

Fraser, B.G. and Williams, D.D. (1998): Seasonal boundary dynamics of a ground water/ surface-water ecotone, *Ecology*, 79(6): 2019-2031.

Frostner, U., and Wittman, G.T.W. (1979) Metal pollution in the aquatic environment, *Berlin Germany, Springer- Verlag.*, pp: 545.

Gardner, W.R. (1957): Some steady state solutions of the unsaturated moisture flow equation with application to evaporation from a water table, *Soil Sci.*, 85: 228-232.

Garg, V. K; Sharma, I.S. and Bishnoi, M.S. (1998): Fluoride in under ground water of Uklana town, District Hisar, Haryana, *Poll. Res.* 17(2): 149-152.

Garg, V.K. and Kaushik, P. (2006): Influence of short-term irrigation of textile mill wastewater on the growth of chickpea cultivars, *Chemistry and ecology*, 22(3): 193-200.

Garg, V.K.; Chaudhary, A.; Deepshikha and Dahiya, S. (1998): An appraisal of ground water quality in some villages of district Jind, *Indian J. Environmental Protection*, 19(4): 267-272.

Gharaibeh, M.A.; Eltaif, N.I. and Bayan Al-Abdullah (2007): Impact of Field Application of Treated Wastewater on Hydraulic Properties of Vertisols, *Water Air Soil Pollut*, DOI- 10.1007/s11270-007-9423-z.

Golia, E.E.; Dimirkou, A. and Mitsios, I.K. (2007): Accumulation of Metals on Tobacco Leaves (Primings) Grown in an Agricultural Area in Relation to Soil, *Bul.l Environ. Contam. Toxicol.*, DOI 10.1007/s00128-007-9111-0.

Goltenboth, F. (1994): Impact of textile factory in Salatiga on Ledok river system, Central Java, *J. Environ. Toxicol.*, South East Asia, pp: 301-317.

Gomez-Serrano, Garcia-Macias, A., Espinosa-Mansilla, A. and Valenzuela-Calahorro (1998): Adsorption of mercury, cadmium and lead from aquoes solution on heat treated and sulphurized activated carbon. *Wat. Res.,* 32:1-4.

GoogleEarth (2006): Software for satellite imagery, available at http://www.google.com.

Gopal, B. (1994): Conservation of inland water in India: An overview. Verh. Internet. Verein. *Hydrobiologia*, 384: 267.

Govindan, V.S. and Sundarlingam, V.S. (1979) Studies on treatment of textile mill waste water by stabilization pond method. *J. Pollution Control*, 5 (2):137-145.

Gray, C. W. and Mclaren, R. G. (2006): Soil factors affecting heavy metal solubility in some New Zealand soils, *Water, Air and Soil Pollution*, 175: 3-14.

Groff, K.A. (1993): Textile waste, *Environmental Research*. 65: 421.

Gupta, R.K., Singh, R.R. and Abrol, I.P. (1989): Influence of simultaneous changes in sodicity and pH on hydraulic conditions of an alkali soil, *Soil Science,* 147: 28-33.

Harper, H.H.; Yusuf, Y.A. and Wanielista, M.P. (1984): Fate of heavy metals in stromwater management system, In: *Lake and Reservoir Management, USEPA, Washington*, pp: 329-334.

Hart, B.T. (1982): Trace metals in natural waters, *Speciation Chem. Australian,* 49: 260-265.

Hedge, V.S.; Shalini, G. and Kanchanagouri, D.G. (2006): Provenance of heavy minerals with special reference to Ilmenite of the Honnevar beach, central west coast of India, *Current Science*, 91 (5): 644-648.

Helena, B.A.; Vega, M.; Barrado, E.; Parado, R. and Fernandez, L. (1999): A case of hydro-chemical characterization of an alluvial aquifer influenced by human activities, *Water, Air and Soil Pollution*, 112: 365-387.

Hesse, P.R. (1994): A textbook of soil chemical analysis, *CBS Publishers and distributors*, 485, Bholanathnagar, Shahdhra, Delhi-110032, pp: 520.

Hitz, H.R.; Huber, W and Rud, R.H. (1978): The absorption of dyes on activated sludge,

Journal of society of dyers and Colorists, February: 71-76.

Horing, R.H. (1976): Characterization and treatment of textile dyeing wastewaters, In: Proceedings of national technical conference, *American association of textile chemists and colorist*, pp: 100-104.

Hoston, A.K. (1965): An index number system for rating water quality, *J. Wat. Poll. Cont. Fed.*, 37(3): 300-306.

http//:www.engg.ksu.edu as access on 16 november, 2006

Huang, J.; Huang, R.; Jiao, J.J. and Chen, K. (2007): Speciation and mobility of heavy metals in mud in coastal reclamation areas in Shenzhen, China, *Environ. Geol.*, DOI 10.1007/s00254-007-0636-7.

Hynes, H.B.N. (1970): The ecology of running waters, *Liverpool University Press, Liverpool, 4th impression*: 1-555.

Ireland, M.P. (1983): Heavy metals uptake and tissue distribution, In: Earthworm ecology- from Darwin to vermiculture (Ed.- Satchell, J.E., *Chapman and Hall*), pp: 135-147.

IUPAC (1994): Atomic weights of the elements, 1993, International Union of Pure and Applied Chemistry, *Pure Appl. Chem.*, 66: 2423.

Jain, C.K. (2004): Metal fractionation study on bed sediments of river Yamuna, India, *Wat. Res.* 38: 569-578.

Jayabaskeran, K. J. Sree Ramulu U. S. (1996): Distribution of heavy metals in soil of various sewage farms in Tamil Nadu, *J. Indian Soc. Soil. Sci.*, 44: 401-404.

Jha, M.N. and Pandey, P. (1984): Impact of growing eucalyptus and soil monocultures on soil in natural sal area of Doon valley, *Ind. For.*, 110: 16-18.

Judlins, J.F. and Hornsby, J.S. (1978): Color removal from textile dye waste using magnesium carbonate, *Journal of Water Pollution Control Federation*, 50: 2446-2456.

Kalra, Y.P. and Maynarol, D.G. (1991): Methods manual for forest soil and plant analysis. *For. Can., Northwest Reg. North. For. Cent. Edmonton, Alberta. Inf. Rep. Nor. X-319,* pp: 1-65.

Kanwar, J.S. (1961): Quality of irrigation water as an index of suitability for irrigation purposes, *Potash Review*, 13: 1-13.

Karle, K.K.; Bhusal, S.S.; Gunjal, P.S. and Kuchekar, S.R. (1992): Studied on ground water quality in Pravaranagar area of Ahmednagar district, *Poll. Res.* 11(2): 65-68.

Kashem, M.A. and Singh, B.R. (1999): Heavy metal contamination of soil and vegetation in the vicinity of industries in Bangladesh, *Water, Air and Soil Pollution*, 115: 347-361.

Kataria, H.C. (1996): BOD and COD contents in bore well water of Bhopal (M.P.), *Natcon*, 8(1): 69-72.

Kataria, H.C.; Gupta, S.S. and Jain, O.P. (1995): Water quality of bore wells in B.H.E.L. area of Bhopal, *Poll. Res.* 14 (4): 455-462.

Katz, M. (1975): The effect of heavy metals on fish and aquatic environment. (Ed.- Krenkel, P.A.), *Pregamon Press, New York*, pp: 637-645.

Kaushik, M.P. (2006): Vanaspati Vigyan, Prakash Prakashan, Muzaffarnagar, 834.

Khan T.I., Marwari Richa, Singh N. (2003): Impact of textile wastewater on *Solanum melongena* var-Fl- Hybrid Kanhaiya in pot experiment with special emphasis on analysis of heavy metals. *Dimensions Polln*, 2: 108-116.

Khurshid, Zaheeruddin and Mohd. Usman Shabeer (1997): Degradation of water quality due to heavy metals pollution in Faridabad district, Haryana, India, *Poll. Res.* 16(1): 41-43.

Korfali, S.I. and Davies, B.D.E. (2004): The relationship of metals in river sediments (Nahr-Ibrahim, Lebanon) and adjacent floodplain soil, *the CIGR J. of scientific research and development*, manuscript LW 04 010, 6: 1-22.

Krebs, R.; Gupta, S.K.; Furrer, G. and Schulin, R. (1999): Gravel sludge as an immobilizing agent in soils contaminated by heavy metals: A field study, *Water, Air and Soil Pollution*, 115: 465-479.

Krishna, A. K. and Govil, P. K. (2004) Heavy metal contamination of soil around Pali industrial area, Rajasthan, India, *Environmental Geology*, 47: 38-44.

Krull, R. and E. Dopkens (2004): Recycling of dye house effluents by biological and chemical treatment, *Water Sc. And Tech.* 49(4): 311-317.

Kudesia, V.P. (1992): Water Pollution, *Pragati Prakashan, Meerut*, pp: 407.

Lofts, S.; Spurgeon, D.J.; Svendsen, C. and Tipping, E. (2004): Deriving soil critical limits for Cu, Zn, Cd, and pH: A method based on free ion concentration, *Environ. Sci. Tech.*, 38: 3623-3631.

Lokeshwari, H. and Chandrappa, G.T. (2006): Impact of heavy metal contamination of Bellandur Lake on soil and cultivated vegetation, *Current Science*, 91(9): 622-627.

Lokeshwari, H. and Chandrappa, G.T. (2006): Impact of heavy metal contamination of Bellandur Lake on soil and cultivated vegetation, *Current Science*, 91(9): 622-627.

Loska, K. and Wiechula, D. (2002): Speciation of cadmium in the bottom sediment of rybnik Reservoir, *Water, Air Soil Pollut.*, 141: 73-89.

Lung, W. (1990): Speciation analysis – why and how? *Fresenius J. Anal. Chem.* 337: 557-564.

Malik, D.S. and Bharti, P. K. (2007): Soil quality of irrigated agricultural fields in textile industrial area of Panipat city, *Asian Journal of Experimental sciences,* 21 (2): 445-451.

Malik, D.S.; Bharti, P.K. and Grover, S. (2006): Alteration in surface water quality near textile industries at Panipat (Haryana), *Environment Conservation J.*, 7(2): 65-68.

Malik, D.S.; Bharti, P.K; Kamboj, N. and Yadav, R. (2007): Quantification of heavy metals migration in ground water regime due to discharge of textile industrial effluents in Panipat area, Haryana, *Pollution Research*, 26 (4): 123-125.

Malik, D.S.; Yadav, R. and Bharti, P.K. (2004) Accumulation of heavy metals in crop plants through irrigation of contaminated ground water in panipat region, *Environmental Conservation Journal* 5 (3): 101-104.

Manahan, S. (1984): Environmental Chemistry, Brooks/Colei, CA, USA, pp: 638.

Manchanda, H.R. (1990): Significance of the type of salinity for growing pulses under saline conditions, *Indo-Pak workshop on Soil Salinity and Water Management,* Feb, 10-14, pp: 2-3.

Mani, V.; Kaur, H. and Mohini, M. (2005): Toxic metals and environmental pollution, *J.*

Ind. Poll. Cont., 21(1): 101-107.

Martin, J.M. and Whitfield, M. (1983): The significance of the river input of chemical elements to the ocean, In: Wong, C.S.; Boyle, E.; Bruland, K.W.; Burton, J.D. and Goldburg, E.D. (Eds.), Trace metals in sea water, *Plenum Press, New York*, pp: 324-331.

Martin, M.H. and Cougherty, P.J. (1982): Biological monitoring of heavy metals pollution, *Applied Science Publishers*, pp: 463.

Masters, G.M. (1998): Introduction to environmental engineering and science, *Prentice-Hall India*, pp: 460.

Mathess, G. (1974): Heavy metals as trace constituents in natural and polluted ground water, *Goel mijnbouw, New Jersy, USA*, 53: 149-155.

McBride, M., Sauve, S. and Hendershot, W. (1997): Solubility control of Cu, Zn, Cd, and Pb, in contaminated soils, *Euro. J. Soil Science*, 48: 337-346.

Mico, C; Recatal, L.; Peris, M. And Sanchez, J. (2007): A comparison of two digestion methods for the analysis of heavy metals by flame atomic absorption spectroscopy, *Spectroscopy Europe*, 19 (1): 23-26

Mido, Y. and Satake, M, (1995): Chemicals in the environment, *Discovery Publishing House, New Delhi,* pp: 491.

Millar, C.E. and Turk, L.M. (2002): Fundamentals of soil science, Biotech Books, Delhi-35, pp: 462.

Minhas, P.S. and Khosla, B.K. (1986): Solute displacement in a silt loam soil as affected by the method of water application under different evaporation rates, *Agric. Wat. Mgmt,* 12: 63-75.

Mohan, R.; Chopra, N. and Chowdhary, G.C. (1998): Heavy metals (Fe, Pb, Cd, Zn) in the ground water of Naini industrial area, Dist. Allahabad, U.P., *Poll. Res.* 17(2): 167-168.

MPCA (2001): Effects of Land Use on Ground Water Quality, St. Cloud Area, Minnesota – Short Report, *Minnesota Pollution Control Agency,* Ground Water Monitoring and Assessment Program, pp: 1-29.

Muller, G. (1979): Schwermetalle in den sedimenten des Rheinsveranderungen seit, *Umschau*, 79: 778-783.

Nasr, S.M.; Okbah, M.A. and Kasem, S.M. (2006): Environmental assessment of heavy metal pollution in bottom sediments of Aden port, Yemen, *International Journal of Oceans and Oceanography*, 1(1): 99-109

National Research Council (NRC) (1989): Contaminated marine systems- assessment and remediation, *National Academy Press, Washington*, D.C. pp: 185.

Navarro, A. and Font, X. (1993): Discriminating different sources of ground water contamination caused by industrial waste in the Besos River Basin, Barcelona, Spain, *J. Applied Biochemistry,* APPGEY, 8: 277.

Nedunuri, K.V.; Govindaraju, R.S.; Erickson, L.E. and Schwab, A.P. (1995): Modeling of heavy metal movement in vegetated, unsaturated soils with emphasis on geochemistry, In: Proceedings of the 10th Annual Conference on Hazardous Waste Research, pp: 57-66.

Nongkynrih, P.; Dkhar, P.S. and Khathing, D.T. (1996): Micronutrients elements in acid alfisols of Meghalaya under rice cultivation, *J. Soil Si.*, 44(3): 455-457.

Nriagu, J.O. and Pacyna, J.M. (1988): Quantitative assessment of worldwide contamination of air, water and soil with trace metals, *Nature*, 333: 134-139.

Numberg, H.W. (1984): The volumetric approach in trace metal chemistry of natural waters and atmospheric precipitation, *Analyst. Chim. Acta*, 164: 1-21.

Obiri, Samuel (2007): Determination of Heavy Metals in Water from Boreholes in Dumasi in the Wassa West District of Western Region of Republic of Ghana, *Environ Monit Assess,* 130: 455–463

Padmavathiamma, P.K. and Li, L.Y. (2007): Phytoremediation Technology: Hyper-accumulation Metals in Plants, *Water Air Soil Pollut.*, DOI- 10.1007/s11270-007-9401-5.

Palanivelu, K.; Priya, M.N.; Selvan, A.M. and Natesan,U. (2006): Water quality assessment in the tsunami affected coastal areas of Chennai, *Current Science*, 91 (5): 583-584.

Prasad, S. (2003): Fundamentals of biostatistics (biometry), *Emkey Publication, Delhi-51*, pp: 168.

Pujari, G.K. and Sinha, B.K. (1999): Studies on the water and soil quality of some villages of Attabira area irrigated by Bargarg main canal originated from Hirakund reservoir of Orissa, *J. of Env. and Poll.*, 6(1): 71-76.

Rao, K.V.G.K.; Gupta R.K. and Kamra, S.K. (1987): Reclamation of waterlogged high SAR saline soil, CSSRI, Karnal, A feasibility report for *CIRB, Hissar, CSSRI, Karnal*, pp: 21.

Rhoades, J.D. (1987): Use of saline water for irrigation, *Wat. Qual. Bull.*, 12: 14-20.

Richards, L.A. (1954): Diagnosis and improvement of saline and alkali soils, US Deptt. Agri., edited Handbook, No. 60: 160.

Saxena, M.M. (1994): In: Environmental analysis water, soil and air, *Agro Botanical Publishers.* pp: 1-180.

Schroeder, W.H. (1989): Development in the speciation of mercury in natural waters, *Trends Anal. Chem.* 8: 339-342.

Sharma, D.R. (1978): Testing of a model for prediction sodium hazards of irrigation waters, *J. Indian Soc. Soil Sci.*, 27: 204-208.

Sharma, D.R. and Parihar, S.S. (1973): Effect of depth and salinity of ground water on evaporation and soil salinization, *Indian J. Agric. Sci.*, 43: 582-586.

Shrivastava V.S. and Patil B.H. (2003): Metallic and some physico-chemical studies of soil and aquatic sediments, *Eco Env Conserv*, 9(1): 75-77

Singh, B. and Bhumbla, D.R. (1968): Effect of quality of irrigation water on soil properties, *J. Res.* (Punjab Agri. Univ.), 5: 166-171.

Singh, B. Rana, D.S. and Bajwa, M.S. (1977): Salinity and sodium hazards of underground irrigation waters of Bhatinda district (Punjab), *Indian J. Ecol.*, 4: 32-41.

Singh, K.N.; Bains, S.S. and Dayanand (1969): Salinity problem in high water table areas- An appraisal, *Indian J, Agron.*, 14: 31-34.

Singh, K.S. and Sharma, R.P. (1971): Studies on the effects of saline irrigation waters on physico-chemical properties of some soils of Rajasthan, *J. Indian Soc. Soil Sci.*, 18: 345-356.

Singh, T.B.; Jadon, S.P.S. and Mishra, G.J. (1994): Degradation of water and soil quality of Parwanoo area with respect to heavy metals, *IJEP*, 14 (4): 282-287.

Srinivasan, M. and Murali, M. (1996): Some studies on effect pollutants on properties of soils, *IJEP*, 16(7): 522-523.

Tan, K.H. and Nopamornbodi, O. (1981): Electron microbeam analysis and scanning electron microscopy of soil-root interfaces, *Soil Sci.*, 131: 100-106.

Taylor, S.R. (1964): Abundance of chemical elements in the continental crust – A new table, *Geochim. Cosmochim. Acta.* 28: 1273-1275.

Trevors, J.T. and Saier Jr., M.H. (2007): Regulation of Pollution, *Water Air Soil Pollut*, DOI 10.1007/s11270-007-9344-x.

Trivedi, R.K. and Goel, P.K. (1984): Chemical and biological methods for water pollution studies Karad, *Environmental publication,* pp: 1-251.

USEPA (1990): Operation and quality control manual, Environmental Protection Agency (EPA), Athens, GA 30613.

Va´zquez, N.N.; Gil, M.A.; Esteves, J. L. and Narvarte, M. A. (2007): Monitoring Heavy Metal Pollution in San Antonio Bay, Rý´o Negro, Argentina, *Bull. Environ. Contam. Toxicol.,* DOI 10.1007/s00128-007-9084-z.

Walker, D.J.; Bernal, M.P. and Correal, E. (2007): The Influence of Heavy Metals and Mineral Nutrient Supply on *Bituminaria bituminosa*, *Water Air Soil Pollut*, DOI 10.1007/s11270-007-9422-0.

Walker, R. (1970): The metabolism of azo compounds: a review of the literature, *Food Cosmetics Toxicology*, 8: 659-661.

WHO (2006) Standards for drinking water, available at http//:www.lenntech.com

Williums, D.R. (1972): Metals, Ligands and Cancer, *Chemical Review*, 72 (3): 203-213.

Wint, A. (1981): The disposal of toxic wastes, In: Industrial Effluent Treatment Vol-I (Eds.- Watler, J.K. and Wint, M.), pp: 1-19.

Yadav, R.K.; Goyal, B.; Sharma, R.K.; Dubey, S.K. and Minhas, P.S. (2002): Post-irrigation impact of domestic sewage effluent on composition of soils, crops and ground water- a case study, *Environment International*, 28: 481-486.

Yuandong, Z.; Shirong, L. and Jiangming, M. (2006): Water-holding capacity of ground covers and soil in alpine and sub-alpine shrubs in western Sichuan, China, *ACTA Ecologica Sinica*, 26(9): 2775-2782.

Zheng, G.; Yue, L.; Li, Z and Chen, C. (2006): Assessment on heavy metals pollution of agricultural soil in Guanzhong District, *J Geographical Sciences*, 16, (1): 105-113.

6

VOHs and PAHs Level in Edible Plants *(Vernonia amydalina, Telfera occidendalis and Amaranthus spinosus)* grown in a Garden Soil near Automobile Mechanic Workshop in Choba, Port-Harcourt Metropolis, Nigeria

—Charles Ikenna Osu, Nigeria

ABSTRACT

*Three different edible plants (*Vernonia amydalina, Telfera occidendalis and Amaranthus spinosus*) were analyzed to investigate the concentrations of volatile organic hydrocarbons (VOHs) and polycyclic aromatic hydrocarbon (PAHs) components. Identification and quantitative analysis of the VOHs and PAH components were achieved by gas chromatography. The results obtained showed that the PAH components present in the samples ranged from 32.50 ± 0.10 – 54.67 ± 0.10 μg /kg, Naphthalene; 8.50 ± 0.01 – 12.70 ± 0.05 μg /kg, Fluorene; 17.60 ± 0.01 – 77.80 ± 0.20 μg /kg, Phenanthrene; 21.00 ± 0.02 – 2.15 ± 0.01 μg /kg, Anthracene; 30.10 ± 0.02 – 88.10 ± 0.01 μg /kg,Fluoranthene; 21.30 ± 0.01 – 87.60 ± 0.40 μg /kg,Pyrene; 1.37 ± 0.01 – 16.70 ± 0.10 μg /kg, Benz(a)anthracene; 0.98 ± 0.01 - 1.74 ± 0.10 μg /kg. Benzo(k)fluoranthene; 5.70 ± 0.02 – 6.50 ± 0.01 μg /kg, benzo(a) pyrene; 2.45 ± 0.02 – 4.70 ± 0.02, benzo(c)phenanthrene. analysed. Benzo(k)fluoranthene, benzo(a)pyrene and benzo(c)phenanthrene were not detected in sample B. VOHs were not detected in all the samples.*

***Key Words:** VOHs, PAHs, plants, toxicity, health.*

Introduction

Volatile organic hydrocarbons (VOHs) and polycyclic aromatic hydrocarbons (PAHs) are pollutants of major environmental concern in urban and industrial areas. Polycyclic aromatic hydrocarbons (PAHs) are a family of chemical compounds with a molecular structure consisting of at least two fused aromatic (benzene) rings in linear, angular or cluster arrangements. By definition they contain carbon and hydrogen atoms although nitrogen, sulfur, chlorine and oxygen may readily substitute into the benzene ring to form heterocyclic aromatic compounds, commonly grouped with the PAHs. The PAH family includes 660 substances indexed by the National Institute of Standards and Technology (Sander and Wise 1997). Approximately 30 to 50 of them commonly occur in the environment (Grimmer 1983, US DHHS 1995). PAHs are formed as a result of incomplete combustion of organic matter through the condensation of ethylenic radicals in the gas phase to form the larger polycyclic compounds (Lane 1989, Strosher 1996). They have a relatively low solubility in water, but are highly lipophilic. When dissolved in water or adsorbed on particulate matter, PAHs can undergo photodecomposition when exposed to ultraviolet light from solar radiation. In the atmosphere, PAHs can react with pollutants such as ozone, nitrogen oxides and sulphur dioxide, yielding diones, nitro- and dinitro-PAHs, and sulphonic acids, respectively. PAHs may also be degraded by some microorganisms in the soil (WHO, 1987; ASTDR, 1994). PAHs pollutants have high molecular mass. PAHs of 4 and more condensed aromatic rings are considered to be more dangerous than two and three rings PAHs in view of their potentials (Tuhackova *et al.*, 2001). PAHs are formed mainly as a result of pyrolytic process, especially the incomplete combustion of organic materials during industrial and other human activities, such as processing of coal and crude oil, combustion of natural gas, including for heating, combustion of refuse, vehicle traffic, cooking and tobacco smoking as well as in natural processes such as carbonization. Natural sources include release in forest or bush fires and from volcanic eruptions. Most environmental PAHs are products of incomplete combustion or pyrolysis of fossil fuels (Holbrook, 1990; Zou, 2003).

Krauss et al. (2005) compared atmospheric and biological sources of plant loads by PAHs in a tropical area. Thiele and Brümmer (2002) confirmed the formation of PAHs in soil by plant material decomposition. They observed formation of 4–6 nuclei PAHs predominantly. The behaviour and distribution of individual PAHs compounds of different molecular weights in the environment can differ markedly. Brandt et al. (2002) presented the information on low availability of compounds with a high value of Kow partition coefficient (octanol/water) for plants.

Holoubek (2005) specifies the uptake of PAHs by plants via the uptake by roots from the soil so-lution (depending on the plant water regime and the content of lipid compounds in the root), the absorption of PAHs on root surface, the absorption of volatilized PAHs (from the soil) on the shoot and the absorption of PAHs on leaves of plants. PAHs are known as highly Stable Contaminants of plants and foodstuffs, including various sources such as contaminated soils, polluted air and water., made of cooking, food processing,

Pseudo- curring with smoking flavor agents or wood generation etc. (Simko, 2005; Reink et al., 2007).

In the past decade PAHs have attracted the attention of many researchers throughout the world because of the growing body of evidence showing that plants can be used as quantitative and qualitative indicators of PAH levels in the environment.

The term of BTEX reflects that benzene, toluene, ethylbenzene and three isomers of xylene. They are some of the volatile organic hydrocarbons (VOHs) that make up a significant percentage of petroleum products and are found in petroleum derivates such as gasoline. BTEX are used as gasoline and aviation fuel additives. They are also used extensively in manufacturing processes such as in the production of synthetic materials and consumer products, like synthetic rubber, plastics, nylon, insecticides, solvent for paints, coatings, gums, oils, resins, inks, plastics, printing pesticides and leather industries. Usually they are often found together at contaminated sites.

Because of their polarity and very soluble characteristics. BTEX will be able to enter the soil and groundwater systems and cause serious pollution problems (Mihelic et al., 1999). The release of BTEX's to the environment is influenced by their fate and transport mechanisms. They are common environmental contaminants. These compounds will tend to be dissolved in the water phase or evaporated into the air spaces of the soil because of the relatively high water solubility, low K_{ow}(octanol-water partition coefficient) values. They are not attenuated very much by the soil particles or constituents because of their high relative hydrophilic nature and can be transported several kilometers downstream the source. BTEX appearance in soil and groundwater can be remediated by volatilization, dissolution, sorption (Bedient, 1994) and degradation by microorganisms (Schreiber and Bahr, 2002); natural attenuation (MacDonald, 2000) or in situ remediation (Cunnigham *et al.*, 2001).

The present study was carried out to determine the concentrations of volatile organic hydrocarbons (VOHs) and polycyclic aromatic hydrocarbons (PAHs) components present in different edible plants (*Vernonia amydalina, Telfera occidendalis and Amaranthus spinosus*) grown in a garden located at automobile mechanic workshop in Choba district area, Port-Harcourt metropolis, Nigeria.

Materials and Methods

Sampling collection

The currently study was performed in the framework of the full-area monitoring of the several hydrocarbons compounds quantities in the Choba district area of Port-harcourt metropolis during the period of 2011. In this study, 3 different edible plants grown in a garden located at automobile mechanic workshop in Choba district area, Port-harcourt metropolis were monitored. The plant samples were collected in August, 2011 and labeled A, B, and C which represent: *Vernonia amydalina, Telfera occidendalis and Amaranthus spinosus* respectively and taken to laboratory for analysis.

Sample analysis for Hydrocarbons

The leaves of the plant samples before hydrocarbon analysis were rinsed quickly with distilled water to remove the contaminant on the plant surfaces, blotted with tissue paper, and immediately weighed. The samples were chopped up, macerated in the mixed petroleum ether and acetone (4:1, v/v), and homogenized with anhydrous Na2SO4 using a mortar and pestle. Maceration and homogenization were repeated several times until no colorful substances remained in the plant materials. The plant residues were further extracted in a Soxhlet apparatus for an additional 4 h. The solutes in extracts were analyzed using a Thermo Finningan U.S. Trace GC Ultra gas chromatography system with an Flame Ionization Detector (GC-FID) equipped with a TriPlus AS auto sampler, with nitrogen as the carrier gas.

Results and Discussion

Table 6.1: PAHs components content (µg/kg) in Telfera Occidentalis, Veronia Amydalina, and *Amaranthus spinosus* grown in in a Garden located at Automobile Mechanic Workshop in Choba district Area

PAH Components (µg/kg)	Sample A	Sample B	Sample C
Naphthalene	41.40 ± 0.02	32.50 ± 0.10	54.67 ± 0.10
Fluorene	8.50 ± 0.01	10.20 ± 0.02	12.70 ± 0.05
Phenanthrene	17.60 ± 0.10	77.80 ± 0.20	43.30 ± 0.03
Anthracene	21.00 ± 0.02	2.15 ± 0.01	19.80 ± 0.07
Fluoranthene	88.10 ± 0.01	30.10 ± 0.02	99.10± 0.20
Pyrene	61.70 ± 0.40	21.30 ± 0.01	87.6 ± 0.40
Benz(a) anthracene	16.70 ± 0.10	1.37 ± 0.01	13.50 ± 0.10
Benzo(k) fluoranthene	1.74 ± 0.10	ND	0.98 ± 0.01
Benzo(a) pyrene	5.70 ± 0.02	ND	6.50 ± 0.01
Benzo(c) phenanthrene	4.70 ± 0.02	ND	2.45 ± 0.02
Total	**267.14 ± 0.80**	**175.42 ± 0.37**	**340.60 ± 0.99**

A = Telfera Occidentalis, B = Veronia Amydalina and C = Amaranthus spinosus

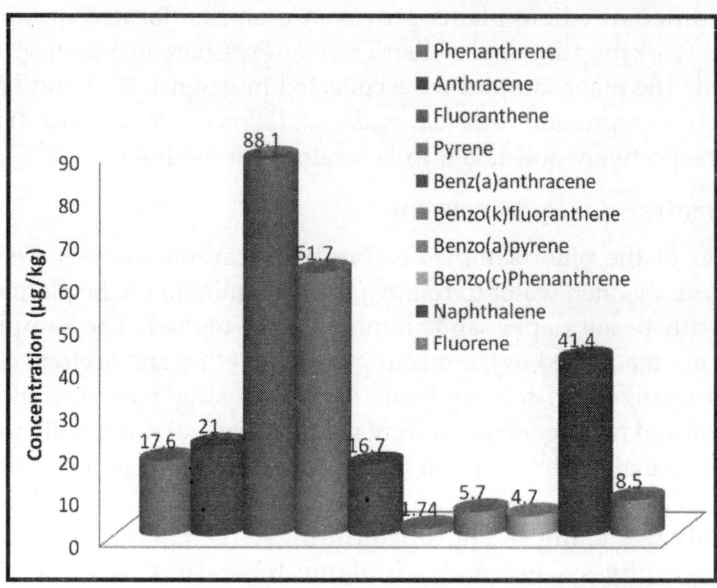

Fig. 6.1: PAH components level (mg/kg) in Telfera Occidentalis grown in a garden located at automobile mechanic workshop in Choba district Area

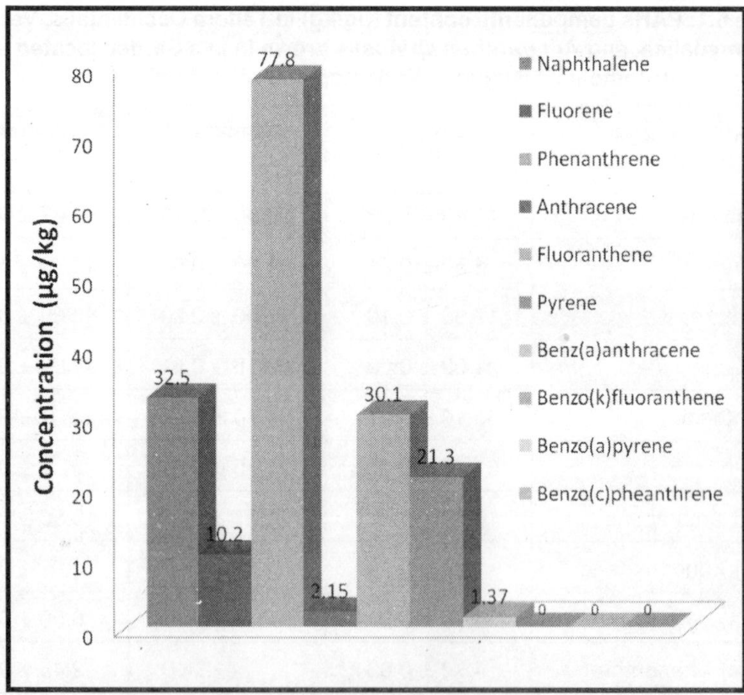

Fig. 6.2: PAH components level (mg/kg) in Veronia Amydalina grown in a garden located at automobile mechanic workshop in Choba district area

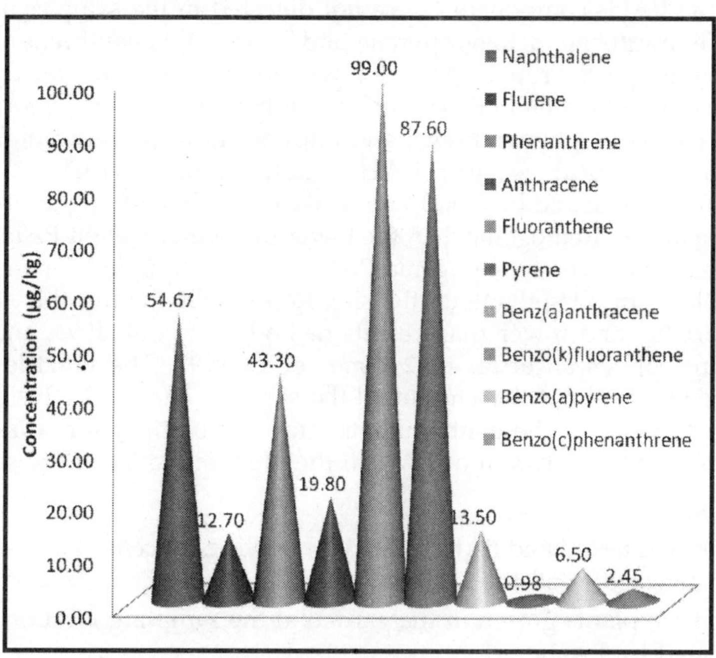

Fig. 6.3: PAH components level (mg/kg) in Amaranthus spinsus grown in a garden located at automobile mechanic workshop in Choba district area

Table 6.2: BTEXs content (µg/kg) in *Telfera Occidentalis* and *Veronia Amydalina* grown in a garden located at automobile mechanic workshop in Choba district area

Samples	Sample A	Sample B	Sample C
BTEXs	ND	ND	ND

ND = not detected.

The concentrations of PAH components (µg/Kg dry weight) in Telfera Occidentalis, Veronia Amydalina, and *Amaranthus spinosus* grown in a garden located at automobile mechanic workshop in Choba district area was presented in table 1 and figure 1-3. The PAHs components ranged from 32.50 ± 0.10 – 54.67 ± 0.10 µg /kg, Naphthalene; 8.50 ± 0.01 – 12.70 ± 0.05 µg /kg, Fluorene; 17.60 ± 0.01 – 77.80 ± 0.20 µg/kg, Phenanthrene; 21.00 ± 0.02 – 2.15 ± 0.01 µg /kg, Anthracene; 30.10 ± 0.02 – 88.10 ± 0.01 µg / kg,Fluoranthene; 21.30 ± 0.01 – 87.60 ± 0.40 µg/kg,Pyrene; 1.37 ± 0.01 – 16.70 ± 0.10 µg /kg, Benz(a)anthracene; 0.98 ± 0.01 - 1.74 ± 0.10 µg /kg, benzo(k)fluoranthene; 5.70 ± 0.02 – 6.50 ± 0.01 µg/kg, benzo(a) pyrene; 2.45 ± 0.02 – 4.70 ± 0.02, benzo(c)phenanthrene. The total PAHs concentration ranged from 175.42 ± 0.37 – 340.60 ± 0.99 µg/kg. Sample C had the highest total PAHs concentration (340.60 ± 0.99). The soils of this location were contaminated by PAHs at varying concentrations (Osu and Asuoha, 2010).

Some of the PAHs components were not detected in the samples analysed. Benzo(k)fluoranthene, benzo(a)pyrene and benzo(c)phenanthrene were not detected in sample B. From the table 1, it was observed that the concentrations of the low molecular weight PAHs such as naphthalene, pyrene, fluoranthene, fluorene, chrysene, phenanthrene, and anthracene were found higher than the high molecular weight PAHs such as benzo(k)fluoranthene, benzo(a)anthracene and benzo(a)pyrene. Also, PAHs with higher molecular weight are more carcinogenic than the lower molecular weight PAHs (Moret and Conte, 2000). The carcinogenic PAH levels in samples depend on the time and level of oil spillage on the site. Results obtained in this study are highly variable and lower than results of Lodovici et al. 1994, and higher than results of *Ignesti* et al. 1992, Jones et al. 1992. The volatile organic hydrocarbons were not detected in all the samples analyzed. This is due to the characteristics of the contaminants such as volatilization, dissolution, degradation and adsorption of PAH to the organic matter of the soil.

Conclusion

All the samples tested had PAHs content in varying concentrations and BTEX were not detected in all the samples.

The edible plants grown in the garden at the sampling location were all contaminated by PAHs.

REFERENCES

Agency for Toxic Substances and Disease Registry (ATSDR). Toxicological profile for polycyclic aromatic hydrocarbons (PAHs). Atlanta, G.A: U.S. Department of Health and Human Services, Public Health Service 1994.

Bedient, Philip B. Groundwater Contamination,Transport and Remediation, Prentice Hall PTR 1994.

Brandt C.A., Becker J.M., Porta A. (2002): Distribution of poly-cyclic aromatic hydrocarbons in soil and terrestrial biota after a spill of crude oil in Trecate, Italy. Environmental Toxicology and Chemistry, *21*: 1638–1643.

Cunningham, J.A., Rahme, H., Hopkins, GD, Leborn, C., Reinhard, M. Enhanced in situ Bioremediation of BTEX Contaminated Ground Water by Combined Injection of Nitrate and Sulfate. Environ. Sci. Technol. 2001; 35, 1663 – 1670.

Grimmer G. (1983) Environmental carcinogens: Polycyclic aromatic hydrocarbons. CRC Press, Boca Raton, FL. 261 pp.

Holbrook, D.J. Carcinogenesis, in: Haddad, L. M and Chester, J.F. (Eds.): Clinical Management of poisoning and drug overdose, 2nd ed, W.B. Saunders Co. Philadelphia, PA, 1990; 508 – 521.

Holoubek I. (2005): The chemistry of the environment IV. Poly-cyclic aromatic hydrocarbons (PAHs). Available at: http://recetox.muni.cz/index.php?id=23

Ignesti G., Lodovici M., Dolara P., Lucia P. & Grechi D. (1992) Polycyclic aromatic hydrocarbons in olive fruits as a measure of air pollution in the valley of Florence (Italy). Bull. Environ. Contam. Toxicol. 48, 809-814.

Jones K. C., Sanders G., Wild S. R., Burnett V. & Johnston A. E. (1992) Evidence for a decline

Krauss M., Wilcke W., Martius C., Banderia A.G., Garcia M.V.B., Amelung W. (2005): Atmospheric versus biological sources of polycyclic aromatic hydrocarbons (PAHs) in a tropical rain forest environment. Environmental Pollution, *135*: 143–154.

Lane D. A. (1989) The fate of polycyclic aromatic compounds in the atmosphere and during sampling. In "Chemical analysis of polycyclic aromatic compounds." T. Vo-Dinh (Ed.), J. Wiley & Sons. pp. 31-58.

Lodovici M., Dolara P., Taiti S., Carmine P. D., Bernardi L., Agati L. & Ciapepellano S. (1994)

McDonald, J.A. Evaluating Natural Attenuation for Groundwater Cleanup. Environ. Sci. Technol. 2000; 34, 346A – 353A.

Mihelic, J. R., Luthy, R. G. (1998). Microbial degradation of acenaphthene and naphthalene under dinitrification conditions in soil-water systems. Appl. Environ. Microbiol. 54, 1188 -1198.

Moret, S. and Conte, L.S. 2000. Polycyclic aromatic hydrocarbon in edible fats and oils: Occurence and analytical methods. J. Chromatogr. A., 882: 245-253.

Osu Charles .I. , Asuoha, Adaku, N. Polycyclic Aromatic Hydrocarbons (PAHs) and Benzene, Toluene, Ethylbenzene, and Xylene (BTEX) Contamination of Soils in Automobile Mechanic Workshops in Port-Harcourt Metropolis, Rivers State, Nigeria. Journal of American Science 2010;6(9):242-246

Polynuclear aromatic hydrocarbons in the leaves of the evergreen tree *Laurus nobilis*. Sci. Total Environ. 153, 61-68.

Reinik, M., Tamme, T., Roasto, M., Juhkam, K., Tenno, T. and Kus, A. 2007. Polycyclic aromatic hydrocarbons (PAHs) in meat products and estimated PAH intake by children and the general population in Estonia. Food Additives and Contaminants, 24(4): 429–437.

Sander L. C. & Wise S. A. (1997) Polycyclic aromatic hydrocarbon structure index. Natl. Inst. Stand. Technol. Special Publication 922. US Gov. Print. Office, Washington, DC. 105 pp.

Schreiber, ME, Bahr, JM. Nitrate–Enhanced Bioremediation of BTEX – Contaminated Ground Water. Parameter Estimation from Natural-Gradient Tracer Experiments. J. contm. Hydrol. 2002; 55, 29 – 56.

Simko, P. 2005. Factors affecting elimination of polycyclic aromatic hydrocarbons from smoked meat foods and liquid smoke flavorings. Mol. Nutr. Food Res., 49: 637-647.

Strosher M. (1996) Investigations of flare gas emissions in Alberta. ARC Report, Calgary, AB., 111 pp.

Thiele S., Brümmer G.W. (2002): Bioformation of polycyclic aro-matic hydrocarbons in soil under oxygen deficient conditions. Soil Biology and Biochemistry, *34*: 733–735.

US Department of Health Human Services (US DHHS) (1995) Toxicological profile for polycyclic aromatic hydrocarbons. Georgia, USA.

World Health Organization Regional Office for Europe Polynuclear aromatic hydrocarbons (PAHs). In: Air quality guidelines For Europe. 1987; 105 – 117.

Zou, Y.L., Zhan, W., Atkinskon, S. The characterization of polycyclic aromatic hydrocarbons emission from burning of different firewood species in Australia, Environmental pollution, 2003; 124: 283 – 589.

7

Soil and Sediment Quality Assessment at Larsemann Hills, Antarctica

—*Pawan Kumar 'Bharti', India*

ABSTRACT

The Larsemann Hills (Lat. 69°202 –69°302 S and Long. 75°552 –76°302 E) is an ice-free coastal oasis with exposed rock and low rolling hills. The Larsemann Hills contain hundreds of freshwater lakes of varying sizes, depth and biology. An environmental study is being conducted at Larsemann Hills in East Antarctica to evaluate the soil and sediment quality. Geographically, the study area (Bharti Island) is situated on Latitude 69° 24' 00.0" S and 76° 10' 00.0" E on southern part of globe. The soil and sediment samples were collected from various locations of different Islands/Peninsulas like Bharti Island, Fisher Island, McLeod Island, Broknes peninsula and Stornes peninsula.

The aim of this study is to assess the general characteristics, metal content, radiation contamination analysis of soil and sediment. The soil and sediment quality of different islands was also conducted to assess the level of various constituents in soil. The present work is aimed towards developing base line data for the local environmental settings and to evaluate the impacts of various activities on the environmental components during the construction work of third Indian scientific station (Bharti) in Antarctica.

Introduction

Antarctica is the most precious asset on the earth and is the last heritage of human kind. Antarctica is the only area on earth planet which is strictly devoted to scientific research and the continents of extremes come to be known as the "Continent of Science". It is the nature biggest laboratory on earth where no outside anthropogenic interference has taken place over the centuries till recent times. Being at a unique geographic location, it offers unique opportunities for Scientists to conduct number scientific research experiments. Antarctica is attracting world attention because of the tremendous biological species in surrounding seas and likelihood of vast hydrocarbons. Even though it is difficult to survive at Antarctica, still Scientists all around the worlds have been engaged in pursing the exciting scientific research investigations. The investigations are essential not for the exploitation of natural resources buried under the region but for the preservation of environment and ecology on earth; especially in the light of climate change.

Antarctica is the coldest, windiest, driest, whitest, highest (averagely) and least accessible continent on the earth. Ice is covered here continuously for the last 25 million years. Antarctica is the 5th largest continents on the earth. Antarctica has no government and is considered no mans-land. Antarctica is the most fragile, vulnerable and pristine environment on the earth.

The Larsemann Hills is an ice-free area of approximately 50 km^2, located halfway between the Vestfold Hills and the Amery Ice Shelf on the south-eastern coast of Prydz Bay, Princess Elizabeth Land, East Antarctica (69°30′S, 76°19′58"E). The ice-free area consists of two major peninsulas (Stornes and Broknes), four minor peninsulas, and approximately 130 near shore islands. Nella Fjord further divides the eastern-most peninsula, Broknes, into western and eastern components. The closest significant ice-free areas are the Bølingen Islands (69°31′58"S, 75°42′E) 25 km to the south-west and the Rauer Islands (68 °50′59"S, 77°49′58"E) 60 km to the north-east[1]. Broknes is one of very few coastal areas of Antarctica that remained partially ice-free through the glaciating period, and sediments deposited there contain continuous biological and palaeoclimate records dating back c. 130 000 years.

The Larsemann hills area was first discovered by a Norwegian expedition led by Christensen in 1935. Subsequently, visits were made by several nations during the last 50 years, but human activity of a significant or sustained nature did not occur until the mid-1980s[2].

However, from 1980 to 1990 saw rapid infrastructure development in the area: an Australian summer research base, a Chinese year-round research station (Zhongshan) and two Russian research stations (Progress I and Progress II) were established within approximately 3 km of each other on eastern Broknes[3].

Study Area

A major feature of the climate of the Larsemann Hills is the existence of persistent, strong katabatic winds that blow from the northeast in summer days. Daytime air temperatures from December to February frequently may exceed 4°C, with the mean monthly temperature a little above 0°C[4]. Mean monthly winter temperatures are between –15°C and –40°C. Pack ice is extensive inshore throughout summer and the fjords and bays are rarely ice-free. Precipitation occurs as snow and is unlikely to exceed 250 mm water equivalent annually[5]. Snow cover is generally deeper and more persistent on Stornes than Broknes, due to northeasterly prevailing winds and the perennial sea ice held in by the islands offshore from Stornes.

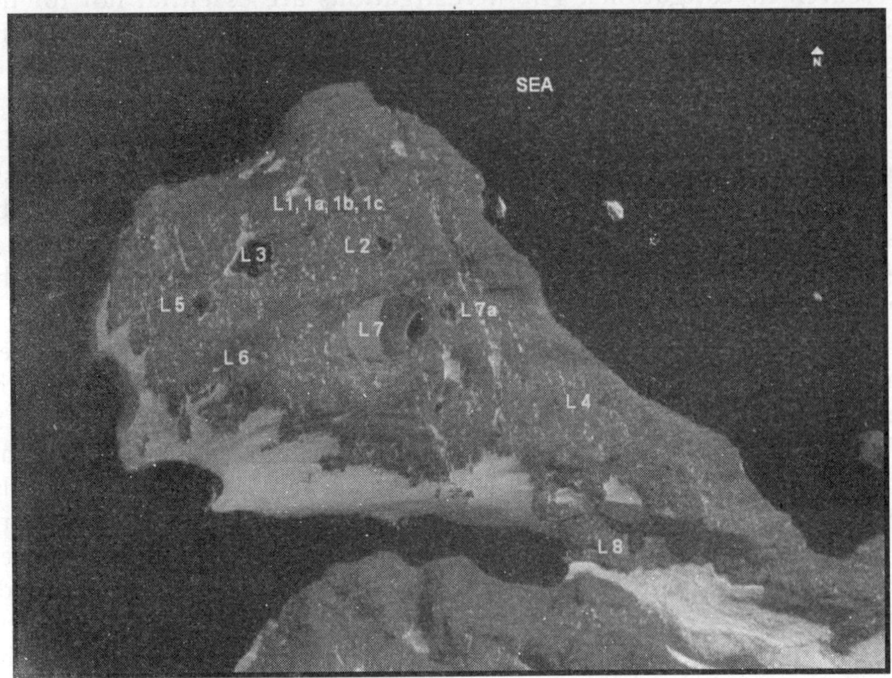

Fig. 7.1: Map showing the Sampling Sites at the Larsemann Hills, Ingrid Christensen Coast, East Antarctica

Environmental Research

A scientific study is being conducted in various island and peninsulas of Larsemann Hills. Soil and sediment samples were collected from different locations. All the samples were collected, preserved, transported and analysed by using standards methods (APHA, 2005). Different Indian standards were followed for different study aspects. IS: 2720 was followed for the assessment of edaphic quality. Dr. Pawan Kumar Bharti, scientist from Shriram Institute for Industrial Research, Delhi was the only environmentalist during the XXX expedition to Antarctica. These scientific tasks were performed during the expedition:

— Ambient Air Quality
— Indoor Air Quality
— Lake and Sea water quality
— Soil quality

— Study of bed sediments
— Generator Stack monitoring,
— Indoor Noise level,
— Ambient Noise level,
— Machinery Noise level,
— Drilling and Blasting Noise level
— Lichen patches and Moss community assessment
— Collection of Planktonic diversity and Benthos from Lake water.
— Fuel consumption and pollution load.
— Solid waste generation, handling, separation and disposal practices and % composition.
— Ash analysis
— Waste oil analysis

Fig. 7.2: Impressions on Rocks after losing soil particles due to the weathering and strong winds at the Larsemann Hills, east Antarctica.

Edaphic Environment

Soil and sediment samples were collected from different locations covering important aspects of physical and chemical properties of soil quality therein and by adopting established sampling procedures given in the IS 2720 specifications. Undisturbed soils and sediments samples representative of the area was collected by means of auger. Besides physico-chemical parameters many heavy metals and radiation contamination was also monitored.

Fig. 7.3: Soil and Sediment Samples inside the Ship during Expedition

Soil pollution is defined or can be described as the contamination of soil of a particular region. Soil pollution mainly is a result of penetration of harmful pesticides and insecticides, which on one hand serve whatever their main purpose is, but on the other hand, bring about deterioration in the soil quality, thus making it contaminated and unfit for use. Insecticides and pesticides are not to be blamed alone for soil pollution, but there are many other leading causes of soil pollution too.

Soil pollution results from the buildup of contaminants, toxic compounds, radioactive materials, salts, chemicals and cancer-causing agents. The most common soil pollutants are hydrocarbons, heavy metals (cadmium, lead, chromium, copper, zinc, mercury and arsenic), herbicides, pesticides, oils, tars, PCBs and dioxins.

The intensity of all these causes on a local or regional level might appear very small and you may argue that soil is not harmed by above activities if done on a small scale. However, thinking globally, it is not your region or my place, which will be the only sufferer of soil pollution.

Table 7.1: Soil Quality Characteristics and Methodology

Sl.No.	Parameters	Unit	Protocol/Method
1.	pH	-	IS:2720 (Part-26)
2.	Conductivity	μS/cm	Conductivity meter
3.	Sodium as Na_2O	% by mass	ICP-OES
4.	Potassium as K_2O	% by mass	ICP/AAS/APHA 21st Ed.
5.	Calcium as CaO	% by mass	ICP/AAS/APHA 21st Ed.
6.	Magnesium as MgO	% by mass	ICP/AAS/APHA 21st Ed.
7.	Iron as Fe_2O_3	% by mass	ICP/AAS/APHA 21st Ed.
8.	Aluminium as Al	% by mass	ICP/AAS/APHA 21st Ed.
9.	Phosphorus as P_2O_5	Mg/kg	ICP/AAS/APHA 21st Ed.
10.	Cadmium as Cd	Mg/kg	ICP/AAS/APHA 21st Ed.
11.	Chromium as Cr	Mg/kg	ICP/AAS/APHA 21st Ed.
12.	Zinc as Zn	Mg/kg	ICP/AAS/APHA 21st Ed.
13.	Manganese as Mn	Mg/kg	ICP/AAS/APHA 21st Ed.
14.	Copper as Cu	Mg/kg	ICP/AAS/APHA 21st Ed.
15.	Chloride as Cl	% by mass	Volhard method
16.	Sulphate as SO_4	% by mass	IS: 2720 (Part-27)
17.	Radiation contamination as Cs-137	Bq/kg	AERB Guidelines

Radiation

Radiation contamination was also monitored in collected soil and sediment samples. The radiation parameters are given below:

Table 7.2: List of Radiation Parameters Analysed in Soil Samples

Sl.No.	Radiation Parameter	Requirement
1.	Gross Alpha (including Ra 226)	<0.5 bq/l
2.	Gross Beta particle activity	<1.9 bq/l
3.	Cesium 137 content	<1.9 bq/l

Conclusion

The environmental assessment studies carried out at Indian Scientific Base, located in Antarctica throws light on the status of air, water and soil quality and waste generated. After completion of sample analysis, the report should be submitted to Antarctica centre, which will be beneficial among the SCAR or other regulatory authorities of Antarctica. Furthermore, the environment assessment and monitoring work will be beneficial while predicting the long term impacts to Antarctica. The data will be the baseline and reference for the further study in future.

REFERENCES

http://www.esri.com/news/arcnews

Antarctica: Fact sheet, september200,page-14, http://www.antarctica.ac.uk

http://www.eia.doc.gov/emeu/cabs antarrctica.html.

Draft Comprehensive Environmental Evaluation for the concept of upgrading the Norwegian Summer Station Troll in Dronning Maud Land, Antarctica to permanent station, 2004, Norwegian Polar Institute, Polar Environmental Centre, Tromsa, Norway.

Report of the Norwegian Antarctic Inspection under Article VII of the Antarctica Treaty and Article 14 of the Protocol on Environmental Protection to the Antarctica Treaty, January 2001.

Erich R, Gundlach; John J, Gallagher; John Hatcher & Tom Vinsor. Planning and Hazards Oil Spill Response in Antarctic's. International Oil Spill Conference 2000, 241-244.

Malik, D.S. and Bharti, P.K. (2010): Textile Pollution. *Daya Publishing House, Delhi*, pp: 383.

Sharma, B.; Bharti, P.K.; Pal, N.; Singh, R.K.; Niyogi, U.K. and Khandal, R.K. (2011): Waste management practices at Indian research station 'Maitri', East Antarctica, In: 'Proceedings of Brainstorming session on Polar sciences' published by Indian Meteorological Department, MoES, Govt. of India, pp: 67-76.

Bharti, P.K. (2011): Environmental monitoring and assessment during the construction of Indian Scientific Base (Bharti Station) in Antarctica, In: Climate Change and Biodiversity (Eds.- Khanna et al), Biotech Books, Delhi.

Bharti, P.K. (2011): Assessment of Lichen patches and Moss communities in the vicinity of Larsemann Hills, East Antarctica, In: Climate Change and Biodiversity (Eds.- Khanna et al), Biotech Books, Delhi.

Bharti, P.K. (2011): Environmental research in Antarctica, In: Climate Change and Biodiversity (Eds.- Khanna et al), Biotech Books, Delhi.

8

A Brief Note on Soil Quality Evaluation near Solid Waste Dumping Site at Haridwar City

—*Sandeep Gupta, India*
—*Triloki Nath Vaish, India*
—*A.K. Chopra, India*

Introduction

Soil is derived from the Latin word solum, which means floor or ground. As a Verb soil means to make dirty, as in the case of soiled dishes or clothing. The Soil is the covering of the solid crust of the earth's land mass. Soil is made up of broken rock materials of varying degree of fineness and changed in varying degree from the parent rocks by the action of different agencies, such that the growth of vegetation and porosity of rocks .This soil word are known with different names as a scientist calls soil, a geologist calls fragmented rock, and an engineer calls earth, while an economist may call land but there are two basic concepts of the soil.

(*a*) According to the first concept, soil is a natural body, biochemically weathered and synthesized product of nature. In other words, pedology considers soil as a natural entity, a biologically weathered and synthesized product of nature. Pedologists define a soil that includes the study of soil origin, its classification and its description.

(*b*) According to the second concept the soil is considered to be a natural habitat for plants and other living organisms and justifies soil studies primarily on this basis. In other words, Edaphology consider the soil as a natural habitat for plant. Edaphalogy is the study of soil from the standpoint of higher plants. Thus Edaphologist covers the study of soil in relation to growth, nutrition and yield of crops.

Soil is a natural body which is a synthesized product of nature and formed by biochemical and weathering process. In other words, pedology considers soil as a natural entity, a biologically weathered and synthesized product of nature. The eternal truth about the soil and water is that these are the two significant capitals of mankind and the natural forests are the mothers of river and the factories for manufacturing soil. The soil provides homes and ideal environment conditions for living beings. The soil is considered to be a natural habitat for plants and other living organisms and justifies soil studies primarily on that basis. In other words, Edaphology consider the soil as a natural habitat for plant. Life on earth depends directly on the living soil and the aquatic eco- system of rivers without fertile soil and the microbial fauna that inhabit it, food would not grow, dead things would not decay and nutrients would not be recycled.

Yet the earth's soil is being stripped away, rendered sterile and contaminated with toxic chemicals at a rate that can not be sustained. Almost all soils contain gravel, coarse sand, fine sand, silt and clay, but the final texture and the property of a soil sample is decided by the type of particles which predominate.A typical soil contains a large number and varieties of elements, trace elements, inorganic and organic compounds. The oxygen, silicon, aluminum, calcium, magnesium, sodium, potassium and iron etc are the elements which are present in the soil. The trace elements present in the soil include cobalt, boron, iodine, cadmium, arsenic, zinc and barium etc. The inorganic compounds present are chlorides, sulphates and oxides, while the organic compounds derived from the dead remains of plants and animals and animal excreta are present in various stages of decomposition.

The organic matter in the soil comes from the remains of plants and animals. As new organic matter is formed in the soil, a part of the old organic matter is mineralized. The original source of the soil organic matter is plant tissues. Under natural conditions the tops and roots of trees, grasses and other plants supply large quantities of organic residues. Thus, higher plant tissues are the primary source of organic matter. Animals are usually regarded as secondary sources of organic matter. Various organic manures such as farmyard manure, compost, green manure etc that are added to the soil from time to time, further it is a store of soil organic matter.

The soil consists of four major components, i.e., mineral matter, organic matter, soil air and soil water. All these components can not be separated with much satisfaction because they are present very intimately mixed with each other. The mineral matter forms the bulk of soil solids and a very small amount of the soil solids is occupied by organic matter.

Volumetric composition of mineral (inorganic) soil is.

1. Mineral Matter	45 percent
2. Organic Matter	5 percent
3. Soil Water	25 percent
4. Soil Air	25 percent

In fact soil is a mixture of various inorganic and organic chemical compounds. The chief inorganic constituents of soil are the compounds of Ca, Al, Mg, Fe, Si, K and Na. Small amounts of the compounds of Mn, Cu, Zn, Co, B, I and F etc. are also present in the soil. Soil solution also contains complex mixtures of minerals as carbonates, sulphates, chlorides, nitrates and also the organic salts of Ca, Mg, K, and Na etc. The chief organic component of soil is humus, which contains the large numbers of organic compounds such s amino acids, proteins, aromatic compounds, sugar, alcohols, fats, oils waxes, resins, tannins, lignin, pigments, pureness and many other. As a result, humus is a black coloured, homogeneous complex material.

Physically, the soil consists of stones, large pebbles, dead plant twigs roots leaves and other parts of the plants, fine sand, silt, clay and humus-derived from the decomposition of organic matter. About 50% of the organic matter in the soil is alive in the organic matter of the portion of the soil. The living part of the organic matter consists of plant roots, bacteria, earthworms, algae, fungi, nematodes, actinomiceties and many other living organisms including rodents and insects. There is a three phase system in which the mineral and organic matter forms the solid phase, the water containing salts and some gases in solution the liquid phase, and the various gases, the gaseous phase. Each phase contains a number of constituents which make the whole system highly complex. The system is never in equilibrium, because of continuous changes taking place in the soil.

As is evident from the volume composition of the soil, the soil contains about 50% solid space (45% mineral matter + 5% organic matter) and 50% pore space (25% soil water +25% soil air). The portion of air and water will vary under natural conditions depending on the weather, climate, and environmental factors. The four major components of the soil (Mineral matter, organic matter, water and air) exist mainly in an intimately mixed condition which encourages various reactions within and between the groups and gives optimum conditions for the crop growth.

With the increase of Human population, humans are indiscriminately using non-degradable and toxic substances and their needs are also touching to the zenith for luxurious life. It has resulted in unwanted heap of substances, which does not assimilate in environment rather it makes environment unhygienic. Rapid urbanization coupled with increased population has brought in an environmental problem in the developing countries. In India huge tonnages of solid refuse are being produced from the urban areas, which need to be disposed off in a manner that should be economically viable and environmentally acceptable.

Review of Literature

Subbiam and Asija (1956) reported majority of the soils from different rivers showed that the available N value below 125 ppm and are decreased as per limits. Krishnamoorthy in 1958 observed that the high iron requirements of rice crop might not be met from the black clay loams, which are dominantly in character, since the iron under arable conditions would have been held in the clay lattices in an unavailable form. Datta et al in 1963 observed that in most of the soils from shallow, medium and deep ravines it was observed that the contents of phosphorus were less than 10 ppm the soils and it falls in the category of phosphorus deficient soils. Battawar & Rao in 1969 has been estimated that out of 326.12 million hectares of total geographical area of the country, about 80.93 M ha are severely affected by erosion. Subramaniam in 1966 reported the cause of the annual loss of about 6,000 million tones of fertile top soil which has been estimated to contain 5.37 million tones of N, P and K worth about 700 crores.

Ponnamperuma in 1966 observed that a period of submergence of 2 to 3 weeks appeared to be necessary for obtained better dry matter production for rice grown under low land conditions for the first time. Green maturing with in 2 to 3 weeks of submergence was found to further enhance dry matter production. Submergence of the soils for the first time led to aluminum concentration of 1.2 to 1.64 ppm which, if not removed through drainage it might be toxic to the rice plant. Silica in leachate was sufficient under submergence for normal growth of rice plant but toxic concentration of aluminium in solution for rice culture. Terman et al. (1973) studied the municipal waste compost and its effects on crop yields and nutrient content in green house pot experiment and found that the compost contained N, P, K and Zn. M.Badrinarayan Rao And J. Venkateswarlu in 1974 reported the absorbed iron, manganese and phosphorus generally increased with period of submergence while potassium decreased after 3 weeks of submergence.

Baldwin (1976) has shown the virus aspect of applying municipal waste to land. Wasiak and Pawlowska (1976) revealed the utilization of municipal waste in agriculture for mutual economic assistance has been revealed. Elsokkary & Lag in1978 reported that the availability of Zn to plants is determined by the dynamic equilibrium involving these different forms rather than its total content present in soil.Takahashi (1979) studied the properties of municipal waste as fertilizer and its effects on soils and crop yield. Baker (1979) worked out the land application of sludge in New York. Chopp et al. (1982) studied the ammonium oxidizing bacteria population and activities in soils irrigated with municipal waste water effluent. Laag (1982) showed the risk of soil pollution around municipal waste incineration plants. Shimizu and Ninaki (1982) studied the quality of municipal waste compost and the decomposition of municipal waste composts in the soil. Subbiah And Manickam etal in 1986 found a sound knowledge about water retention characteristics is important in crop production management.

Water retention characteristics of some of the Andhra Pradesh soil. The relationship between the soil water characteristics at 0.03 and 1.5 Mpa tensions and physicochemical characteristics was studied in 108 horizon- wise soil samples collected from 22 representative pedons in Krishna, Godavari and Sarda river command area of Andhra Pradesh. The water retention was lower in surface horizons over sub-surface horizons. The information available for soils of Krishna, Godavari and Sarada River which is used to generate the data on water retention characteristics of twenty two soil sample. Prasad and Sakal in 1988 observed a negative correlation with pH, $CaCO_3$ and organic carbon content of the soils and also they observed a significant positive correlation between residual Zn and organic carbon content of soil.

P. Rama Krishna Prasad *et. al.* in 1998 found that the cation exchange capacity, clay, silt and exchangeable Mg and Na had significant positive relationship with the available water content and with the water retained at 0.03 and 1.5 M.pa, while the sand had shown negative correlation with all the three water parameters start.

Material and Methods

Study Area

Hardwar (latitude 29º 26' N and longitude 77º 30′ E.) is a holy place located in Uttrarakhand, India and is a major revenue center for trade and commerce. Its average altitude is 250 Mt from the sea level. The annual rainfall is 2315.4 mm and summer temperature ranges between min 16°C to max 41°C while in winter the temperature ranges between min. 40°C to max. 18°C. The total population of Hardwar is 14, 44, 213 and population density is 612 person/ km^2. In normal days around 50,000 visitors (tourists + pilgrims) visit the Hardwar city and generate approx. 22.66 MT/day solid wastes. The number of visitors in Hardwar easily increases from 1, 50,000 to 500,000 on some auspicious bath days while this number of pilgrims may increase up to 50 lacks on specific days of Mhakumbha mahotsava. The waste generated from the central Hardwar that is always packed with the tourist, is dumped near Neel Parvat, Chandi bridge municipal dumping area. The area of experimental sites covers 0.1071 km^2 That may affect the soil and ground water quality as well as affect the health status of the people living in slum area.

Sample Analysis

The preliminary study on the quality of soil and solid waste was conducted in the month of January 2008 because in the winter season the visitor's population decreases in therefore solid waste generation also reduces in Hardwar city. The soil samples were collected by composite sampling method with the help of hand augur which is used to bore the soil up to desired depth. Collection of soil sample were taken during the first week of the month in between 7.00 A.M. to 10 A.M. Firstly the sampling area is to be cleaned up by removing discarded material, refuse, stone etc.

The soil samples were prepared to perform various tests as per the Indian standard method-2006.The analysis of physico-chemical parameters viz. temperature, bulk density, pH, electrical conductivity, available nitrogen, available phosphorus, available potash and organic matter were determined following the standard methods (Trivedi and Goel, 1984 and Hesse, 1994). Nitrogen was determined by Kjeldal method, organic matter following Walkley and Black method (cited in Trivedi and Goel, 1984).

Statistical Analysis

The mean ± S.D. values, percentage change, analysis of variance (ANOVA) one way statistical test and Correlation coefficient (r) of physico-chemical parameters in soil of different experimental and control sites were determined with the help of EXEL (Microsoft Office), SPSS and sigmaplot.

Results and Discussion

The mean values ± S.D of physico-chemical properties (viz. temperature, available nitrogen, available phosphorus and available potash) of different dumping sites of municipal waste dumping area of hardwar. Soil temperature is one of the deciding factors in the process of litter decomposition. The growth of plants is unaffected due to warming of the soil around their roots by the interior heat of the earth (Miller and Turk 2002). In present study, it was observed that the temperature was found minimum 22.31 ± 1.90°C and maximum 24.61 ± 2.19°C among various samples collected from hardwar city. It may be because of presence of more stabilized waste where microbial population is low further the increase of the temperature appears to be due to high metabolic activity of microbes at the initial stage of compost development. The municipal waste makes a covering layer upon the soil, which helps to retain the moisture and provide low oxygen condition to microbes which are responsible for putrefied odour near the municipal waste dumping sites. Chan et al. (1997) have observed the quite higher temperature (33.9°C) in landfill site at Junk Bay in Hong Kong in comparison to the temperature observed in present study at dumping site of Hardwar. The higher temperature at Junk Bay may be due to cover landfill that was covered by soil that had been laid there for about 3 years.

In case of available nitrogen the maximum available nitrogen was (0.32 ± 0.19%) due to presence of stabilized waste (compost) while minimum available nitrogen was (0.24 ± 0.17). This may be due to that presence of more amount of degradable waste material (Humus). As waste is converted in to humus, the nitrogen level might have increased in soil. Therefore decomposed municipal waste has a positive influence on soil productivity by increasing available nitrogen in soil. The application of composts obtained from waste increases the available nitrogen content in soil is in close proximity noticed by Winant et al. (1981), Sotomayor (1979), Schossing (1983), Kowed et al. (1982) Giusquiani et al. (1988) and Chan et al. (1997 for different dumping wastes). Rapid uptake of nitrogen in available form of (NO_3^- & NH_4^+) by the plants takes place only when all wastes get decomposed by microbes and during decomposition of fresh waste maximum nitrates may percolate down up to ground water.

Further in case of available phosphorus it was found minimum (14.35 ± 7.00 ppm,) and maximum was (33.16 ± 20.68 ppm,). This may be due to the difference in pH of soil samples as also studied by Ozores and Obreza et al., (1999) at S-W Florida and also may be due to that the waste contains large proportion of organic material which acts as the source of phosphorus during decomposition of waste and get associated with iron. Thus, it can be said that slightly basic pH increases the available P and affects the soil productivity positively.

In case of the available potash it was found minimum (73.98 ± 14.82 ppm,) and maximum (260.17 ± 173.79 ppm, (+ 437.11 %). This may be due to more amount of urban waste containing ash that comes due to burning of waste containing higher amount of organic matter. As the amount of waste increased, the potassium content might have also increased and because of its cationic behavior might have helped to accumulate K on the upper layer of soil. The higher K content in the soil has also been reported by Martinez (2003) at Spain, Rao and Shantaram (1996) at Amberpet landfill site, Hyderabad and Chan et al. (1997) at Junk bay landfill site, Hongkong. Therefore it may be quoted as a remark that the municipal wastes have a positive effect on soil quality by increasing the K content of the soil.

REFERENCES

Baker, J. (1979). Land application of sludge Municipal waste disposal, New York, Soil-Conservation (USA). 44(9): 4-5.

Baldwin, L.B. (1976). Virus aspects of applying municipal waste to land: symposium proceedings, June 1976/edited by L. b. baldwin, J. m. davidson, J. f. gerber, Gainesville :Center for Environmental Programs, Institute of Food and Agricultural Sciences, Univ. of Florida.

Battawar, h.B.& Rao, Y.P. 1969 ; J. soil Wat. Consery. India, 17(3&4: ,39.

Chan, Y. S. G., Chu L.M and Wong M.H. (1997). Influence of landfill factors on the plants and soil fauna- An ecological perspective. Env. Poll., 97(1-2): 39-44.

Chapman, H.D., Liebig, G.F. Jr., and Vanselow, A.P (1939). Some nutrietional relationships as revealed by a study of mineral deficiency and excess symptoms on citrus. Soil Sci. Society of America, 4, 196-200.

Datta, N.P.,Muhr, G.R.& Donahue, R.L.(1963) ; Soil Testing in India, U.S. Agency for International Development, New Delhi.

Elsokkary & Lag 1978; (1978) J. Acta Agric. Scand. 28, 262.

Giusquiani, P.L, Marucehini, C. and Businelli, M. (1988). Chemical properties of soil amended with compost of urban waste. Plant Soil. 109: 73-78.

Hesse, P.R. (1994). A textbook of soil chemical analysis, CBS Publishers and distributors, 485, Bholanathnagar, Shahdhra, Delhi-110032: 520.

Kowed, R., Bathiyar, M. and Ditter, P. (1982). Effect of refuse compost on the properties and the crop yield of an arable field. Soil and Fertil Absts.: 671.

Krishrnamurthy, K. and Mune Gowda, M.K. 1982. Subabul (Chiguru) Leucarna leucocephala (L) – A multipurpose plan. University of agriculture Science Banglore. UAS. Tech. Series No. 38 (revised).

Laag, J. (1982). The risk of soil pollution around municipal waste incineration plants [mercury, cadmium], Land and Myr (Norway), 6(6): 134-137.

M. Badrinarayan Rao and J, Venkateswarlu. Indian soc. Soil. Vol 22 (1) : 13-18, 1974.

Martinez, F.; Cuevas, G.; Calvo, R. and Walter, I. (2003). Biowaste effects on soil and native plants in a semiarid ecosystem, Journal of Environmental Quality 32(2): 472- 479.

Miller, C.E and Turk, L.M. (2002). Fundamentals of soil science. Biotech. Books, 1123/74, Trinagar, Delhi: 157.

Ozores Hampton, M. and Obreza, T.A. (1999). Composted waste use on Florida vegetable crops: A review In: Warman, P.R.,Taylor, B.R.(Eds.) Preceedings of the international composting symposium (ICS'99), Halifax, Nova Scotia, Canada, Vol.I. CBA Press, Turuo, NS, Canada: 827-842.

P. Ramakrishna Prasad, G.V. Subbaiah, V. Styanarayana and Ch. Srinivas Rao; (1998) J. of the Indian society science Vol. 46 No. 2 pp 171-176.

Ponnamperuma , F.N. (1972) The chemistry of submerged soils. Adv. In Agron. 24; 29-96.

Ponnamperuma, F.N; Tianco, E.M. and Loy, T.A. (1966). Ionic strength of solutions of flooded soils and other natural aqueous solutions form specific conductance. Soil Sci. 102: 408-413

Prasad & Sakal 1988 ; J. Indian Soc. Soil 36, 246.

Rao, Jeevan, K. and Shantaram, M.V. (1995). Effect of urban solid waste application on concentration of micro-nutrients and heavy metals in soil and maize plant parts.I.J.E.P.15 (3): 201-209.

Schoossing, C. (1983). Refuse compost application on dialvial sands and silty marsh soils of Eastern Friesland. Announcements of Deutsche Bodeu Kundlichen society Schaff.38: 697-702.

Shimizu, K.; Ninaki, M. (1982). Studies on the quality of municipal waste composts, 1: The decomposition of municipal waste composts in the soil. Journal of Agricultural Science Tokyo Nogyo Daigaku (Japan). 27(1): 84-94.

Sotomayor, R.I. (1979). Refuse compost as a source of organic fertilizer compared with chemical fertilizer: Part-I Agril. Technica. Chile. 39: 152-157.

Hazra. C.B.1994 Soil fand water conservation aspects of agroforestry on natural resource regeneration and plant production. J.Soil water Cons.India 38:69:89.

Subbiah, B.V.& Asija ; G.L.1956 Curr.Sci.25,259.

Subramaniam 1966 ; J. Soil Wat, Conserv. India,15,4.

Takahashi, K. (1979). Properties of municipal waste as fertilizer and its effects on soils and crop yield, J Sci Soil Manure. Tokyo, Nippon Dojohiryo Gakkai. June 1979. 50 (3): 273-284.

Terman, G.L.; Soileau, J.M. and Allen, S.E. (1973). Municipal waste compost: effects on crop yields and nutrient content in greenhouse pot experiments. Journal of Environmental Quality. 2(1): 84-89.

Trivedi, R.K., and Goel, P.K. (1984). Chemical and biological methods for water pollutions studies. Environment Publication, Karad, New Delhi.

Wasiak, G. and Pawlowska, L. (1976). Utilization of municipal waste in agriculture of the Council for Mutual Economic Assistance countries , New-Roln (Nowe-Roln), Dec 1/15, 25 (23): 22-23.

Winant, W.H., Menser, H.A. and Bennett, O.L. (1981). Effects of sanitary landfill leachate on some soil chemical properties. J. Env. Qual. 10: 318-322.

9

Comparative Evaluation of Different Agro-Industrial Biomass on The Soil Chemical Composition, Growth and Yield of Melon *(Cucumeropis edulis L)*

—*E. I. Moyin-Jesu, Nigeria*

ABSTRACT

*Four field experiments were carried out at Akure in the rainforest zone of Nigeria to determine the effects of different agro-industrial biomass on the soil chemical composition, growth and yield of Melon (*Cucumeropis edulis *L).*

There were three organic fertilizer treatments namely; wood ash, cocoa pod husk and poultry manure applied and a control (no manure, nor fertilizer), replicated four times and arranged in a randomized complete block design (RCB). The economic benefit ratio for using organic fertilizer for melon was calculated.

The results showed that there were significant increases ($P<0.05$) in the leaf, seed weight and average of pods per plant of melon and soil chemical composition under different organic fertilizers compared to the control treatment.

For melon leaf analysis, wood ash treatment increased the % K, and Ca and Mg by 22%, 40% and 50% compared to poultry manure. However, poultry manure increased % leaf N and P by 47% and 3.4% compared to wood ash.

When compared to NPK 15-15-15, wood ash increased the K, Ca and Mg by 39%, 97% and 94% respectively except %N and P.

For seed analysis, all the values of nutrients in the melon seeds were greater than that of the leaf chemical composition wood ash treatment had the highest values of seed K, Ca and Mg followed by cocoa husk and poultry manure respectively.

For growth parameters, wood ash increased leaf area, and vine length of melon by 28.0% and 14% compared to that of cocoa husk. When compared to NPK 15-15-15, it increased the leaf area and vine length by 18.7% and 5.5% respectively.

For the melon seed yield, wood ash had the highest seed yield value (kg/ha) followed by poultry manure, cocoa husk, NPK 15-15-15 and control treatments. The same trend was observed for the average number of fruits while NPK 15-15-15 delayed melon fruit formation.

For the soil chemical composition, wood ash increased soil Ca, Mg and pH by 72%, 53% and 7% respectively compared to poultry manure treatment. It also decreased the soil bulk density by 3% compared to poultry manure. However, NPK 15-15-15 fertilizer increased soil N, P and K by 27%, 66% and 31% compared to wood ash. The soil K/Ca, P/Mg and K/Mg ratios were higher in NPK 15-15-15 fertilizer than that of organic fertilizers.

R^2 value of 0.876 was obtained from the multiple regression analysis between melon seed yield, soil N, P, K, Ca, Mg, O.M and pH. Interestingly, N contributed R^2 value of 0.45 out of the total R^2 value respectively 51%.

Wood ash treatment had the highest benefit cost (BC) ratio of 2.4 followed by poultry manure (1.97) and cocoa husk (1.169) respectively while NPK 15-15-15 had < 1 BC value.

Wood ash applied at 6t/ha was recommended because it had the best BC ratio value, leaf, seed yield and leaf nutrients.

Keywords: *Agro-Industrial Biomass, soil fertility and melon yield.*

Introduction

Feeding the rapidly growing population in sub-Saharan Africa has become a major developmental problem to policy makers, agricultural experts and international agencies. This is because populations are increasing in the region where, ironically, the soils have low inherent fertility and are fragile, highly weathered and characterized by low activity clays.

Moyin-Jesu (2007) reported that intensive farming in the western countries relied heavily on pesticides and chemical fertilizers while on the other hand, traditional African farmers tackle the problems of infertile soils by practicing the shifting cultivation of mixed crops.

With the rapid demographic and economic changes in Africa, the cultivated areas had expanded into marginal soils with reduced fallow periods and this had resulted into gradual degradation of large areas of land and reduced crop yields. The practice of using high chemical fertilizers input for agricultural production has not been widely adopted by farmers in tropical Africa including Nigeria because they are very expensive to purchase and destroy soil properties on continuous use (Folorunso *et al* 2000).

Agboola (1982) reported that many agricultural wastes were generated in the tropical countries but few quantities of them, were returned to the soil for fertility maintenance and sustainable crop production.

Melon is an annual creeping crop which belongs to the family cucurbitaceae and its seeds contain high content of oil which are ground and used in domestic soup preparation. The seeds also contain minerals such as K, Ca, Mg and vitamins B_{12} which are useful for body and reproductive growth while the pulp which is bitter is used for the treatment of constipation, dysentery and other ailments (Olaofe *et al*, 2000).

Most of the past research work on melon centred on the use of inorganic fertilizers such as NPK 15-15-15, Urea, Single Super Phosphate and Triple Super Phosphate fertilizers (Ojeniyi, 1998 and I.I.T.A, 2001). However, there is scarcity of research work on growing melon crop using wood ash, cocoa husk and poultry manure as soil amendment; thus, there is a strong justification for the research work on melon using agro-industrial biomass to improve soil fertility maintenance.

The objectives of this research are (i) to determine the effect of wood ash, cocoa husk and poultry manure on the growth and yield of four crops of melon (ii) to determine the effect of these agro-industrial biomasses on the leaf, seed and soil chemical composition.

Materials and Methods

Source and Preparation of Organic Materials

Cocoa pod husk and wood ash were obtained from the cocoa plantations and cassava processing unit of the Federal College of Agriculture, Akure Nigeria respectively. Poultry manure was collected from the college livestock unit.

The organic materials were processed to allow decomposition and rapid release of nutrients to crops. The dried cocoa pod husk was ground with a hammer mill while the wood ash was sieved to remove pebbles, burnt charcoal and wood. The poultry manure was stacked to allow mineralization process.

These methods of preparation of organic materials were simple and could be readily carried out by farmers. Nevertheless, if farmers did not prepare the organic materials before application, it should not change the final results except that the nutrients release would be slower than after preparation.

Chemical Analysis of Organic Materials

The processed forms of the three organic materials were analyzed for the determination of nutrients using a wet digestion method using 25-5-5ml of 16M HNO_3 – 18M H_2SO_4 – 11M $HClO_4$ acids respectively. The filtrates collected were used for the determination of percentage P, K, Ca, Mg and micronutrients (mg/kg). The P content was evaluated using a vanado-molybdate colorimeter (CORNING Colorimeter 253, Corning Limited Halstead, Essex England). The K and Ca concentrations were quantified by flame photometry, (Jenway Flame photometer model PFP7, Jenway Limited, Felsted Dunmow, Essex CM 6 3 LB, United Kingdom). The Mg and Micronutrients were determined by atomic absorption spectrophotometry

(A.O.A.C., 1970). The % N was determined using a microkjedahl method (Jackson, 1964). The data on the chemical analysis of the organic fertilizers are presented in Table 1.

Soil Analysis before the Experiment

Sixty soil core samples were randomly taken from the entire field at 0-15cm depth before planting or residue application. They were bulked together in polythene bags, air-dried and sieved with a 2mm sieve for routine analysis.

The soil pH was determined in a 1:1 soil/water suspension and 2:1 $CaCl_2$ soil suspension using a glass/calomel electrode system, Jenway 3015 pH meter, Jenway Limited, Felsted Dunmow, Essex England, CM 63 LB. (Crockford and Nowell, 1956).

Organic matter was determined by Walkley and Black (1934) method through chromic acid digestion. Soil nitrogen was extracted through addition of 5ml of concentrated H_2SO_4 and selenium catalyst, then distilled with NaOH and titrated against 0.01M HCl (Jackson, 1984).

Bray P1 extractant and the amount in the extract was measured with Murphy and Riley (1962) blue colouration method on a spectronic 20 (Bausch and Lomb spectronic 20 (Bausch and Lomb spectronic 20, the Bausch and Lomb France S. A., Boite Postate 3, F 78320 Les Mensi Saint Denis, France) at 882 Um.

The exchangeable bases (K, Ca, Mg and Na) were extracted with 1M NH_4OAC pH 7 and the amount in the extracts were determined using atomic absorption spectrophotometry, (Novaspec 11 visible spectrophotometer, pharmacia Biotech (Biochron Ltd.) Cambridge, England). The exchangeable acidity (H^+ and Al^{3t}) was measured from 0.1M HCl extracts by titrating with 0.1M NaOH (McLean, 1965). Micronutrients (Mn, Fe, Cu and Zn) were extracted with 0.1M HCl (Ogunwale and Udo, 1978) and measured with Perkin Elmer atomic absorption spectrophotometer, Perkin Elmer AAS (Model 372), Perkin Elmer Ltd., Williams Street Wellesley, MAO 2481-4078, USA.

Determination of Soil Physical Properties

The physical properties of the soils on the site were determined before the field experiment. The soil bulk density (mgm^{-3}) was determined by a core method (Ojeniyi, 1988) and porosity was calculated from the values of bulk density. The mechanical analysis of the soil was done by the hydrometer method (Bouycous, 1951) and percentage sand, silt and clay were read on a textural triangle to determine the soil texture.

Field Experiments

The experiments were carried out at Akure in the rain forest zone of Nigeria (elevation 10m, 7^o15^1 N, 5° 15^1). The soil is a sandy clay loamy (Skeletal, Kaolinitic, isohyperthermic been continuously cropped for 8 years and the four field experiments were conducted in 2003 and 2004 cropping seasons with each one consisting of four months.

The annual rainfall amount and air temperature in the study area were 1450mm and 26.7°C in 2003 and 1460mm and 27.3°C in 2004 respectively.

The field site was cleared, ploughed and harrowed to maintain optimal tilth for the crop. Each plot size was 5m × 5m (25m^2). There were three organic fertilizer treatments namely; wood ash, cocoa pod husk and poultry manure, in-addition to 400 kg ha^{-1} NPK 15-15-15 fertilizer per crop (800kg ha^{-1} for two crops) and the control (no manure, no fertilizer) treatments.

The organic materials were applied at 6 t ha^{-1} per crop (24t ha^{-1} per two crops), replicated four times and arranged in a randomized complete block design (RCB). The choice of 400kg NPK 15-15-15 was based on the recommendation of Agboola (1982) and the choice of 6t ha^{-1} for organic fertilizers was based on the work of Moyin-Jesu (2002) for growing arable crops. The data on the total quantities of the organic fertilizers and amount of nutrients in them for this experiment are presented in Table 9.2.

Melon (*Cucumeropsis edulis* L) seeds were obtained form Ondo State Agricultural Development Agency (ADP). The seeds were planted per hole at a spacing of 90 x 60cm (92 stands per plot 25m^2). Weeding was promptly carried out at 2, 4 and 6 weeks after planting while the crop was sprayed with Nuvacron (a.i 400grams/litre monocrotophus; Ciba Geigy Chemical Company, Basel Switzerland at the rate of 5ml per 15 litres of water starting from second week after planting and this was repeated at sixth week after planting.

Ten plants were randomly sampled from each plot and tagged for determination of growth parameters at one week interval till six weeks after planting. The growth parameters were leaf area, and stem girth.

At 10 weeks after planting, the melon fruits were harvested, depulped and after five days, the seeds were removed from mucilage, dried and weighed for seed yield. The harvest of melon pods from the remaining plants in the plots were weighed and combined with the earlier harvested sampled plots to obtain the gross yield of the crop.

Analysis of leaf and seed samples of melon

At four weeks after planting, leaf samples were taken from the melon crop under different fertilizer application using secateur. Two grammes of sampled leaves were weighed into crucible, dry ashed in a muffle furnace at 450°C for 6 hours. The ash was made into solution with distilled water, filtered and the contents analysed for N, P, K, Ca and Mg. (AOAC, 1990).

Likewise, after the harvest the sample of dried melon seeds were shelled and dry ashed in a muffle furnace at 450°C for 6 hours. The ash was also made into solution and analysed for melon seed N, P, K, Ca and Mg (A.O.A.C. 1990).

Soil Analysis after the field Establishment

At the end of each field experiment on melon, 15 soil cores were collected from the 0-15 depth in each treatment plot of 25m^2 (5m x 5m) and bulked together. The soil samples were aid-dried and passed through 2mm sieve for routine chemical analysis while the procedure for the analysis of soil pH, O.M, %N, P, K, Ca and Mg were as described earlier.

Statistical Analysis

The data for soil, growth and yield of melon in 2003 and 2004 were subjected to Analysis of Variance (ANOVA). Variables for which significant treatment effects were found and characterized further using Duncan Multiple Range Test (DMRT) (d=0.05). Steele *et al* (1977). Step wise regression coefficient (R^2) was calculated to determined the contribution of each variable (N, P, K, Ca, Soil pH and soil organic matter) to the relationship between melon yields and soil fertility.

Determination of Economic benefit cost ratio and net income of melon using fertilizers

For the determination of benefit cost ratio using the organic fertilizers to grow melon, the gross income from the sales of melon seeds yield (naira) were calculated. The variable cost include the cost of preparing and application of the organic fertilizers, cost of weeding, spraying of nuvacron, harvesting of melon, cost of shelling and bagging, transport cost of purchasing NPK fertilizers (8 bags) and cost of land preparation.

The net income (profit) is calculated as;

Net income = Gross income – variable income while economic benefit cost ratio is calculated using formula.

$$BC = \eta\varepsilon \, Bt$$

$$t = 1(1+r)t$$

$$\eta \;\; \varepsilon \;\; Ct$$

$$t = 1(1+r)t$$

Where Bt = Benefit income or gross income, r = discount rate of 15% existing in the country and Ct = Cost of production (variable cost).

The BC ratio determines the profitability of using organic fertilizers for optimum production of melon. A market survey of the prices for melon was carried out in the study area. 1kg of melon was sold for N45.00 ($0.32).

Results

Chemical analysis of the agro-industrial biomass

The chemical composition of the agro-industrial biomass used for the experiments are presented in Table 9.1. Among the materials, poultry manure had the wood ash had the highest values of K, Ca, Mg, Fe, Zn, Mn, Cu followed by cocoa husk and poultry manures.

The poultry manure had the least C/N ratio of 6.93 followed by cocoa husk (11.1) and wood ash (12.1). The nutrient contents of each fertilizer treatment plus the quantity of each agro-industrial biomass applied per crop and year is presented in Table 9.2. The wood ash and poultry manure had the highest amount of nutrients especially N and P contents.

The synthetic NPK fertilizer supplied moderate amount of N, P and K contents but added minimal levels of Ca and Mg to the soil.

Initial soil physical and chemical properties before planting melon

The physical and chemical properties of the soils before treatment application are presented in Table 9.3. According to the established critical levels for soils in Southwest Nigeria, the soil is acidic and low in soil organic matter (SOM) compared to critical levels of 3% SOM (Agboola and Corey, 1973) and 0.15% total nitrogen, considered optimum for crops (Sobulo and Osiname, 1981).

The available P was less than 10mg/kg P considered adequate for crop production (Agboola, 1982). Exchangeable K, Ca, mg and Na values were much lower than the critical level of 0.2 mmol/kg; crops grown on the soils were expected to respond to K, Ca, Mg and Na application. The micronutrients values were more than the established critical levels of 5mg/kg Fe, 1.0mg/kg Cu, 5.0mg/kg Mn and 3.0 mg/kg Zn (Adeoye, 1986). The soil bulk density value was 1.65mgm^{-3}.

Effect of agro-industrial biomass on leaf and seed chemical composition of melon

The chemical composition of melon leaf and seeds are presented in Table 9.4 and 9.5 respectively. The agro-industrial biomass increased the melon leaf and seed N, P, K, Ca and Mg significantly ($P<0.05$) relative to the control treatment.

For melon leaf analysis, poultry manure treatment had the highest values of % leaf N and P compared to others while wood ash had the highest values of % leaf K, Ca and Mg.

For instance, wood ash increased the %K, Ca and Mg by 22%, 40% and 50% compared to poultry manure. However, poultry manure increased % leaf N and P by 47% and 3.4% compared to wood ash.

When compared to NPK 15-15-15, wood ash increased the K, Ca and Mg by 39%, 97% and 94% respectively except %N and P where NPK increased %N and P by 62.3% and 8.42%. The control treatment had the least value of melon leaf % N, P, K, Ca and Mg.

For the seed analysis, all the values of nutrients in the melon seeds were greater than that of the leaf chemical composition. Wood ash treatment had the highest values of seed K, Ca and Mg followed by cocoa husk and poultry manure respectively. Poultry manure had the highest values of seed N and P than wood ash and cocoa husk respectively. Seed N in NPK 15-15-15 treatment was slightly lower than the leaf N.

NPK 15-15-15 had lower values of melon seed K, Ca and Mg compared to wood ash, cocoa husk and poultry manure respectively.

For instance, wood ash treatment increased melon seed N, P, K, Ca and Mg by 7.4%, 12.6%, 15.5%, 46.6% and 30% compared to cocoa husk. Poultry manure treatment increased seed N and P by 8% and 10.3% compared to wood ash.

Wood ash increased melon seed N, P, K, Ca and Mg by 7.4%, 12.6%, 15.5%, 46.6% and 30% compared to cocoa husk. Poultry manure treatment increased seed N and P by 8% and 10.3% compared to wood ash.

Wood ash increased melon seed K, Ca and Mg by 19%, 98% and 95% compared to NPK 15-15-15 fertilizer treatment.

Growth and Yield Parameters of melon under different Agro-industrial Biomass

The agro-industrial biomass increased the melon yield and growth parameters; vine length, number of branches and leaf area, weight of melon seeds and average number of pods per plant significantly ($P<0.05$) relative to the control treatment (Table 9.6).

Wood ash treatment increased melon vine length and leaf area compared to cocoa husk, poultry manure and NPK 15-15-15 treatments respectively. For instance, wood ash increased leaf area and vine length by 28% and 14% compared to that of cocoa husk.

When compared to NPK 15-15-15 treatment, wood ash increased the melon vine length and leaf area by 18.7% and 5.5%. However, NPK had the highest average number of branches of melon compared to wood ash, poultry manure and cocoa husk.

For melon seed yield, wood ash had the highest seed yield value (kg/ha) followed by poultry manure, cocoa husk, NPK 15-15-15 fertilizer and control treatments. The same trend was observed for the average number of fruits per plant.

For instance, wood ash increased the seed melon yield by 19%, 27%, 39% and 81% compared to poultry manure, cocoa husk, NPK 15-15-15 and control treatment respectively.

The NPK 15-15-15 fertilizer delayed melon fruit formation and subsequently seed yield when compared to the agro-industrial biomass.

Multiple regression analysis between the melon seed yield, soil N, P, K, Ca, Mg, organic matter (O.M) and pH yielded R^2 values of 0.876 for the four crops (Table 9.7). For instance, the stepwise regression of all the soil variables for the four crops showed that nitrogen specifically contributed R^2 values of 0.45 out of the total R^2 value of 0.876 representing 51%.

Effect of different agro-industrial biomass on the soil chemical composition after harvesting melon

The agro-industrial biomass increased significantly ($P<0.05$) soil pH, soil organic matter (SOM), K, Ca, Mg, %N, available P and bulk density compared to the control treatment (Table 9.8).

Wood ash treatment had the highest values of soil Ca, Mg, pH and bulk density compared to cocoa husk, poultry manure, NPK 15-15-15 and control treatments respectively. However, NPK 15-5-15 treatment had highest values of soil N, P and K compared to others.

For instance, wood ash increased soil Ca, Mg and pH by 72%, 53% and 7% respectively compared to poultry manure treatment. It also decreased the soil bulk density by 3% compared to poultry manure.

When compared to NPK 15-15-15, wood ash increased soil Ca, Mg, pH and O.M by 97%, 82%, 26% and 82% respectively. However, NPK 15-15-15 fertilizer increased soil N, P and K by 27%, 66% and 31% respectively compared to wood ash.

NPK 15-15-15 fertilizer treatment decreased soil pH, O.M and increased bulk density after harvesting melon compared to the initial soil nutrient status. NPK 15-15-15 fertilizer treatment had higher ratio of K/Ca, P/Mg and K/Mg nutrient interaction in the soil than the agro-industrial biomass. For instance, soil K/Ca, P/Mg and K/Mg ratio were 38:1, 2260:1 and 25:1 respectively in NPK fertilizer treatment compared to K/Ca (3:1), P/Mg 148:1 and K/Mg (3:1) under wood ash treatment leading to serious imbalance in P, Ca and Mg nutrients availability to melon crop.

Wood ash decreased the soil bulk density (mgm^{-3}) the most followed by cocoa husk and poultry manure treatments while the NPK fertilizer and control plots had relatively high bulk density values.

Determination of economic benefit cost (BC) and profitability of using agro-industrial biomass for melon seed yield.

Table 9.9 presents the values of economic benefit cost (BC) ratio using agro-industrial biomass on melon seed yield.

Weed ash treatment had the highest benefit cost (BC) ratio, gross income and net income followed by poultry manure, cocoa husk, NPK 15-15-15 and control treatments respectively.

For instance, wood ash increased the BC ratio value of melon seed yield by 18%, 30%, 62% and 86% compared to poultry manure, cocoa husk, NPK 15-15-15 and control treatments.

The highest variable cost under NPK 15-15-15 fertilizer was because of high cost of purchasing 8 bags and transportation cost.

The highest BC ratio and net income of using wood ash treatment on the melon seed yield indicated higher profitability index compared to NPK, control, poultry manure, cocoa husk treatments respectively.

Discussion

The poor growth and yield performances of melon in the control treatment was consistent with the fact that the soil was very low in nutrient contents. This observation was supported by Moyin-Jesu (2002) who had reported poor growth and yield responses of crop in soils not fertilized.

The low values of gross income, benefit cost (BC) ratio less than one and negative net income also supported poor yield performance of melon in the control treatment, indicating poor profitability index or low economic returns for farmers. In addition, the lowest leaf and seed N, P, K, Ca and Mg values were also recorded for melon crop under the control treatment.

Adegeye (2004) reported that any production business which has BC ratio < 1 is not profitable, thus, there is need to ensure better fertilization of soils in the tropics to enhance productivity of crops because the soils are usually low in organic matter (O.M), N, P, K, Ca, Mg, Na and pH.

The fact that NPK 15-15-15 fertilizer improved the vegetative growth of melon is consistent with the better N, P and K status of the soils fertilized with NPK fertilizer which were made more readily available to crops in ionic forms than their organic forms in the agro-industrial biomass which must first change to the mineralized state by micro-organisms (Ojeniyi, 1984). This explains the better soil and melon seed N, P and K nutrients in NPK fertilizer compared to the agro-industrial biomass.

NPK 15-15-15 fertilizer also decreased soil, leaf and seed K, Ca and Mg nutrients in melon and this could be adduced to the nutrients imbalance in the soil as shown by high P/Mg and K/Ca ratio which affected Ca and Mg uptake (Folorunso *et al* 2000).

Furthermore, the low soil O.M, Ca and Mg nutrients in the NPK fertilized plot coupled with the sandy loam texture of the soil, would not allow much retention of the nutrients as a result of erosion. This could be responsible for the reduced yield of melon crops compared to the agro-industrial biomass which improved soil pH, O.M, N, P, K, Ca and Mg, thereby supporting growth and yield performances.

The higher soil K, Ca and Mg nutrients under the agro-industrial biomass constituted better base saturation of the soil and thereby increasing the soil cation exchange capacity, organic matter and pH. Hence, the soils are capable of retaining nutrients and resist erosion better than the NPK fertilized plot. It was observed that NPK 15-15-15 fertilizer delayed the flowering and seed formation in melon compared to the agro-industrial biomass. This could be due to luxury consumption of N and P nutrients which consequently encouraged vegetative growth at the expense of reproductive growth in crops, thereby, delaying flowering and seed formation (Moyin-Jesu 2007).

The best yield performance of melon using the wood ash fertilizer treatment could be attributed to the fact that it had the best values of K, Ca,

Mg, Na, Fe, Zn, Cu and Mn and moderate amount of N and P (Table 1). The positive effect of the balanced nutrient composition of wood ash could explain further the fact that the gross income, net income values and benefit cost ratio were the highest for melon under this treatment signifying higher economic returns and profitability for farmers compared to cocoa husk, NPK 15-15-15 fertilizer and control treatments respectively. The observation was supported by Adegeye (2004) who reported that the higher the benefit cost (BC) values, the better the profitability or economic returns of such business enterprise.

The NPK 15-15-15-15 fertilizer and control treatment had lower values of BC ratio < 1 for NPK fertilizer under melon yield indicated that the use of fertilizer was not profitable considering its high cost of purchase by poor resource farmers and deterioration of soil properties on continuous use. (Moyin- Jesu 2006).

Table 9.1: The Chemical Composition of the Organic Materials used for the Cultivation of Melon

Organic materials	C %	N %	C/N ratio	Available P (mg/kg)	K mg/kg	Ca mg/kg	Mg mg/kg	Na mg/kg	Fe mg/kg	Zn mg/kg	Cu mg/kg	Mn mg/kg
Cocoa pod husk	16	1.44	11	100	21	9.34	7.10	4.4	5.40	1.7	0.55	8.60
Wood ash	18	1.53	12	86	23	9.40	8.50	8.3	6.60	1.83	0.60	12.00
Poultry manure		4.33	6.93	385	9.7	3.32	4.10	2.31	3.78	1.26	0.15	4.10

Table 9.2: Total amount of Nutrients Supplied kg/ha Applications in all the Organic Materials Sources NPK Fertilizers and the Quantities used for the two crops of melon

Fertilizers	N	P	K	Ca	Mg	Total quantities of residues	
						per crop	year
	kg/ha application						
NPK 15-15-15	240	240	240	16	8	400kg/crop	800kg/yr
Cocoa pod husk	346	250	285	638	160	6T/crop	12kg/yr
Wood ash	367	272	262	642	212	6T/crop	12kg/yr
Poultry manure	432	360	159	132	146	6T/crop	12kg/yr

Table 9.3: Soil Physical and Chemical Properties before Planting Melon

Soil parameters	Values
1	2
Soil pH (H_2O)	5.80
Soil pH (H_2O)	5.35
Organic matter (%)	0.55
Nitrogen (%)	0.05

1	2
Available P (mg/kg)	7.38
K^+ (mmol/kg)	0.08
Ca^{2+} (mmol/kg)	0.11
Mg^{2+} (mmol/kg)	0.14
Na^+ (mmol/kg)	1.04
H^+ (mmol/kg)	4.40
Al^{3+} (mmol/kg)	1.47
Fe^{2+} (mgl/kg)	6.10
Cu^{2+} (mgl/kg)	2.05
Mn^{2+} (mg/kg)	1.33
Zn^{2+} (mg/kg)	2.99
Sand (%)	79.50
Silt (%)	14.80
Clay (%)	5.70
Bulk density (mg m^{-3})	1.65
% porosity	41.81
Texture class	sandy loam
USDA Soil classification	Alfisol (Oxic tropodaulf)

Table 9.4: Leaf Chemical Composition (%) of Melon under different Agro-Industrial Biomass

Treatments	%N	%P	%K	%Ca	%Mg
Wood ash	0.75c	0.87b	1.8d	0.1c	0.08d
Cocoa husk	0.65b	0.85b	1.49b	0.07b	0.06c
Poultry manure	1.41d	0.90c	1.40b	0.06b	0.04b
NPK 15-15-15	1.99e	0.95d	1.1c	0.003a	0.005a
Control	0.2a	0.14a	0.13a	0.001a	0.004a

Treatments within each column followed by the same letters are not significant different from each other using Duncan Multiple Range Test at 5% level of significance.

Data are means of 16 observations (four replicates x four crops).

Table 9.5: Chemical Composition (%) of Melon Seeds under different Agro-Industrial Biomass

Treatments	%N	%P	%K	%Ca	%Mg
Wood ash	1.36c	0.87b	1.93e	0.15c	0.10d
Cocoa husk	1.26b	0.76b	1.63d	0.08b	0.07c
Poultry manure	1.48d	0.97d	1.56c	0.07b	0.05b
NPK 15-15-15	1.35c	1.20e	1.40b	0.003a	0.005a
Control	0.3a	0.14a	0.14a	0.002a	0.004a

Treatments within each column followed by the same letters are not significant different from each other using Duncan Multiple Range Test at 5% level of significance.

+Data are means of 16 observations (four crops x four replicates).

Table 9.6: Growth and Yield Parameters of Melon under different Agro-industrial Biomass

Treatments	Vine Length (cm)	Average number of branches	Leaf area (cm^2)	Weight of melon seeds (kg/ha)	Average number of pod per plant
Wood ash	28.35e	7.8c	256.0e	1550e	5.59d
Cocoa husk	24.35c	6.9b	185.3b	1125c	3.14b
Poultry manure	26.75d	14.2e	252.1d	1250d	3.15b
NPK 15-15-15	23.05b	11.98d	242.1c	950b	4.76c
Control	11.9a	3.91a	108.2a	300a	1.62a

Treatments within each column followed by the same letters are not significant different from each other using Duncan Multiple Range Test at 5% level of significance.

+ Data are means of 16 observations (four crops x four replicates).

Table 9.7: Stepwise Regression showing Specific R^2 Contribution of each Soil Properties to the Seed Yield of four Crops of Melon using different Agro-Industrial Biomass

Stepwise number of soil Variables		Specific R^2 values
Step 1	Soil N	0.45
2	Soil P	0.114
3	Soil K	0.087
4	Soil Ca	0.018
5	Soil Mg	0.017
6	Soil O.M	0.153
7	Soil pH	0.037
Total R^2		0.876

+Data are means of 16 observations (four crops x four replicates).

Table 9.8: The Soil Chemical composition after Harvesting of Melon using different Agro-industrial Biomass

Treatments	SOM %	N %	P (mg/kg)	K (mmol/kg)	Ca (mmol/kg)	Mg mmol/kg	pH	Bulk density
Wood ash	2.17	0.19	23.1	0.52	0.58	0.156	7.1	1.46
Cocoa husk	1.93	0.17	22.48	0.50	0.41	0.17	6.8	1.48
Poultry manure	2.50	0.24	36.67	0.20	0.16	0.08	6.6	1.50
NPK 15-15-15	0.40	0.26	67.81	0.75	0.02	0.03	5.25	1.68
Control	0.39	0.03	2.24	0.04	0.02	0.03	5.35	1.73

Treatments within each column followed by the same letters are not significant different from each other using Duncan Multiple Range Test at 5% level of significance.

+Data are means of 16 observations (four crops x four replicates).

Table 9.9: Determination of Economic Benefits Cost (BC) Ratio and Profitability of using different Agro-industrial Biomass for Melon Seed Yield

Treatments BC	Seed yield (kg/ha)	Gross income (N)	Variable Cost (N)	Net income	ratio
Wood ash	1550	69,750	29,000	40,750	2.40
Cocoa husk	1125	50,625	30,000	20,625	1.69
Poultry manure	1250	56,250	28,500	27,750	1.97
NPK 15-15-15	950	42,750	46,000	-3250	0.92
Control	300	13,500	38,200	-24,700	0.35

+Data are means of 16 observations (four crops x four replicates).

Recommendation and Conclusion

It could be concluded from the experiment that wood ash treatment gave the best melon vegetative, soil and leaf nutrients and seed yield performance. This also reflected in having the best values of gross income, net income and BC ratio compared to cocoa husk, poultry manure, NPK 15- 15-15 and control treatments.

It is recommended that for better yield, land utilization and improvement of soil nutrient status, wood ash applied at 6 t/ha gave optimum melon seed yield. This recommendation is important considering the high cost of purchasing NPK 15-15-15 fertilizers by poor resource farmers who are the major producers of food crops in the tropics and also the need to prevent environmental pollution and deterioration of soil properties on continuous use.

REFERENCES

Adeoye, G.O, 1986. Comparative studies of ammonium bi-fluoride chelate extractants for sedimentary soils of South Western Nigeria. Ph. D. thesis, Faculty of Agriculture and Forestry, University of Ibadan, Ibadan, Nigeria.

Adegeye, J.A, 2004. Small scale business, you can start with little or no capital investment. Publ. by Josadeg Nigeria limited, Ibadan, Nigeria ISBN 978-2379-059.

Agboola, A.A., 1982. Soil testing, soil fertility and fertility use in Nigeria. A paper presented at 1st National seminar in Agricultural Land Resources, September 15-18 Kaduna, Nigeria.

Agboola, A.A, Corey, R.B, 1973. Soil testing N, P, K for maize in the soils derived from metamorphic and igneous rocks of Western State of Nigeria. J. West African Sci. Assoc. 17 (2), 93-100.

AOAC ,1970. Official Method of Analysis, 12th ed. AOAC, Arlington, VA.

AOAC 1990. Official methods of Analysis. 16th ed. AOAC, Arlington, VA.

Bouycous, H., 1951. Mechanical analysis of soils using hydrometer method. Anal. Chem. Acta 22, 32-34.

Crockford, L., Nowel, R., 1956. Laboratory Manual of Physical Chemistry. Expl. 31 and 32. John Wiley and Sons, New York.

Folorunso, O.O., Agboola, A. A., Adeoye G. O; 2000. Evaluation of three fertilizer models, P and k needs of maize (*Zea may* L). Jour. of Tech. Educ. NBTE, Kaduna, Nigeria, 1&2: 145-155.

Jackson, M. L., 1964. Soil Chemical Analysis. Prentiice Hall Inc. Englewood Cliffs. New York, Pp. 86-92.

I.I.T.A. 2001. Annual report of International Institute of Tropical Agriculture, Ibadan. (8): 110-120.

McLean, E.O., 1965. Aluminum Pp. 927-932. In: Black, M. C. A. (Ed.), Methods of Soil Analysis part 2, Agron. 9. Amer. Soc. Agron., Madison, WI, USA.

Murphy, J., Riley, J.P., 1962. A modified single solution for determination of phosphate in natural waters. Anal. Glumi-Acta 27, 35-36.

Moyin-Jesu, E.I., 2002. Raising oil palm seedling in urban cities using sole and amended forms of wood ash and sawdust. Jour. Tropical Agricultural Science, Pertanika, Malaysia, 25 (2): 31-37.

Moyin-Jesu, E.I. 2007. Effect of some organic fertilizers on soil and coffee (*Coffee Arabica* L) Leaf Chemical Composition an Growth. University of Khartourn Jour. Agric. Sci 15 (1), 52-70.

Olaofe, O., Adeyemi, F. O., Adediran, G. O. 1994. Amino acid and mineral composition and functional properties of some oil seeds. J. Agric. Food Chem. 42: 878-881.

Ogunwale, J.A., Udo, E.J., 1978. A laboratory manual for soil and plant analysis, Agron. Department, University of Ibadan, Ibadan, Nigeria, Pp. 201-206.

Ojeniyi, S.O., 1984. Compound chemical fertilizer and food crop production. Effects of NPK 15-15-15 fertilizer on pepper, cowpea and maize. Nigeria J. Appl. Sci. 2, 91-95.

Ojeniyi, S. O. 1988. Soil physical properties under maize and cowpea. Nigeria J. Agron. 3, 65-76.

Ojeniyi, S. O. 1988. Use of woodash for soil fertility and crop yield improvement. Paper presented at 24th Ann. Conf. Soil Sci. Soc. of Nigeria, December 7-11, A.B.T.U., Bauchi, Nigeria.

Sobulo, R.A., Osiname, O.A., 1981. Soils and fertilizer use in Western Nigeria, Res. Bull. 11, I.A.R.&T., University of Ife, Nigeria, November 12, Pp. 8-9.

Steele, R.G.D., Torrie, J.H., Dickey, D.A., 1997. Principles and Approach McGraw Hill Companies Inc., Pp. 28-35.

Walkley, A., Black, I.A., 1934. An examination of Degtajaroff method for determination soil organic matter, and a proposed modification of the chromic acid titration method. Soil Sci. 37, 29-38.

10

Heavy Metal in Drain Sediments, River Bed Sediments and Agricultural Soil in around Gajraula Industrial Area, Gajraula, India

—*Pawan Kumar, India*

ABSTRACT

In this modern industrial era, the waste problem in land lies in the leaching process, such as quantum of liquid wastes leachates slowly through the layers of soil beneath and contaminate the water resources deep down the land, however, the problem of soil pollution differs from air and water pollution in the respect of pollutants remains direct contact with the soil for relatively long period. The wide industrialization and increasing consumption pattern has changed the very complexion of soil especially in industrial area. Thus soil is getting heavily polluted day by day by addition of toxic materials.

The concentrations of heavy metals (Cu, Cd, Mn, Fe, Ni, Pb and Zn) were studied in soil and sediments to understand metal contamination due to industrialization in and around Gajraula. All heavy metals analyzed according to APHA (2005) by atomic absorption spectrophotometer. The data revealed concentration of Copper, Cadmium, Manganese, Iron, Nickel, Lead and Zinc in drain sediments, river bed sediments and agricultural soil.

Key words: *Industrial pollution, Heavy metal, accumulation, Gajraula*

Introduction

Gajraula, being a prominent industrial area of western Uttar Pradesh, owes its significance to diverse group of industries, which includes large distillery and its associated chemical units, paper, phosphate fertilizer plant, textiles, pharmaceuticals, dairy and other units. The industrial effluents contain toxic chemicals, hazardous compounds, suspended solids and non-biodegradable materials. The major source of surface and ground water pollution is injudicious discharge of untreated industrial effluents directly into the surface water bodies resulting in surface and ground water pollution (Nasrullah, *et al.*, 2006). The effluents from the industries and sewage of industrial towns have drained collectively through a local drain known as Bagad nallah, which assumes the shape of seasonal river, especially during monsoon. The quality of Bagad river water is a great concern to deteriorate the quality of the surface water and ground water due to releasing their effluent without any adequate treatment and polluting the upper water table through the leaching process in and around industrial area. The quality of composite effluent, ground water, soil and sediments around the industrial area have been affected a lot and causes serious disease among the human beings and other livestock population. The industrial effluents if not treated properly controlled, can pollute and cause serious damage to the surface water, ground water, soil and sediment (Olayinka, 2004).

In the adjoining area of industrial estate, the farmer communities mainly depend on agricultural practices for their livelihood. Agricultural soil requires sufficient irrigation in agricultural fields for high crop production. The bioavailable metal content in soil exerts a decisive impact on soil quality and its use in food production. Hence, the assessment of metal contamination is on vital importance in industrial areas. The drain sediments existing as the bottom of the water column played major role in the pollution status of aquatic system by depositing heavy metals (Forstner, 1985). Contaminants at large contaminated site often share critical properties such as high lipophilicity leading bio-accumulation of food web with a view to understand the heavy metal dynamics. The risk of heavy metal contamination is pronounced in the environment adjacent to large industrial complexes. Many cases of particularly severe metal pollution by atmospheric deposition have been reported from areas surrounding non ferrous metal smelters in many countries Lohani *et al* (2008).

The main goal of present study was to assess the impact of industrial and urban activities on drain sediments, river bed sediments and agricultural soil quality of the area.

Material and Methods

Gajraula city is approximately 115 Km. away from Delhi on national highway NH-24, Delhi-Lucknow road. Gajraula is well known and one of the oldest industrial area of district J.P. Nagar (Uttar Pradesh) situated on globe at a longitude 78° 13′48.75" E and latitude 28° 50′59.26" N at 679 feet above sea level (207 msl). Gajraula industrial area was selected on the basis of existence of large number of industries (chemical units, pulp & paper, phosphate fertilizer plant, textiles, pharmaceuticals, dairy products processing units and others), which discharge a huge amount of wastewater in the form of mixed effluents through different drains into a seasonal river Bagad. The study was carried out in different seasons during April 2008 to March 2009. The samples of drain sediments were collected from composite industrial drain and samples of river bed sediments were collected from river bed sediments. The samples of agricultural soil were collected from agricultural fields around industrial area.

Sampling and Analysis

All samples of soil and sediments were collected from around 5 km from industrial area by grab sampling method in summer, monsoon and winter seasons. Soil and sediments samples (45) were collected from the outer surface of study area the industrial and urban waste sources of pollutants as normally industrial pollutants contaminate the upper layer of soil (0-40 cm). The soil and sediment samples were dried at 60°C for two days. The dried samples were finally powdered by grinding and extracted by aqua regia (HNO_3 + H_2SO_4-3:1) and analyzed by AAS as per APHA (2005).

Results and Discussion

The present study shows that heavy metals pollution in and around Gajraula industrial pollution. Heavy metals concentration was not found in excess because most of the industries in Gajraula industrial area are releasing metals containing effluent. Gajraula industrial area having following most effluent generating industries namely, Jubilent organosys, Insilco fertilizers, Shree Acids and Chemicals and Corel News Print etc. So, Gajroula industrial effluents containing usually organic matter with some heavy metals. Organic matter in industrial waste water alters the physico-chemical characteristics of Bagad River Water and ground water quality. The results obtained for each metal are shown in Table 10.1.

Table 10.1: Heavy Metals (ppm) in Composite Effluent Drain Sediments, River Bed-sediments and Agricultural Soil

	Drain Sediments			River Bed-sediments			Agricultural soil		
Metals	Summer	Monsoon	Winter	Summer	Monsoon	Winter	Summer	Monsoon	Winter
Cu	41.261	34.477	37.313	41.847	44.217	48.136	30.890	26.436	16.616
Cd	4.146	3.530	2.992	5.268	5.033	4.384	3.097	0.957	1.405
Mn	908.661	665.556	837.854	862.344	533.721	604.412	12.915	9.866	5.989
Fe	6890.622	4591.612	5009.730	6192.649	4126.689	5967.195	68.917	24.986	27.701
Ni	59.760	48.321	54.037	48.629	38.152	44.232	9.350	6.645	5.231
Pb	55.464	48.601	43.958	64.976	58.136	44.304	55.378	34.876	23.018
Zn	213.018	171.437	130.847	213.827	209.194	163.347	10.641	15.404	8.792

Copper is sometimes found in insufficient quantity in soil (Miller and Turk, 2002) but it may be added in to soil system by some anthropogenic activities. Copper may accumulate in living organisms and their various body parts (Kudesia, 1992). High amount if heavy metals like Cu and Zn may harm to living organism of existing ecosystem (Aslam *et al.*, 2004). Minimum and maximum values of copper in drain sediment, river bed sediments and agricultural soil were recorded 34.477 ppm in monsoon and 41.261 ppm in summer, 41.847 ppm in summer and 48.136 ppm in winter and 16.616 ppm in winter and 30.890 ppm in summer respectively. Cadmium transfer is due to some other non-point sources of cadmium pollution. During the last decade, the industrial use of Cd has increased and can create both acute and chronic cases of clinically identifiable toxicity in humans. In human, absorption of dietary Cd is limited up to 15% and that of inhaled Cd is high 40% and not absorbed from skin (Mani *et al.*, 2005). Minimum and maximum values of cadmium in drain sediment, river bed sediments and agricultural soil were recorded 2.992 ppm in winter and 4.146 ppm in summer, 4.384 ppm in winter and 5.268 ppm in summer and 0.957 ppm in monsoon and 3.097 ppm in summer respectively. The use of contaminated water into irrigation may be increase the cadmium status in agricultural soil (Mani *et al.*, 2005).

Manganese is one of the most trace elements essential for organism. It has low acute oral toxicity, however, the chronic manganese poisoning leads to progressive deterioration of the central nervous system and system and symptoms resembling to those of Parkinson's disease are observed. Minimum and maximum values of Manganese in drain sediment, river bed sediments and agricultural soil were recorded 665.556 ppm in monsoon and 908.661 ppm in summer, 533.721 ppm in monsoon and 862.344 ppm in summer and 5.989 ppm in winter and 12.915 ppm in summer respectively.

Excess calcium can reduced the activity of iron in soil and soil aeration may influence the availability of iron to plants (Miller and Turk, 2002). Minimum and maximum values of Iron in drain sediment, river bed sediments and agricultural soil were recorded 4591.612 ppm in monsoon and 6890.622 ppm in summer, 4126.689 ppm in monsoon and 6192.649 ppm in summer and 24.986 ppm in monsoon and 68.917 ppm in summer respectively.

Minimum and maximum values of Nickel in drain sediment, river bed sediments and agricultural soil were recorded 48.321 ppm in monsoon and 59.760 ppm in summer, 38.152 ppm in monsoon and 48.629 ppm in summer and 5.231 ppm in winter and 9.350 ppm in summer respectively. Nickel may accumulate in aquatic life but its presence is not magnified along food chains. So, there is not so big fear of nickel toxicity to higher animals including human beings, but agricultural plant health will be affected in contaminated agricultural soil.

Lead is well known to cause harmful health effects; especially children are particularly susceptible to increased levels of lead in their blood (Velea *et al.*, 2009). Lead is the least mobile element among toxic metals, which attributed to binding of the metal to organic matter, Prohic *et al.*, (1997). Minimum and maximum values of lead in drain sediment, river bed sediments and agricultural soil were recorded 43.958 ppm in winter and

55.464 ppm in summer, 44.304 ppm in winter and 64.976 ppm in summer and 23.018 ppm in winter and 55.378 ppm in summer respectively. Lead is deposited mostly in bones and some soft tissues. High concentrations of lead may create toxicity in human (Kudesia, 1992). Similar trend of lead concentration was also reported by Krishna and Govil, (2008) in soil. Minimum and maximum values of zinc in drain sediment, river bed sediments and agricultural soil were recorded 130.847 ppm in winter and 213.018 ppm in summer, 163.347 ppm in winter and 213.827 ppm in summer and 8.792 ppm in winter and 15.404 ppm in monsoon respectively. Zinc salts are relatively non-toxic, but high concentrations may cause health problems like vomiting, renal damage, etc. (Kudesia, 1992). High amount of Zn may harm to living organism of that ecosystem (Aslam *et al.*, 2004).

The present study reveals that there was heavy metals pollution in composite industrial effluents drain sediments, river bed sediments, agricultural soil, which affected the agriculture soil system and latter on, deteriorate the quality of ground water of industrial area at Gajraula. Beside this, the bottom sediment of composite industrial effluent drain and Bagad river stored the heavy metals in high quantities, which have no secure or pre-managed future.

Acknowledgement

The authors are thankful to Prof. A.K Chopra, Dean, Faculty of Life Science, Prof. B.D. Joshi, Coordinator of UGC (SAP) and Prof. D. Bhatt, Head, Department of Zoology and Environmental Science for the facilities provided to carry out research work successfully. The author (Pawan Kumar) is gratefully acknowledged the financial support from UGC, Delhi.

REFERENCES

APHA (2005). Standard methods for the examination of wastewater. *American Public Health Association, Washington, D.C.* pp. 1190.

Aslam, M.M.; Baig, M.A.; Hassan, I.; Qazi, I.A.; Malik, M. and Saeed, H. (2004): Textile wastewater characterization and reduction of its COD and BOD by oxidation. *Electron. J. Environ. Agri. Food Chem.*, 3(6): 804-811.

Forstner, U. (1985): Chemical forms and reactivities of metals in sediments in chemical methods for assessing bioavailable metals in sludge and soils, In: Leschber, R., Davies, R.D. and Hermite, L.P. (Eds). *Elsevier, London*, pp: 1-30.

Krishna, A. K. and Govil, P. K. (2004): Heavy metal contamination of soil around Pali industrial area, Rajasthan, India. *Environmental Geology*, 47: 38-44.

Kudesia, V.P. (1992): Water Pollution. *Pragati Prakashan, Meerut*, pp: 407.

Lohani, M.; Singh, A.; Rupainwar, D. C. and Dhar, D. N. (2008): Seasonal variation in heavy metal contamination in river Gomti at Lucknow city region. *Environmental Monitoring and Assessment*, 147:253-263.

Mani, V.; Kaur, H. and Mohini, M. (2005): Toxic metals and environmental pollution. *J. Ind. Poll. Cont.*, 21(1): 101-107.

Millar, C.E. and Turk, L.M. (2002): Fundamentals of soil science, Biotech Books, Delhi-35, pp: 462.

Nasrullah., Naz, R.; Bibi, H.; Iqbal, M. and Durrani, M. I. (2006). Pollution load in industrial effluent and ground water of Gadoon Amazai Industrial Estate (GAIE) Swabi, NWFP. *Journal of Agriculture and Biological Science,* 1(3):18-24.

Olayinka, K. O. (2004). Studies on industrial pollution in Nigeria- the effect of textile effluents on the quality of groundwater. *Nigerian Journal of Health and Medical Sciences,* 3:44-50.

Prohic, E.; Devis, J. C. and Hansberger, G. (1997): Geochemical patterns in soils of the karst region Cratia. *J. Geochem. Expplor.,* 60:139-155.

Velea, T.; Liliana, G.; Predica, V. and Krebs, R. (2009): Heavy metal contamination in the vicinity of an industrial area near Bucharest. *Environ. Sci. Pollut. Res.,* 16(1): S27-S32.

11

Comparative Evaluation of Traditional Food Legumes as Soil Amendments for Fertility Improvement, Growth, Leaf Minerals Composition and Yield of Maize *(Zea mays L)*

—*E. I Moyin-Jesu, Nigeria*

ABSTRACT

*Two field experiments were carried out at Akure (7°N, 5°10[1]E) in the rainforest zone of Nigeria in 2003 and 2004 to determine the effectiveness of bambara groundnut, pigeon pea and groundnut legumes as soil amendments in improving soil fertility, growth, leaf chemical composition and yield of maize (*Zea mays *L). There were six treatments namely, bambara groundnut, pigeon pea, groundnut legumes, NPK 15-15-15 (400kg/ha) as a reference treatment and a control treatment, replicated four times and arranged in a randomized complete block design. The maize seeds were planted at a spacing of 90x30cm and germinated five days later after which two seeds each of bambara groundnut and groundnut were inter-planted within the maize and between at a spacing of 75x45cm while pigeon pea was planted at a spacing 1x1m between and within maize. The results showed that there were significant increase (P<0.05) in the maize growth, leaf mineral composition and yield of maize under different legumes treatment compared to the control treatment. For maize growth parameters, bambara groundnut treatment had the highest values of maize plant and leaf population while groundnut treatment had the highest values of leaf area and stem girth.*

For instance, bambara groundnut increased the maize plant height by 9%, 12%, 2% and 36% compared to groundnut, pigeon pea, NPK 15-15-15 and control treatments respectively while groundnut increase the leaf area by 1.3%, 1.2%, 2.5% and 13.3% compared to bambara groundnut, pigeon pea, NPK 15-15-15 and control treatments.

For leaf mineral composition, NPK 15-15-15 fertilizer increased the maize leaf N by 9.4%, 15.5%, 12.5% and 99% compared to pigeon pea, groundnut, bambara groundnut and control treatments respectively while groundnut treatment had the highest maize leaf K and Mg. For maize yield, bambara groundnut treatment had the highest maize yield values compared to other. Legumes Bambara groundnut increased maize yield by 2.6%, 3% and 53% compared to groundnut, pigeon pea and control treatments. However, NPK 15-15-15 slightly increased the maize yields over the legumes.

For soil fertility improvement groundnut treatment had the highest values of soil O.M, N, K, and Ca while pigeon pea treatment also had the highest values of soil pH, P and Mg respectively. For instance, groundnut treatment increased soil O.M, N, K and Ca by 16%, 12%, 19% and 4% compared to bambara treatment. NPK 15-15-15 fertilizer decreased soil O.M, pH, Ca and Mg compared to others. The high soil K/Ca, K/Mg and P/Mg ratios in the NPK fertilizer treatment led to an imbalance in the supply of P, K, Ca and Mg nutrients to the crop. Therefore, bambara groundnut intercropped with maize gave the highest grain yield and could effectively substitute for 400kg/ha NPK 15-15-15 in maize production.

Key words: Bambara groundnut, pigeon pea, groundnut, maize yield, leaf chemical composition, soil fertility improvement.

Introduction

Maize (*Zea mays* L) is a staple food crop belonging to the family Graminae and it is consumed by people and livestock. It is also used in agro-allied industries for the production of corn flakes, breakfast cereals, corn oil, glucose starch, silage, animal feeds, straw flour and alcohol.

Among the cereal crops, maize is prepared by boiling and baking, fermented or roasted. It is currently being grown in over 2.5million hectares of from with an estimated production of 2.5 tonnes per hectare (Mustapha, 1991). The average annual maize production in Nigeria is about 2 millions metric tonnes (Oyekan 1990). The rising price of maize (*zea may* L) in Nigeria indicated a higher demand for the crop and efforts meant to increase production of maize have led to intensive cultivation of the same piece of land by the farmers, thus resulting into decline in soil fertility and the resultant effect is the decline in grain yield of maize.

Attempts made in the past to improve the soil fertility through the use of inorganic fertilizers are hindered by high cost of purchase and scarcity at the level of poor resource farmers and destruction of soil properties because of long term use (Folorunso *et al*, 1995). Further researches aimed at increasing soil fertility through the use of solid organic fertilizers have not been fully adopted by farmers because of their bulky nature and difficult in transportation (Moyin-Jesu and Akinwale, 2002).

Therefore, there is need to provide an alternative methods of improving the soil fertility through the use of low cost sustainable biological nitrogen fixation (BNF) plants such as pigeon pea (*cajanus cajan*), Groundnut (*Arachis hypogea*) and Bambara groundnut (*Vigna subturran*). Apart from their food and nutritive values, these food legumes also have the characteristics of fixing atmosphere nitrogen, thus, making it available to the non legume crop. The non legume is either intercropped with or that which follows the legume crop (Moyin-Jesu and Adekayode, 2010).

The objectives of this study area (*i*) to determine the effect of bambara groundnut, groundnut and pigeon pea legumes as soil amendments on the growth and yield of maize (*ii*) To determine their influence on the maize leaf nutrients composition and soil chemical properties.

Materials and Methods

Soil sampling and analysis before planting

Sixty soil core samples were randomly taken form the entire field at 0-15cm depth before planting the legumes. They were bulked together in polythene bags, air-dried and sieved with a 2 mm sieve for routine analysis.

The soil pH was determined in a 1:1 soil/water suspension and 2:1 $CaCl_2$ soil suspension using a glass/calomel electrode system, Jenway 3015 pH meter, Jenway Limited Felsted Dunmow, Essex England, CM63LB (Crockford and Nowell, 1956).

Organic matter was determined by Walkley and Black (1934) method through chronic acid digestion. Soil nitrogen was extracted through addition of 5ml of concentrated H_2SO_4 and selenium catalyst, then distilled with NaOH and titrate against 0.01M HCl (Jackson, 1964). Soil P was extracted using Bray P_1 extractant and the amount in the extract was measured with Murphy and Riley (1962) blue colouration method on a spectronic 20 (Bausch and Lomb spectronic 20) at 882Um.

The exchangeable bases (K, Ca, Mg and Na) were extracted with 1M NH_4OAc pH_7 and the amount in the extracts were determined using atomic absorption spectrophotometry (Novaspec 11 visible spectrophotometer, pharmacia Biotech (Biochron Ltd., Cambridge, England). The exchangeable acidity (H^+ and Al^{3+}) was measured from 0.1M HCl extracts by titrating with 0.01M NaOH (McLean, 1965). Micronutrients (Mn, Fe, Cu and Zn) were extracted with 0.1M HCl (Ogunwale and Udo, 1978) and measured with Perkin Elimer atomic absorption spectrophotometer Perkin Elimer ASS. (model 372), Perkin Elimer Ltd., Williams Street Wellesley MAO 2481-4078 USA.

Determination of Soil Physical Properties

The physical properties of the soils on the site were determined before the field experiment. The soil bulk density (mgm^{-3}) was determined by a core method (Ojeniyi, 1998) and porosity was calculated from the values of bulk density. The mechanical analysis of the soil was done by the hydrometer method (Bouycous, 1951) and the percentage sand, silt and clay were need on a textual triangle to determine the soil texture.

Field Experiments

The experiments were carried out at Akure in the rainforest zone of Nigeria (elevation 10m, $7^{o}15^{1}$N, $5^{o}15^{1}$). The soil is a sandy, clay, loam (skeletal, kaolinitic, isohyperthermic oxic paleustalf (Alfisol) or Ferric Luvisol (FAO). The site had been continuously cropped for 10 years and the experiments were conducted in 2003 and 2004 cropping seasons with each one spanning four months. The annual rainfall amount and air temperature in the study area were 1450mm and 26.7°C in 2003 and 1460mm and 27.3°C in 2004 respectively.

The field site was cleared, ploughed and harrowed to maintain optimal tilth for the crop, and each plot size is $25m^2$. There were three legumes treatment namely groundnut, bambara groundnut, pigeon pea, in-addition to 400kg/ha NPK 15-15-15 per crop (800kg/ha for two crops 2003 and 2004) and the control (no fertilizer nor legumes) replicated four times and arranged in a randomized complete block design. The choice of 400kg ha^{-1} NPK 15-15-15 was based on the work of Moyin-Jesu (2002) for growing arable crops.

Two maize seeds were planted at a spacing of 90x30cm and germinated five days later. After which, two seeds each of bambara groundnut and groundnut (*Archis hypogeai*) were inter planted within the maize and between at spacing of 75cmx45cm while pigeon pea was planted at a spacing 1m by 1m between and within the maize plant. NPK 15-15-15 fertilizer was applied at two weeks after planting maize.

Hand weeding was done thrice starting from the 2nd and continued at 5.7 and 9 weeks after planting. Five maize plants were sampled in each plot for the measurement of plant height, stem girth, leaf area and leaf population at weekly interval until 7th week after planting. The maize plants tasseled between 7th and 9th weeks after planting. At 15th week after planting, the maize cobs were harvested, dehusked labeled and oven dried at 70°F to attain 13% moisture content, shelled and the grain yield was determined for each treatment.

Sampled grains of maize from each treatments was ground into powdery form by hammer mill. 2 grammes of the processed grains was weighed into crucibles each, dry ashed at 400°C for 6 hours in muffle furnace. After cooling, the ashed samples were made into solution and their nutrient contents N, P, K, Ca, Mg were analysed as described by A.O.A.C (1970).

Soil Analysis after the Experiment

Soil samples were taken from each treatment plot, air-dried, sieved with 2mm sieve and analysed for soil pH, O.M, N, P, K, Ca, Mg as described earlier.

Statistical Analysis

The average data for soil, growth parameters vegetative parameter and grains yield for the two crops of maize in 2003 and 2004 were subjected to Analysis of Variance (ANOVA) and the treatment means were also separated using Duncan Multiple Range Test at 5% level of significance (Gomez and Gomez, 1984).

Results

Soil Analysis before the Experiment

Table 1 presents the soil chemical composition before the experiment. The soil nitrogen content is 0.14% which is lower than the 0.15% optimum level recommended for optimum maize production. Sobulo and Osiname (1981). The soil pH (H_2O) 6.68 and pH (2:1 $CaCl_2$) 6.67 showed that the soil was slightly acidic.

The % soil organic matter is 0.52% which was far less than 3% recommended for crop production in South Western Nigeria Agboola and Corey (1973). The available soil P is 5.80 which is less than 10mg/kg soil P recommended for optimum crop production. Agboola and Corey (1973). The soil K, Ca and Mg contents were very low below the recommended critical values of 0.2 mmol/kg.

Effect of different Leguminous Fertilizer Treatments on the Growth of Maize

There were significant increases ($P<0.05$) in the maize plant height, leaf area, leaf population and stem girth under different leguminous fertilizers compared to the control treatment (Table 2).

Bambara groundnut treatment had the highest values of maize plant height and leaf population while groundnut treatment had the highest value for leaf area and stem girt respectively. For instance, bambara groundnut treatment increased the maize plant height by 9%, 12%, 2% and 36% respectively compared to groundnut, pigeon pea, NPK 15-15-15 fertilizer and control treatments respectively. In addition, groundnut treatment also increased the maize leaf area by 1.3%, 1.2%, 2.5% and 13.3% respectively compared to bambara groundnut, pigeon pea, NPK 15-15-15 and control treatments respectively.

Effect of different legumes treatments on the yield of maize grains

There were significant increase ($P<0.05$) in the maize yield grains (kg) under different legume treatments and NPK fertilizer compared to the control treatment (Table 3). Among the legumes, bambara groundnut treatment had the highest values of maize yield compared to other treatments. For instance, bambara groundnut increased the maize yield by 2.6%, 3% and 53% compared to groundnut, pigeon pea and control treatments.

However, NPK 15-15-15 fertilizer treatment increased the maize yield by 2.7%, 5.7% and 5.2% compared to bambara groundnut, pigeon pea, groundnut treatments respectively.

Effect of different Legumes Treatments on the maize leaf Mineral Composition

The legumes and NPK 15-15-15 fertilizer treatments increased significantly (P<0.05) the maize leaf N, P, K, Ca and Mg compared to the control treatment (Table 4). NPK fertilizer treatment increased most maize leaf N and P while groundnut increased most the maize leaf K and Mg respectively. For instance, NPK 15-15-15 fertilizer increased the maize leaf N by 9.4%, 15.6%, 12.5% and 99% compared to pigeon pea, groundnut bambara groundnut and control treatments respectively.

Among the legumes, groundnut increased most the leaf P and K compared to others while pigeon pea also had the highest value of leaf Ca. There was higher leaf K/Mg, K/Ca and P/Mg ratio under NPK fertilizer compared to the groundnut, bambara groundnut, pigeon pea. For instance, maize leaf K/Ca, leaf K/Mg and leaf P/Mg ratios under NPK fertilizer treatment were 73:1, 110:1 and 17:1 respectively compared to 5:1, 39:1 and 5:1 under pigeon pea treatment.

Effect of different Legumes on the Soil Chemical Composition after the Experiment

There were significant increases (P<0.05) in soil N, P, K, Ca, Mg, pH and O.M under different legume treatments compared to control treatment (Table 5). Among the legume treatments, groundnut treatment had the highest values of soil O.M, N, K and Ca while pigeon pea treatment also had the highest values of soil pH, P and Mg respectively. For instance, groundnut treatment increased soil O.M, N, K and Ca by 16%, 12%, 19% and 4% compared to bambara groundnut treatment.

NPK 15-15-15 fertilizer treatment decreased soil O.M, pH, Ca and Mg compared to others. For example, NPK 15-15-15 fertilizer decreased significantly (P<0.05) soil O.M, pH, Ca and Mg by 90%, 20%, 98.9% and 85% respectively compared to groundnut treatment. However, NPK 15-15-15 fertilizer increased soil P and K by 22% and 42% compared to groundnut treatment.

There were higher soil K/Ca, K/Mg and P/Mg ratios under NPK fertilizer than the legumes. For instance, soil K/Ca, K/Mg and P/Mg ratios in NPK fertilizer were 101:1, 76:1 and 934:1 compared to 1:2, 3:1 and 41:1 respectively under groundnut treatment respectively.

Discussion

The least value of growth and yield parameters in maize (plant height, leaf area, stem girth yield) in the control experiment could be due to initial soil nutrient status resulting from continuous cropping of the site and loss of exchangeable bases. This observation supported that of Moyin-Jesu (2003) who reported poor growth and yield performance of crops on soils that were not fertilized. This was also confirmed by the fact that the soil and leaf chemical composition were also the least in the control treatment, therefore, fertilizer is needed for improvement in the soil nutrient status to enhance growth and yield of crops.

The increase in growth and yield performances of maize under the bambara groundnut and groundnut legume were due to the fact that they fixed nitrogen into the soil for crop growth. This assertion was supported by the observation that there were corresponding increases in soil and leaf N, P, K, Ca, Mg, soil pH and O.M under these legumes which helped in improving soil productivity for future. Nitrogen helps plant to grow vegetatively and increases yield while phosphorus maintains healthy activities of all plant tissues such as oxidative phosphrylation (Oyeniyi, 1984). Adu-Daaph, 1994 and Moyin-Jesu 2007 also reported that K is essential for carbohydrate formation, and promotion of meristematic tissue.

The highest increase in growth and yield maize under NPK 15-15-15 fertilizer was attributed to its quick release of N, P and K in mineralized forms than the organically forms of N, P and K in the legumes and organic manures. This observation agreed with Moyin-Jesu (2009) who reported better responses of kolanut seedling growth parameters in NPK 15-15-15 fertilized treatment than the organic manures. However, the long term benefits of increased soil nutrient status and physical properties improvement by the legumes were added advantages for continuous cultivation of the land without soil fertility depletion. This had been reported by Moyin-Jesu and Adekayode (2010) who noted that growing maize in rotation or intercropped with legumes maintain soil fertility and prevent yield declines associated with small holder cropping system in Zimbabwe.

People *et al* (1989) also corroborated this observation by reporting that since Nitrogen is the most limiting plant nutrient in arable farming in the tropics and also, the most expensive element as a mineral fertilizer, there is a great need for biological nitrogen fixation by legumes to reduce cost of fertilizer input and maintain crop yields.

The observed lower yield of maize intercropped with pigeon pea plants compared to bambara groundnut and groundnut legumes could be as a result of competition for light, nutrients because of fast growing and drought resistant nature of pigeon pea. This made it to have growth advantage over maize and consequently lower yield. The result was supported by Willey *et al* (1980) who reported that the erect and fast growing habit of pigeon pea made it to suppress associated growing crop.

Nevertheless, pigeon pea also increased significantly the soil N, P, K, Ca, Mg, pH and O.M showing that it is a good soil amendment but it is not suitable for maize intercrop because of its erect growing habit. However, it is suitable for increase in maize yield grown in the subsequent growing season when the legume plant might have been harvested.

The high K/Ca, K/Mg and P/Mg ratios in the soils fertilized with NPK 15-15-15 might cause nutrient imbalance and ultimately affected the uptake of soil K, Ca and Mg for crop growth. This will cause serious dislocation in the soil equilibrium without continuous application of the inorganic fertilizer. Moyin-Jesu (2004) had reported serious nutrient imbalance in soils used for cultivation of budded rubber in the field under NPK 15-15-15 fertilizer treatment.

Table 10.1: Soil Fertility Status before Planting

Soil parameters	Values
Soil pH (H_2O)	5.45
Soil pH 0.01M $CaCl_2$	5.32
Organic matter (%)	0.69
Nitrogen (%)	0.07
Available P (mg/kg)	5.06
Exchangeable bases	
K^+ (mmol/kg)	0.10
Ca^{2+} (mmol/kg)	0.11
Mg^{2+} (mmol/kg)	0.09
Al^{3+} (mmol/kg)	1.45
Fe (mg/kg)	8.50
Zn (mg/kg)	3.75
Mn (mg/kg)	1.80
Cu (mg/kg)	2.00
Sand (%)	79.10
Silt (%)	15.20
Clay (%)	5.70
Soil bulk density (mgm^{-3})	1.60
% porosity	41.81

Table 10.2: Effect of different legumes on the Growth Parameter of Maize

Treatments	Plant Height (cm)	Stem girth	Leaf area (cm)	Leaf population (cm^2)
Control	57.90^{a}	3.00^{a}	290.30^{a}	9.20^{a}
Bambara groundnut	90.97^{e}	5.60^{b}	330.70^{c}	10.00^{e}
Groundnut	82.90^{c}	5.90^{d}	334.95^{d}	9.30^{b}
Pigeon pea	79.80^{b}	5.50^{bc}	331.10^{c}	9.40^{c}
NPK 15-15-15	88.90^{d}	5.60^{bc}	326.60^{b}	9.60^{d}

Treatment means within each column followed by the same letters are not significantly different from each other using Duncan Multiple Range Test at 5% level.

Interestingly, the legumes (groundnut, bambara groundnut and pigeon pea) increased soil properties in balanced forms such as soil pH, O.M, N, P, K, Ca and Mg unlike in NPK 15-15-15 where there was a reduction in soil pH, O.M, Ca and Mg. Besides, the yields from bambara groundnut, groundnut and pigeon pea served as additional source of food and income to farmers, apart from that of maize. Thus, it is profitable to grow them.

Table 10.3: Effect of different Legumes Crops on the Yield Parameters of Maize (*Zea mays* L)

Treatments	Maize Grain yield per plant (g)	Maize Grain yield Kg/ha
Control	69.75	697.5a
Bambara groundnut	148.5	1485d
Groundnut	144.7	1447c
Pigeon pea	143.9	1439d
NPK 15-15-15	152.6	1526e

Treatment means within each column followed by the same letters are not significantly different from each other using Duncan Multiple Range Test at 5% level.

Table 10.4: Effect of different Legumes on the Leaf Chemical Composition of Maize

Treatments	% N	% P	% K	% Ca	% Mg
Control	0.03[a]	0.02[a]	0.05[a]	0.04[a]	0.05[b]
Bambara groundnut	2.80[c]	0.38[b]	2.99[c]	0.37[b]	0.06[b]
Groundnut	2.70[b]	0.44[c]	3.11[d]	0.44[c]	0.07[c]
Pigeon pea	2.90[d]	0.37[b]	2.77[b]	0.50[d]	0.07[c]
NPK 15-15-15	3.20[e]	0.52[d]	3.30[e]	0.045[a]	0.03[a]

Treatment means within each column followed by the same letters are not significantly different from each other using Duncan Multiple Range Test at 5% level.

Table 10.5: Effect of different Legumes on the Soil Chemical Composition after Planting

Treatments	Soil pH (H_2O)	Org. % matter (%)	Available K		Ca	Mg mmol/kg	
			Nitrogen	P(mg/kg)			
Control	5.30a	0.32a	0.03a	3.14a	0.05a	0.07a	0.08a
Bambara groundnut	6.90c	2.57b	0.36bc	26.49b	1.42b	2.71b	0.71b
Groundnut	6.87c	3.06d	0.41e	29.23c	1.75c	2.82c	0.70b
Pigeon pea	7.01d	2.79c	0.33b	29.97c	1.71c	2.71b	0.77c
NPK 15-15-15	5.47b	0.30a	0.39d	37.37d	3.03d	0.03a	0.04a

Treatment means within each column followed by the same letters are not significantly different from each other using Duncan Multiple Range Test at 5% level.

Conclusion and Recommendation

The use of convectional legumes as soil amendments increased significantly the growth and yield of maize. It is recommended that bambara groundnut intercropped with maize gave the highest yield. This is against the backdrop that convectional legumes such as bambara groundnut and groundnut could effectively substitute for 400kg/ha NPK 15-15-15 fertilizer in sustainable production of maize in the study area.

In-addition, the legumes are cheaper to obtain, environmentally friendly and prevent yield decrease associated with small holder cropping system.

REFERENCES

Adu-Daaph, H.K, Cobbira, J. and Asare, E.O. 1994. Effect of cocoa pod ash on the growth of maize. Journal of Agric. Science Cambridge 132: 31-33.

Agboola, A. A. and Corey R. B. (1973): Soils testing, N, P, K, fore maize in the soil derived from metamorphic and igneous rocks of Western State of Nigeria. Jour. West African Sci. Ass. 17(2): 93-100.

Bouycous, J. (1951): Hydrometer method for soil particle size analysis. Agron. Jour. 54:464-465.

Crockford, L. and Nowell, R. (1956): Laboratory manual of physical chemistry. John Wiley and Sons, N. Y. 1956: Expts., 31 and 32: 58-59.

Folorunso, O. O., A. A. Agboola and Adeoye G. O. (1995): Use of Fractional Recovery Model to calculate the Potassium (K) needs of maize. Nigeria Journal of Technical Education.

Jackson, M. L. (1958): Soil Chemical Analysis Englewood Cliffs. New York. Prentice Hall Inc.

McLean, E. O. (1965): Aluminum P 927-932. M.C.A. Black Eds.: Methods of soil analysis parts. Agronomy 9, Amer. Soc. Agronomy, Madison, Wisconsin, U.S.A.

Moyin-Jesu, E. I. and Akinwale .O. (2002): Use of plant tonic fertilizers for soil fertility improvement, leaf chemical composition and yield of pop corn/maize intercrop. Discovery and Innovation Journal, Kenya 14(3&4).

Moyin-Jesu, E. I. (2003): Incorporation of agro-industrial biomass and their effects on four successive crops of Amaranthus. Pertanika Jour. Trop. Agric. Sci. 26(1):35-40.

Moyin-Jesu, E. I. (2004): Effect of different organic fertilizers on the soil fertility, leaf chemical composition and growth of budded rubber. Pertanika Jour. of Tropical Agricultural Sci. 24(2): 91-100. Malaysia.

Moyin-Jesu, E. I. (2007): Evaluation of different organic fertilizers on the soil fertility, leaf chemical composition and growth performance of coffee seedlings. African Jour. Sci. and Tech. UNESCO (21): 1-6.

Moyin-Jesu, E. I. (2009): Evaluation of sole and amended organic fertilizers on soil fertility and growth of Kola seedlings (*Cola acuminate*). Pertanika Jour. Trop. Agric. Sci. 32(1): 17-23.

Moyin-Jesu, E. I. and Adekayode, F. O. (2010): Use of long yam bean as soil amendment for the growth, leaf chemical composition and yield performance of White yam (*Dioscorea rotundata* L). Journal of America Science.

Murphy, J. and Riley, J.P. (1962): A modified single solution method for determination of phosphate in natural waters. Analytical Glumi Acta, 27:31-36.

Mustapha, S. (1991): Maize production policy in Nigeria. A paper

presented at the official launching of Maize Growers Association of Nigeria held at I.I.T.A, June 3, 1991.

Ogunwale, J. A. and E. J. Udo (1978): A laboratory manual for soil and plant analysis. Agronomy Dept. Univ. of Ibadan, Nigeria: 201-206.

Ojeniyi, S. O. (1984): Compound chemical fertilizer and food production, effect of NPK 15-15-15 fertilizer on pepper, cowpea and maize. Nigeria Jour. Applied Science 2:91-95.

Ojeniyi, S. O. (1998): Use of woodash for soil fertility and crop yield improvement. A paper presented at the 24th Annual Conference of Soil Science Society of Nigeria. Eds. .O. Babalola. ABTU, Bauchi, Nigeria, pp.12-16.

Oyekan .L. (1990): Dowry mildew of maize in Nigeria; Epidermology distribution and importance. A paper presented at the Ministry Review Technology Meeting (MRTM) of Ondo Agric. Development Project held in Akure Nigeria.

Peoples, M.B., A. W. Faizah, B. Rekasem and D. F. Heridge (1989): Methods for evaluating nitrogen fixation by nodulated legumes in the field. ACIAR monograph no.11, Canberra: 76.

Sobulo, R. A. and Osiname, O. A. (1981): Soils and fertilizer use in Western Nigeria. Research Bulletin No.11, I.A.R. & T., University of Ife.

Walkley, A. and I. A. Black (1934): An examination of degtajaroff method for determining soil organic matter and a proposed modification of the chronic acid filtration. Soil Sci. 37:29-38.

Willey, R. W., Rao, M. R. and Natargan.M. (1980): Traditional cropping systems with pigeon pea and their improvement. Pp.1124. In Y.L. Nene and V. Kumble (eds.) Proc. Inter Workshop on pigeon pea Vol., Patanchery ICRISAT, India.

Index